THE BLACK ART
OF MULTIPLATFORM
GAME PROGRAMMING

JAZON YAMAMOTO

Cengage Learning PTR

CENGAGE
Learning·

Professional • Technical • Reference

Australia • Brazil • Japan • Korea • Mexico • Singapore • Spain • United Kingdom • United States

CENGAGE
Learning®

Professional • Technical • Reference

The Black Art of Multiplatform Game Programming
Jazon Yamamoto

Publisher and General Manager, Cengage Learning PTR: Stacy L. Hiquet

Associate Director of Marketing: Sarah Panella

Manager of Editorial Services: Heather Talbot

Senior Acquisitions Editor: Emi Smith

Senior Marketing Manager: Mark Hughes

Project Editor: Kezia Endsley

Copy Editors: Kezia Endsley, Reem Halabi, and André LaMothe

Technical Editors: Carlos Yamamoto, André LaMothe, and Francesco De Simone

Videographer/Scriptwriter/Editor and Producer: Jazon Yamamoto

Interior Layout: MPS Limited

Cover Designers: Jazon Yamamoto, André LaMothe, and Luke Fletcher

Proofreaders: Stacie Saenz LaMothe, Francesco De Simone, and Gene Redding

Indexer: Sharon Shock

For product information and technology assistance, contact us at **Cengage Learning Customer & Sales Support, 1-800-354-9706.**

For permission to use material from this text or product, submit all requests online at **cengage.com/permissions**.

Further permissions questions can be emailed to **permissionrequest@cengage.com**.

All trademarks are the property of their respective owners.

Library of Congress Control Number: 2014932082

ISBN-13: 978-1-305-11038-0

ISBN-10: 1-305-11038-2

Cengage Learning PTR

20 Channel Center Street

Boston, MA 02210

USA

Cengage Learning is a leading provider of customized learning solutions with office locations around the globe, including Singapore, the United Kingdom, Australia, Mexico, Brazil, and Japan. Locate your local office at: **international.cengage.com/region**.

Cengage Learning products are represented in Canada by Nelson Education, Ltd.

For your lifelong learning solutions, visit **cengageptr.com**.

Visit our corporate website at **cengage.com**.

Printed in the United States of America
1 2 3 4 5 6 7 16 15 14

I dedicate this book to my mother.

ACKNOWLEDGMENTS

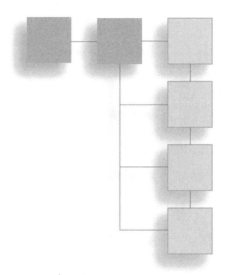

First, I would like to thank my parents for being supportive and encouraging me to follow my dreams and pursue happiness. My mother has always been a nurturing pillar of support and my father is a man worth looking up to. I would also like to thank my brother for guiding me and giving me advice. He has always watched over me and I really appreciate it.

I want to thank my mentor, André LaMothe, for pushing me into doing this. I can't even begin to explain how much he inspired me to make this happen. I read his books as a teenager and frequented his forums on a daily basis. He was always helpful and made sure he gave the best advice he could. I feel privileged to have the opportunity to work with him.

Next, I would like to thank all my friends and family. I would like to thank Reem Halabi for being of great help and a fun person to work with. A special thanks goes to my cousin Juan Manuel Soto who I consider to be my brother. If I were to list all the people that I'd like to thank, I'd be sitting here all night! Also, I want to give a shout out to Day[9] for everything he does and for helping me be a better gamer.

Finally, I would like to thank everyone at Cengage. Working with them has been a great experience since day one. I want to give a personal thanks to Senior Acquisitions Editor Emi Smith and Project Manager/Copy Editor Kezia Endsley for all the effort they put into this and all the great advice they gave me. Another thanks goes to Technical Editor/Proofreader Francesco De Simone, who has a great attitude and a keen eye for detail.

ABOUT THE AUTHOR

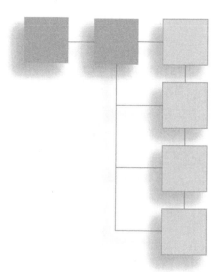

Jazon Yamamoto is a self-taught computer programmer currently pursuing a degree in computer engineering. He began programming at the age of 13 when his father first bought him a book on Visual Basic programming. He quickly moved into C++ and began learning about DirectX and OpenGL. Aside from being a programmer and a student, he is also an avid gamer and an amateur musician.

CONTENTS

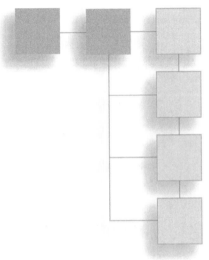

FOREWORD BY ANDRÉ LAMOTHE

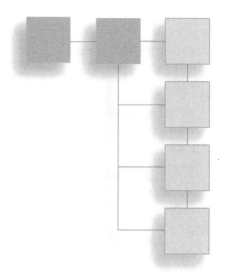

Wow. How did we get from there to here? I think about the early 1970s when I played the first Pong game in the arcade and finally wore my parents out into buying me an Atari 2600. Video games for me have always been a magical experience. Even now, 30 years later, and after developing and publishing hundreds of games myself under my former company Xtreme Games LLC, games are still magical to me. When I play a game, for a moment, I am taken to another world with simpler rules and goals, and the experience is never the same.

The first moment I played Pong, I was mesmerized by the thought of creating a functioning meta-world and creating anything I could imagine. This passion and obsession followed me for a long time as I learned how to develop games by reading anything I could about game development (which was very little at the time). Most game programming in the early days was do-it-yourself, in the real sense of the phrase. We had to figure it out ourselves; there were no books, no classes, and no one to ask. You just sat at the computer and coded day and night. Figuring out algorithms like how to draw a line was a milestone. I remember years later realizing that I literally re-invented Bresenham's algorithm! This was half the fun, figuring things out for myself. I couldn't just "Google" something, or even go to the library to find a solution. Game coding just wasn't widely published or disseminated.

Then in the 1980s, things got really crazy. Video games, in particular arcade games and home consoles, exploded. I actually met other people who knew what I was talking about! Of course, the sheer amount of work to develop a game was hard for most of my friends to stick with, and in the end, only three people in high school ever finished a game and published it on a BBS or on the shareware channels of the day.

By the 1990s, game development was getting serious. It was turning into a "science," and people with PhD's in math, physics, computer science, and so forth started getting into it, and computer graphics, hardware acceleration, and computing power in general seemed to be driven by the single goal of customers wanting to play games! Then of course, we all remember when *Wolfenstein 3D* and *DOOM* came out. Those games showed that anyone with a PC could make something amazing. This was when I decided to start writing books about game development. My first book *Tricks of the Game Programming Gurus* was published in 1994 and was a work of love and passion, and probably the hardest thing I ever did. I didn't have anyone to guide me, no help, just me and the desire to write a book to put down all the years of experience making games and show others how to do it. And remember, there was *no* "Internet" yet; that didn't happen for a couple more years! So, writing a book was a very manual process, and writing a game book was very challenging since just getting information was very hard. I remember, I wanted to put a CD-ROM in the book, which was totally unheard of at the time. I convinced SAMS Publishing to do it since I wanted to use the CD-ROM to put the tools, games, art, and sound assets for programmers, so they didn't have to download them. Most people had a 1,200-9,600 baud dial-up connection to a BBS, CompuServe, or AOL, so downloading megabytes would take forever. Having a CD-ROM with the book was huge!

Even though the book wasn't perfect, it was a best seller instantly. I knew I had something here. The public was dying for books on this subject, and there were hundreds of thousands of programmers out there who wanted to learn how to make games. So, I was off and running, and I wrote book after book. My last one is my personal masterpiece—*Tricks of the 3D Game Programming Gurus*—about software rasterization and 3D. The book IMO is still relevant since math is math, and if you don't have hardware acceleration, then you need to understand how to write a 3D engine yourself. Of course, I did write other books after this, but not really about game programming. For example, there's *The Black Art of Video Game Console Design*, but that's about hardware design and another story…

Then I was approached by a publisher to become Series Editor for a new game programming series under Prima Tech. I thought, "Awesome, I can basically have other authors write books that I don't have time to, but I know people will enjoy and I can get the word out there even more about game programming with all my ideas that are still in my head." So, for half a decade I came up with ideas, titles, and guided countless authors in writing their first books (in many cases) on game development. It was both an exhausting and exhilarating experience. In the end, the company was acquired (a couple times), and settled into Thomson Course Technology, where I passed the torch on to them and they went on their own with what I had created over the years. But, I will always be proud of the dozens of books that I came up with, and were able to make into reality with their resources.

My focus is now on gaming hardware and developing embedded gaming systems and teaching others how to do the same, but I still dabble in game development and writing of course—it will never be out of my system. And with that in mind, I am always looking for someone who has the talent and the stamina to write a game development book and see if I can help him or her actually make it real. One such person who came into my sites a few years ago was Jazon Yamamoto. I saw him post on my `XGameStation.com` site, and I noticed that he was very mature for his age, and instead of *talking* about what he was going to do, he would actually *do* something and post a link to a screenshot, or a game he was working on, and so on. This is the first thing I look for, people who *do* things and don't just talk about doing things. So, I watched quietly for years, waiting for him to learn enough. Once in a while I would guide him in a personal email or correspondence about how to do something in the game or demo he was currently developing.

Then one day, he posted an article he had written about game programming. It was something simple, maybe about plotting pixels or drawing sprites, but I noticed that he had talent. He could communicate complex and abstract ideas much better than most engineers twice his age. Sure, he needed to hone his skills, but I knew he had the right stuff to write a book. And I thought this would be a great experience for him, and a great calling card for college and work, since he was only 19–20 years old at the time.

So, we started talking about ideas, and I dropped the bomb on him. I told him, we are going to write a book. Well, to be more precise *you* are going to write the book, and I am going to edit it, guide you, and make it rock. I could sense his excitement as well as sheer terror. The moment in life where you finally have to put your money where your mouth is—most people crumble, run, and hide. But, Jazon said, "Okay, let's do it." Of course, in my head I was thinking of the scene from *Star Wars* when Luke tells Yoda he isn't afraid, and Yoda responds, "You will be... you WILL be...".

We started on the book, and over the period of a year, there were many re-starts and edits, but finally Jazon got the pattern and plowed thru the writing, demos, editing, and all the other billion little things that have to be done to finish a book. Also, an idea I have always wanted to try was to make screen recordings and little "video tutorials" in one of my books. So, to my knowledge, this is the first game development book ever whereby the author himself made videos summing up each chapter, so I think this will be pretty cool. Definitely check them out for each chapter on the Cengage website downloads page.

So, in conclusion, if you're looking for a book to get you started on C/C++ game programming and you don't know that much about DirectX or aren't sure you want to lock yourself into Windows, this book is perfect. The book uses a generalized approach and of course the SDL (Simple Direct Media Library), which works on Windows, Linux, and Mac OS to name a few, so it's a great introduction and sampler of game programming. It allows you to immediately leverage your skills on all the major platforms. And, unlike most of my books, this one is only a few hundred pages and not 1,000-1,500. You can actually read it in a few days!

Sincerely,

André LaMothe

"Sometime in the early 21st Century..."

INTRODUCTION

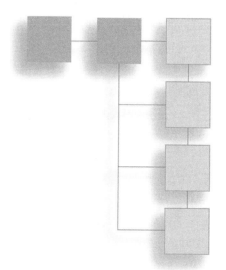

This book was written to teach the creation of 2D games using SDL 1.2. The goal of this book is to take an amateur programmer, and give him/her the ability to create complete arcade-style video games. The first half of this book focuses on learning the features of SDL, and their possible applications. The latter half focuses on more advanced techniques used in game creation. This book is divided into 13 chapters, and each chapter deals with a different aspect of game programming. Reading each chapter and understanding the concepts thoroughly should provide any aspiring game programmer a strong foundation. As an extra feature, the final chapter covers SDL 2.0 and the future of the library.

WHO SHOULD READ THIS BOOK

This book was written for anybody who has ever played a game and wanted to write one. It is accessible to complete beginners, but intermediate users can still learn from it. Any beginner programmer will be able to jump straight into this book.

OUTLINE OF THE CHAPTERS

Every chapter in this book is unique and each is vastly different from the next. Here is a brief rundown on what each chapter covers.

Chapter 1: Setting Up Your Workstation

This chapter covers the procedure of setting up a work environment on Windows and Linux. At the end of this chapter, you will be able to compile SDL programs in both operating systems.

Chapter 2: Entering the Digital Domain

This chapter covers first contact with SDL. Here, you take small steps to make a window, draw images on that window, and eventually make what's called a game loop.

Chapter 3: Tapping Into the World of Graphics

This chapter is the first milestone. Here, I cover graphics using SDL in great detail. By the end of this chapter, you will be able to draw primitive graphics, draw different images with transparency, and even animate images.

Chapter 4: Interacting with the Matrix

This chapter deals with mouse and keyboard input. You'll use these to manipulate elements in your program. By the end of this chapter, you will be able to input commands into your programs via keyboard and mouse.

Chapter 5: Blasting Music and Sound Effects

This chapter deals with audio. Here, you learn how to play ambient music and sound effects. These combined elements make games more entertaining.

Chapter 6: Your First Playable Video Game

This chapter is the next milestone of the book. Here you use what you've learned so far to craft a simple video game. This game is fully functional and actually quite entertaining.

Chapter 7: Rethinking the Paddle Game

This chapter covers video game creation to a finer extent. Here, you implement features such as menus and pause screens to make your games feel more complete.

Chapter 8: Designing a Game Engine

This chapter marks the turning point of this book. Here, I start dealing with advanced topics of game programming, such as game engines and engine extensions. By the end of this chapter, you will have a simple game engine that you'll build upon in the following chapters.

Chapter 9: Crafting Levels with Tile Maps

This chapter covers the creation of levels using tile maps. Tile mapping is a popular technique for implementing levels in a video game and a highly flexible one as well. By the end of this chapter, you will be able to create awesome levels.

Chapter 10: Forging Worlds with Scene Management

This chapter covers the art of scene management. In short, this chapter teaches you how to create a virtual world with characters that can interact with each other. Combined with tile maps, the knowledge acquired in this chapter will grant you the ability to create alternate realities for your players.

Chapter 11: Inside the Mass Production Zone with Factories and Scripts

This chapter covers aspects of software engineering that are very useful for game creation. Factories and scripts are put to good use to help speed up the creation of video games.

Chapter 12: The Final Frontier

In this chapter, you take everything you have learned and apply it to make a complete video game similar to something you could find in an arcade. This video game will be complete, but highly extensible. Upon completing this chapter, you will be able to make quality games in an efficient and elegant manner.

Chapter 13: SDL 2.0 and the Future

This is an added feature. Here, I cover SDL 2.0 and the future of the library. This chapter specializes in the new features of the library, and how you can use them to their full potential.

CONVENTIONS USED IN THIS BOOK

`Monospace font` is used to indicate filenames, directories, keywords, events, functions, and other words that are typed in as code.

Anything you type into a program or screen appears in **bold**.

Code lines appear in the following font:

`sound = Mix_LoadWAV(filename);`

Variables like *filename* are placed in italic because they are placeholders. In this case, the file's name would be placed here, which would be a string.

This book comes with companion files that must be downloaded and installed. The directory of installation is referred to as `BAMGP\`.

 Whenever I discuss the video tutorials that you can view from the website, you'll see this icon to remind you about this unique and helpful feature, exclusive to this book.

Tip

Important tidbits of information that can make your life easier and your gaming efforts more fun and productive are shown in these tip boxes.

CONTENTS OF THE DOWNLOADABLE FILES

The downloadable files contain the source code to the games and programs created in this book. I recommend browsing through those before reading each chapter so you know what to expect. The downloadable files also contain the SDL library files and tools that can be used to make games. Everything you need to get started can be obtained from **http://cengageptr.com/Topics/TitleDetail/1305110382**. Simply locate the "Companion Downloads" link and click on it to be redirected to a download page. Alternatively, the files can also be downloaded from **http://www.jazon-yamamoto .com/bamgp**. They are contained in a .ZIP file named `BAMGP.zip`. Download the .zip file and extract it anywhere on your hard drive. This will make it easier to explore and experiment with the files in the future. As mentioned, I refer to the root directory of the files as `BAMGP\`. Figure FM.1 contains a directory tree of the contents of `BAMGP\`.

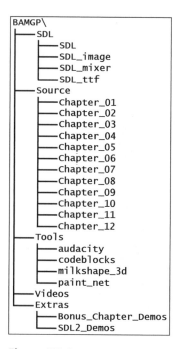

Figure FM.1
The BAMGP\ directory tree.
© Jazon Yamamoto.

Source Code

The source code to every demo or game can be found here. Due to the nature of SDL, this code can be built using Windows, Linux, Mac OS, and pretty much anything that can compile C++ applications. The demos from the first few chapters usually only contain one source file. The demos from the latter chapters are much larger and contain more source files.

Video Tutorials

Every chapter in this book has a video tutorial to go along with it. Video tutorials explain some things in more detail or demonstrate how to modify the source code that comes with each chapter. Be sure to check these out since they contain information that cannot be conveyed through the text.

The SDL 1.2 Library Files

These are the development files. They are required to compile SDL applications.

QUESTIONS OR COMMENTS

Please send any comments, corrections, or questions about the book to the following email address:

info@jazon-yamamoto.com

The website for the book, with information, updates, corrections, and source code, is available at:

http://www.jazon-yamamoto.com/bamgp

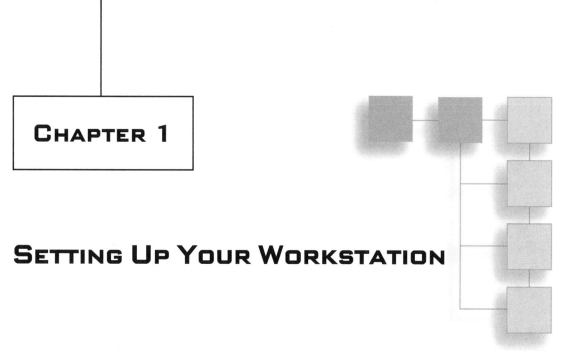

CHAPTER 1

SETTING UP YOUR WORKSTATION

In the beginning, computers were not fun to program. Programmers were given specific hardware, and they had to write specific code for it. A program created to run on a computer would function only on that computer. If the same program had to run on a different computer, it had to be rewritten to address the specific procedures required by the new computer. This was tedious, time consuming, and costly, but operating systems rose to address this issue. An operating system (OS) is a layer of software designed to run on different machines. Machines made with different hardware, but using the same OS, could now run the same programs without the need to rewrite them. Programmers rejoiced when they were finally able to write a program that would run on many different machines.

The problem today is that there are hundreds and hundreds of OSs to work with, and most of them have their own way of rendering graphics, playing sounds, reading input, and so on. It's common for programs to be recoded multiple times to run on different machines (this is called *porting*). The game *Doom* by Id Software has been ported to run on almost any OS that can handle it! To port games more easily, code libraries were built that could abstract all the OS-specific procedures so that programs could run on multiple OSs using the same code base. The Simple DirectMedia Layer (SDL) is a library that was originally designed to simplify the process of porting games. This library is powerful, robust, and easy to learn. Although it was originally used to port games, SDL has also proven to be very well suited for creating video games from the ground up. Today, it runs on over 20 OSs and makes a great multiplatform game development library.

WHAT IS A VIDEO GAME?

Before making them, take a minute to consider what video games really are. At their simplest, video games are computer programs that present the users with a challenge. This challenge could be anything, such as shooting down enemy spaceships or hunting down trolls. Video games usually have a reward system, like awarding a high score to a player for playing well or giving a player a cutscene for beating the game. They can be simple and addictive or complicated and compelling. They have changed over the decades, but the fact that remains is that video games have to be fun. A video game can make use of the newest technology available and still not be as fun as Atari's *Pong*. In other words, the fun factor is the most important aspect of a video game.

It can be hard to point out which video game was the first one ever created. Many people believe it's Atari's *Pong*, since it was the first to hit the masses, but *Computer Space* was created earlier by the same company, and even before that, there was *Space Wars,* which ran on gigantic PDP-1 machines. If a video game could be defined as an electronic game that uses a graphical display as means of presenting the gameplay to the user, then the first video game would be *Tennis for Two* by William Higinbotham. Higinbotham was an American physicist working at the Brookhaven National Laboratory. He realized that the lab's visitors' day needed more interactive demonstrations. In 1958, he created *Tennis for Two* to entertain the visitors with a novel piece of technology. This game simulated tennis from a side view and even calculated accurate ball trajectories. The game proved to be popular, and it paved the way to a new form of entertainment. At the time, this was the only video game in the world, but today video games are everywhere. You can play them on televisions, computers, handheld consoles, and even cell phones. Taking their popularity into consideration, it's safe to say that video games are here to stay.

WHAT YOU NEED TO KNOW TO USE THIS BOOK

For reading this book, I recommend moderate knowledge of C++. The first half of the book uses C to make it easier to demonstrate how SDL works, but the second half uses C++ to make more flexible and reusable code. C++ coders shouldn't have too much of a hard time, while it's recommended for C coders to brush up on the basics of C++. In general, most of the code will be simple and easy to understand, and the more complicated parts will be covered in greater detail.

For the mathematical aspect of programming, algebra should be enough. Geometry, trigonometry, and calculus will definitely help, but they aren't completely necessary. In fact, a grand majority of the math used throughout this book is simple adding, subtracting, multiplying, and dividing!

The one thing that is absolutely necessary for game programming (and pretty much everything else in life) is problem-solving skills. Video games are all about challenges, and programming them is not too different from playing them.

THE TOOLS YOU NEED TO GET STARTED

To get started, you need a computer running an operating system that SDL supports. Two popular options are Microsoft's Windows and the legendary Linux. You also need an appropriate compiler and the SDL library files. There is a multitude of free compilers on the web, and the SDL library files themselves are free, so you can make games without paying a single penny (provided you already have a functional computer).

REVISITING THE COMPANION FILES

All of the files necessary to set up a game development environment can be obtained from the following web page: **http://cengageptr.com/Topics/TitleDetail/1305110382**. Simply locate the "Companion Downloads" link and click on it to be redirected to a download page. Alternatively, the files can also be downloaded from **http://www .jazon-yamamoto.com/bamgp**. They are contained in a .zip file named BAMGP.zip. Download the .zip file and extract it anywhere on your hard drive. This will make it easier to explore and experiment with the files in the future. As a convention, I will refer to the root directory of the files as BAMGP\. Figure 1.1 contains a directory tree of the companion files for this book.

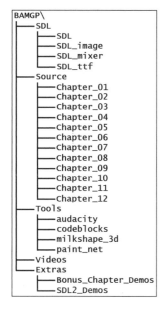

Figure 1.1
The BAMGP\ directory tree.
© Jazon Yamamoto.

SETTING UP ON WINDOWS

Setting up on Windows should be a relatively painless process. Windows makes for a great development system since there are plenty of tools out there to program games on it. If you're using Windows and don't know how to set up SDL with a compiler, make sure you read this section carefully (you may skip this section if you're using Linux).

Step 1: Downloading a Compiler

The first thing you need is a C++ compiler. For windows, I recommend using Code::Blocks because it's free and easy to use. Code::Blocks is available for download at **www.codeblocks.org**. Make sure that you download the Windows binary release that comes with MingW (MingW stands for Minimalist GNU for Windows). In reality, MingW is the compiler and Code::Blocks is just an IDE (Integrated Development Environment) that you can use with different compilers. If you download the version that does not come with MingW, you will have to install MingW manually. To avoid complications, just make sure you get the version that comes packaged with MingW.

Tip

Many people prefer Microsoft's Visual Studio Express Edition, but I stay away from it because when it comes to distributing programs, other computers need to download and install runtime libraries to run them. This could be really annoying, so it's best to avoid the issue as a whole.

Run the program as an administrator immediately after it downloads. To do so, right-click on the icon and select Run as Administrator. You will be asked for permission. Simply accept and you should be greeted with something resembling Figure 1.2.

Figure 1.2
The Code::Blocks Setup wizard.
© Jazon Yamamoto. Source: Code::Blocks Studio.

Click Next and you should see a license agreement like the one shown in Figure 1.3.

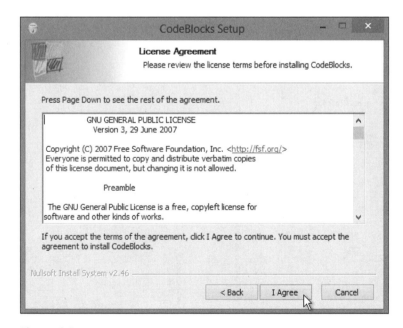

Figure 1.3
The license agreement.
© Jazon Yamamoto. Source: Code::Blocks Studio.

Click on I Agree and you should see some installation options, as shown in Figure 1.4. In this window, make sure that the option to install the MingW Compiler Suite is checked.

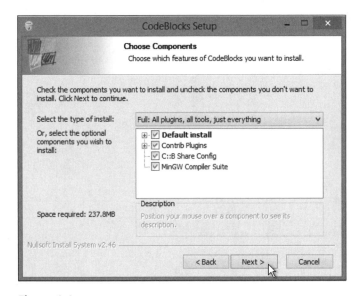

Figure 1.4
The component selector.
© Jazon Yamamoto. Source: Code::Blocks Studio.

Next, the setup window should resemble Figure 1.5.

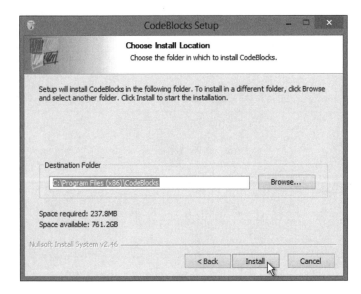

Figure 1.5
The install path.
© Jazon Yamamoto. Source: Code::Blocks Studio.

You will be asked to enter the path in which you want to install Code::Blocks. You can change this path, but I recommend installing on the default path. Once you have decided on the path, click Next. The window should now resemble Figure 1.6.

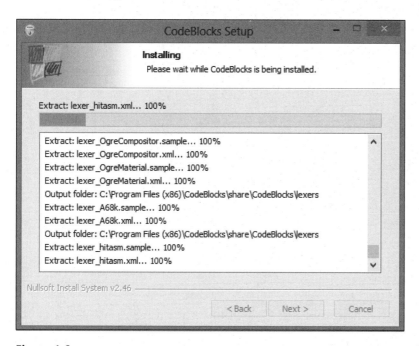

Figure 1.6
The installation process.
© Jazon Yamamoto. Source: Code::Blocks Studio.

This window indicates that Code::Blocks is installing. Once the bar fills up, Code::Blocks will be completely installed. If you have multiple compilers installed, you might see a list of compilers that Code::Blocks has detected. If so, simply press OK. If all the steps were performed correctly, you should see a window similar to Figure 1.7.

Figure 1.7
The installation is complete.
© Jazon Yamamoto. Source: Code::Blocks Studio.

Now, run Code::Blocks and you should see Code::Blocks running in all its glory, as demonstrated in Figure 1.8.

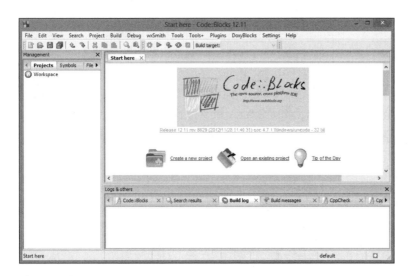

Figure 1.8
Code::Blocks is running.
© Jazon Yamamoto. Source: Code::Blocks Studio.

If all the steps were performed correctly, Code::Blocks should be running on your computer.

Step 2: Setting Up SDL

Setting up SDL is easy, but you must be careful when doing so. One mistake can ruin the whole installation, and you will have to start all over again. First, you have to download the SDL libraries from **www.libsdl.org**. You will need the "SDL 1.2 Development" library, which is located in the Downloads section of the site. Make sure you download the development libraries that are configured for MingW (see Figure 1.9). This book uses a 32-bit version of SDL. This version will work on 32-bit systems as well as 64-bit systems. Some releases of SDL come with an x86 folder and an x64 folder. Each folder contains a different version of SDL. Always use the x86 folder since that one contains the 32-bit version.

The MingW development libraries

Figure 1.9
The download link on the SDL website.
© Jazon Yamamoto. Source: Google Inc.

Once you have downloaded the file, create a folder on the C drive of your computer (or any drive that is convenient) and name it **SDL**. (See Figure 1.10).

Tip

I chose to install SDL on my C:\ drive for the sake of simplicity, but you can install it on any drive and any directory.

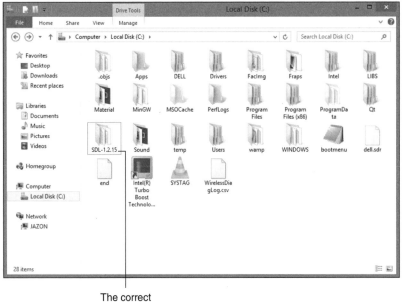

The correct
SDL folder

Figure 1.10
The SDL folder in the C:\ drive.
© Jazon Yamamoto. Source: Microsoft Inc. Used with permission from Microsoft.

The next step is to extract the contents of the file you downloaded to the folder you just created (see Figure 1.11).

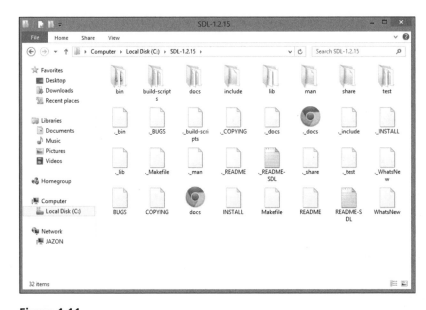

Figure 1.11
SDL after extraction.
© Jazon Yamamoto. Source: Microsoft Inc. Used with permission from Microsoft.

Tip

SDL may come in a compressed file, and you may need to download a third-party program to extract SDL. If so, you can use a free trial of WinRAR to do this. Just make sure you purchase a license for WinRAR if you plan to keep on using it after the trial expires.

There are several more libraries that you will need. These libraries are actually extensions of SDL that give you more tools to work with images, sound, and fonts. They can be downloaded from **http://www.libsdl.org/projects/SDL_ttf/release-1.2.html**, **http://www.libsdl.org/projects/SDL_image/release-1.2.html**, and **http://www.libsdl .org/projects/SDL_mixer/release-1.2.html**. There are several different distributions, so make sure you download the development binaries that are configured for Win32 development (see Figure 1.12).

The ones you want to download end with the letters VC. These are actually configured for Visual C++, but they work on MingW as well. Also, make sure they are the SDL 1.2 files and not the SDL 2.0 files. The names of the files are `SDL_image-devel-1.2.12-VC.zip`, `SDL_mixer-devel-1.2.12-VC.zip`, and `SDL_ttf-devel-2.0.11-VC.zip`.

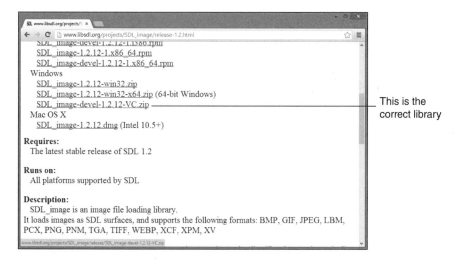

Figure 1.12
The `SDL_image` development library configured for Win32.
© Jazon Yamamoto. Source: Google Inc.

After extracting each of those files, they should each contain a folder called `include` and a folder called `lib`. Copy the files in the `lib` folder that have a `.lib` extension and paste them in the `lib` folder in your SDL directory. Next, copy the files in the `include` directory and paste them in the folder called `SDL`, which is located in the `include` folder of your SDL directory (see Figure 1.13). There are also DLL files in the lib folder, and these are going to be necessary later on, so do *not* lose them.

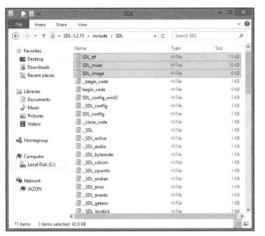 

Figure 1.13
Installing the extension libraries into the SDL directory.
© Jazon Yamamoto. Source: Microsoft Inc. Used with permission from Microsoft.

With SDL installed, your next step is to configure Code::Blocks.

Step 3: Configuring Code::Blocks

This is probably the easiest of all steps. First of all, open Code::Blocks and click on Settings → Compiler and Debugger, as shown in Figure 1.14.

Figure 1.14
The Settings menu.
Source: Code::Blocks Studio.

Then, click on Global Compiler Settings → Linker Settings. In the Other Linker Options box, type `-lmingw32 -lSDLmain -lSDL -lSDL_image -lSDL_ttf -lSDL_mixer`, as demonstrated in Figure 1.15. This list doesn't have to be on the same line. You can put each item in a separate line. Just make sure you type them exactly as they appear.

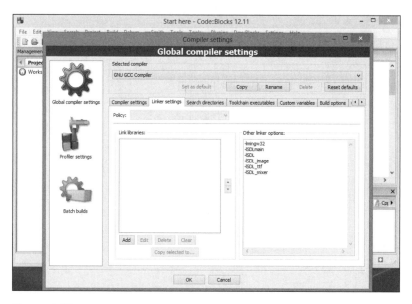

Figure 1.15
The linker settings.
Source: Code::Blocks Studio.

After that, go to the Search Directories tab. Under the Compiler tab, click on Add and add the `C:\SDL\SDL-1.2.15\include` directory, as illustrated in Figure 1.16.

Figure 1.16
The search directories.
Source: Code::Blocks Studio.

You can also use the Browse button to locate the folder. Upon adding the path, you should see something resembling Figure 1.17.

Figure 1.17
The include directories.
Source: Code::Blocks Studio.

Now go to the Linker tab and add to the libraries the following path: `C:\SDL\`
`SDL-1.2.15\lib` (see Figure 1.18).

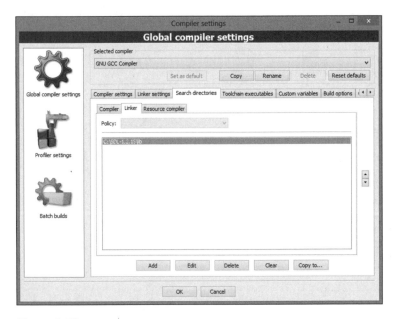

Figure 1.18
The `lib` directory.
Source: Code::Blocks Studio.

Next, press OK at the bottom of the window. SDL should be ready to run on your Windows environment.

Step 4: Creating a Project

To create a project, click on File → New → Project. You should see a window resembling Figure 1.19.

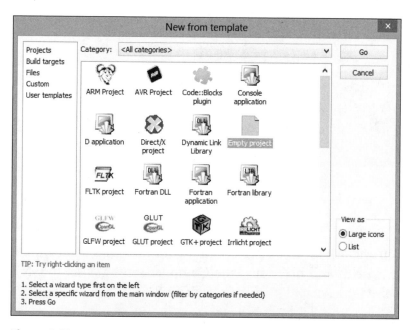

Figure 1.19
The project wizard.
Source: Code::Blocks Studio.

Click on Empty Project and then click on Go. You should see a new window greeting you with information about creating new projects. Click Next. The window will ask you for a directory and a project name. For the project name type **Test**. For the directory, type the folder in which you want the project files to be stored. I made a folder called SDLGames on my Desktop and selected that folder as my directory to store the project files, but you can put it anywhere you want (see Figure 1.20).

Figure 1.20
Naming the project.
Source: Code::Blocks Studio.

Click Next and the program will ask for a few project configurations. Clear the Output Dir and Objects Output Dir fields and make sure the Compiler setting is set to GNU GCC Compiler. When you're done, click Finish (see Figure 1.21).

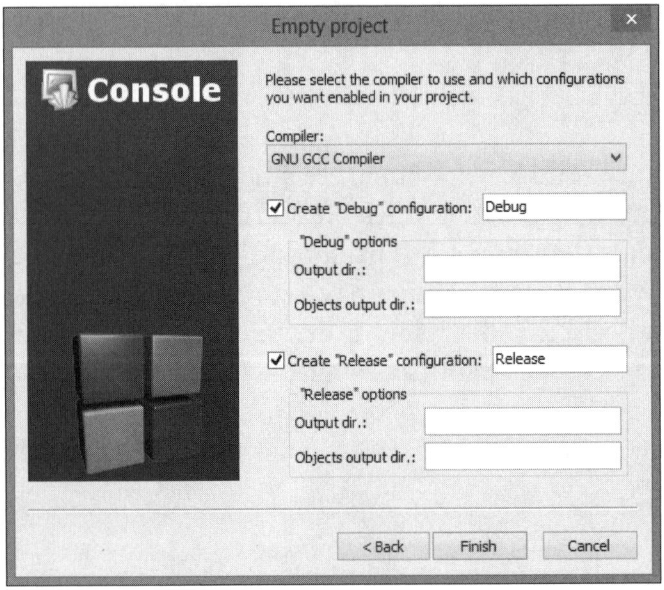

Figure 1.21
The final step in creating a new project.
Source: Code::Blocks Studio.

Now you'll add the main file to your project. To add a file to the project, click on File → New → Empty File, and a message box will ask if you want to add the file to the project. Click Yes, and it will inform you that the file must be saved first. Save the file as main.cpp and click OK. Keep in mind that you have to manually type the extension .cpp when saving the file. The next thing you will see is a window resembling Figure 1.22.

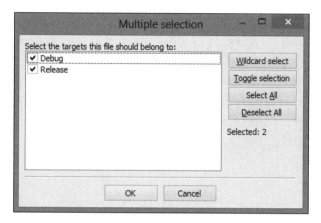

Figure 1.22
The Multiple Selection dialog.
Source: Code::Blocks Studio.

Tip

Files ending with the .cpp extension are C++ source files, whereas files ending in .c are standard C files. And of course, .h files are headers.

Leave the default settings on it as they are and click OK. Whenever you're ready, type the code from Listing 1.1 into the main.cpp file.

Listing 1.1: The First SDL Program for Windows

```cpp
#include <SDL/SDL.h>

int main(int argc, char* args[])
{
    SDL_Init(SDL_INIT_EVERYTHING);
    printf("Windows FTW!!!");
    SDL_Quit();

    return 0;
}
```

Tip

You don't have to type the code from Listing 1.1 by hand. You can copy the file `main.cpp` from `BAMGP\`. It is located under `Source\Chapter_01\1_1_Test\`. In Code::Blocks, you have to add the file to the project by clicking on Project → Add Files and selecting the `main.cpp` file. If you don't add the file, Code::Blocks won't find it, and the program won't compile.

Click on Build → Build and Run and you should see the project compile successfully. If you see a message box that says, "The program can't start because `SDL.dll` is missing from your computer...", go to `C:\SDL\SDL-1.2.15\bin`, copy the file `SDL.dll`, and paste it in your project folder (see Figure 1.23). By including the `SDL.h` file, you made your program dependent on the `SDL.dll` file. In Windows, these files must be present in the same directory as the program for the program to run. Remember that you also installed extensions of SDL, so if a program uses any of them, make sure to include the appropriate DLL files in the program's directory. Table 1.1 lists the SDL libraries and their required DLL files.

Tip

It is actually possible to add the `bin` directory's path as an environment variable in Windows. Doing so enables programs to run without having the `.dll` file in the same directory. Of course, for development this is a good strategy, but when you want to distribute the game, you should always copy all the required `.dll` files into the game `.zip` for distribution, so your users can run the game without problems.

Figure 1.23
The `SDL.dll` file in your project's directory.

Source: Windows 8 File Explorer, © Microsoft Corporation. Used with permission from Microsoft.

Table 1.1   SDL Libraries and Their Dependencies

SDL Library Header File	DLL Dependencies
SDL.h	SDL.dll
SDL_image.h	SDL_image.dll, libpng12-0.dll, libtiff-3.dll, jpeg.dll, and jzlib.dll
SDL_ttf.h	SDL_ttf.dll, libfreetype-6.dll, and zlib1.dll
SDL_mixer	SDL_mixer.dll, libogg-0.dll, libvorbis-0.dll, libvorbisfile-3.dll, mikmod.dll, and smpeg.dll

© Jazon Yamamoto.

When you run the program, you should see something resembling Figure 1.24.

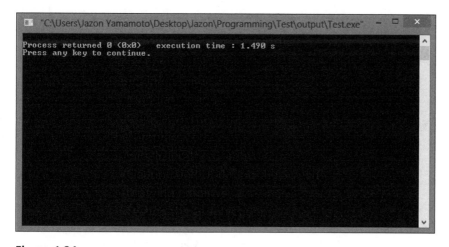

Figure 1.24
The program's successful execution.
Source: Notepad, © Microsoft Corporation. Used with permission from Microsoft.

If you noticed, the console did not print the string Windows FTW!!!. This is because in Windows, using printf with SDL actually outputs the string to a text file named stdout.txt in the project's directory (see Figure 1.25).

Tip

You can run the program by opening `test.exe`, which should also be located in the project's directory if compilation was successful.

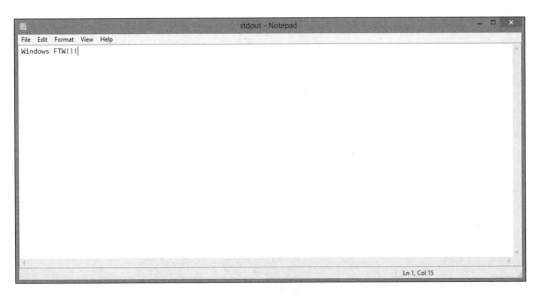

Figure 1.25
Your program's debug output.
Source: Notepad, © Microsoft Corporation. Used with permission from Microsoft.

If you didn't get this far, go back and make sure all the steps were performed correctly. Also, remember that if you successfully compiled the application, it's possible to run it by going to the project's directory and opening `test.exe`. If you ever want to share a game you made with your friends, you can just give them the executable file along with any other dependencies on a flash drive.

Setting Up on Linux (Ubuntu 12.04)

Linux is one of the most stable operating systems out there. It rarely crashes, and there is a huge community of developers that continues to integrate Linux into new hardware. Linux runs on almost anything that has microchips (the funny thing is that I'm barely even exaggerating). Setting up on Linux is a much simpler process than setting up on Windows. If you don't plan to develop for Linux, you can skip this section. This book focuses on Ubuntu 12.04. At the time of writing this, Ubuntu 13.10 is the newest version, but version 12.04 is known as the "long term support" version. This means that 12.04 will be supported by the Linux community for a relatively long time. Nevertheless, the methods described in this book will work across different versions of Ubuntu, but your mileage may vary.

Tip

Linux is known to have issues when it comes to supporting different hardware and programs coded in SDL. Even though this is rare, just keep it in mind.

Step 1: Setting Up SDL

It's a bit easier to set up SDL on Linux before setting up the compiler. First, open the Ubuntu Software Center. This program can be found in the launcher to the right (see Figure 1.26). If you are unable to find it, you can search for it by opening the Dash. The Dash can be opened by clicking on the icon in the launcher with an Ubuntu logo on it. Here, you can search for any program that has already been installed on Linux.

Figure 1.26
Opening Ubuntu Software Center.
Source: Ubuntu, © Canonical Ltd.

Next, search for Synaptic Package Manager on the search bar at the top-right corner of the window. Once the search results are displayed, install it by selecting it and clicking on the Install button to the right, as shown in Figure 1.27. Note that Older Ubuntu distributions come with Synaptic Package Manager preinstalled. If you're running an older version of Ubuntu, you may be able to run the program without having to install it.

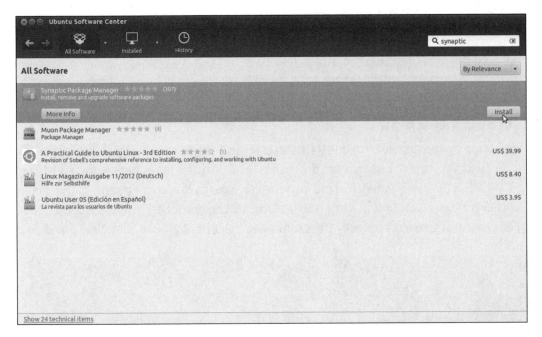

Figure 1.27
Installing Synaptic Package Manager.
Source: Ubuntu, © Canonical Ltd.

The next step is to run Synaptic Package Manager. This can be done by clicking on the icon on the launcher or searching for it in the Dash. In the manager, search for the libraries listed next in the order they appear, and mark each of them for installation, as demonstrated in Figure 1.28.

- libsdl1.2debian
- libsdl1.2-dev
- libsdl-image-1.2
- libsdl-image-1.2-dev
- libsmpeg0
- libsmpeg-dev
- libsdl-mixer1.2
- libsdl-mixer1.2-dev
- libsdl-ttf2.0
- libsdl-ttf2.0-dev

Tip

Use the Quick Filter to find the libraries faster.

Figure 1.28
Selecting the packages you need to use.

Source: Synaptic Package Manager, © 2001–2004 Connectiva S/A, © 2002–2012 Michael Vogt.

Next, apply the changes (see Figure 1.29).

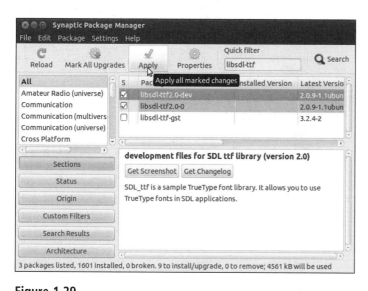

Figure 1.29
Applying the changes to your environment.

Source: Synaptic Package Manager, © 2001–2004 Connectiva S/A.

A window will pop up and ask for permission to apply the changes. Click Apply to continue (see Figure 1.30).

Figure 1.30
Finalizing your selection.
Source: Synaptic Package Manager, © 2001–2004 Connectiva S/A.

The packages should download and install (see Figure 1.31).

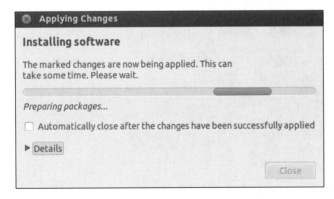

Figure 1.31
Downloading and installing software.
Source: Synaptic Package Manager, © 2001–2004 Connectiva S/A.

Once the installation is complete, a message box will appear. Click Close, and exit the Package Manager (see Figure 1.32).

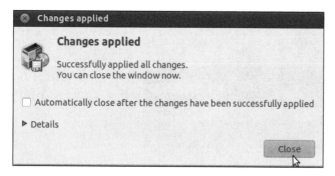

Figure 1.32
The packages have been successfully installed.
Source: Synaptic Package Manager, © 2001–2004 Connectiva S/A.

If you get to the screen shown in Figure 1.32, SDL should be fired up and ready to go!

Step 2: Setting Up Eclipse

To set up Eclipse, open the Ubuntu Software Center. Here, You will need to install a total of three programs. There is a need to install three programs because Eclipse doesn't support C++ out of the box. Eclipse started out as a Java IDE but eventually evolved as a well-rounded tool that can be used with multiple languages. The first program you need is GNU C++ Compiler. To do so, type **g++** in the search bar and it should be one of the top results. For reference, see Figure 1.33. Click on Install once you find the compiler.

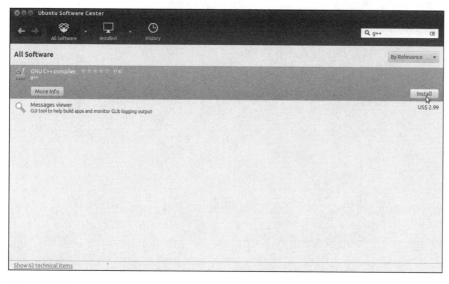

Figure 1.33
Installing GNU C++ Compiler.
Source: Ubuntu Software Center, © Canonical Ltd.

Once GNU C++ Compiler is installed, search for Eclipse and click on Install (see Figure 1.34).

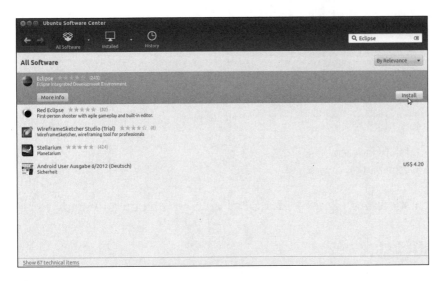

Figure 1.34
Installing Eclipse.
Source: Ubuntu Software Center, © Canonical Ltd.

Next, search for `eclipse-cdt` and install the C/C++ Development Tools for Eclipse (see Figure 1.35).

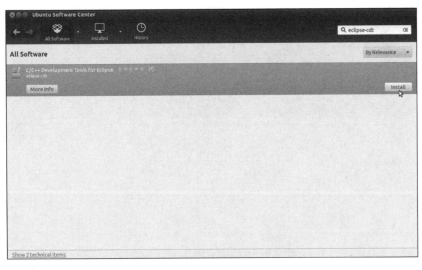

Figure 1.35
Installing the C/C++ development tools.
Source: Ubuntu Software Center, © Canonical Ltd.

With this, Eclipse should be ready.

Step 3: Creating a Project

Open up Eclipse. If you're greeted with a screen prompting you to select a workspace, just click OK to use the default one. Next, click on File → New → Project. You should see something resembling Figure 1.36. Click on C/C++ → C++ Project and press Next.

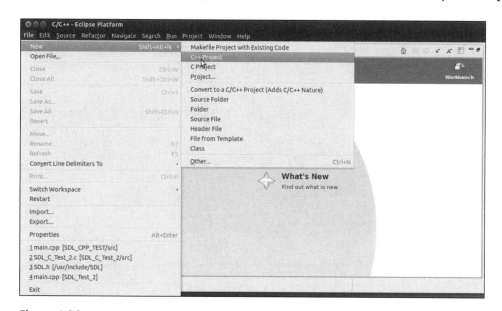

Figure 1.36
Creating a C++ project.

Source: Eclipse, © The Eclipse Foundation.

In the next window, select Empty Project under Project Type and enter **Test** as the project name. Make sure that under Toolchains, Linux GCC is selected. Click on Finish (see Figure 1.37).

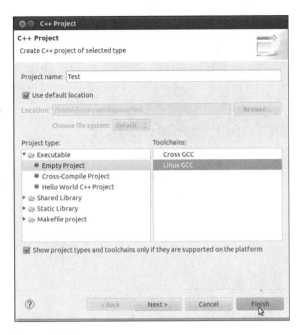

Figure 1.37
Naming a project.
Source: Eclipse, © The Eclipse Foundation.

Now, click on Project → Properties from the top menu bar. In the left panel of the properties window, navigate to C/C++ Build → Settings. Select the Tool Settings tab and in the GCC C++ Linker section, select Libraries. In the small panel to the right, click on the Add button (see Figure 1.38).

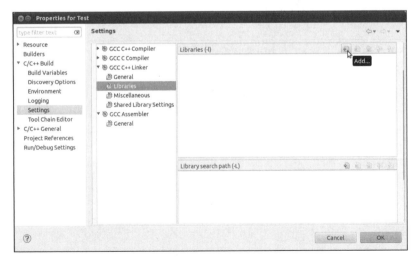

Figure 1.38
Adding the library dependencies.
Source: Eclipse, © The Eclipse Foundation.

In the textbox, type **SDL** without spaces before or after. Then, click OK (see Figure 1.39).

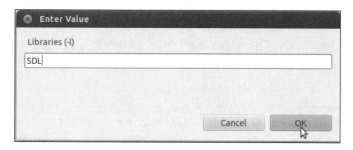

Figure 1.39
Adding SDL to the list of libraries.
Source: Eclipse, © The Eclipse Foundation.

After adding SDL, you may also add SDL_image, SDL_mixer, and SDL_ttf. These are not necessary for this example, but they will be necessary when programming games that make use of those libraries. Figure 1.40 displays what the Libraries panel should look like after adding all the necessary libraries.

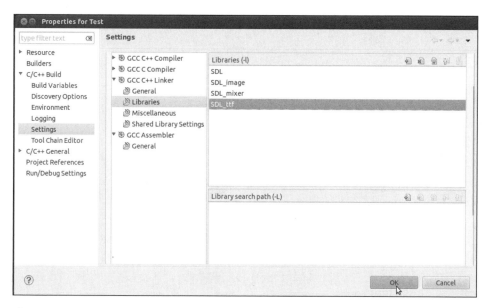

Figure 1.40
SDL in the library list.
Source: Eclipse, © The Eclipse Foundation.

Eclipse is now configured for use with SDL. It is important to note that you must do this step every time you create a new project.

Step 4: Testing

Click on File → New → Source File and a new window will be displayed. In the Source File section, type **main.cpp**, as shown in Listing 1.2, and click Finish (as shown in Figure 1.41). Remember that the `.cpp` extension must be typed in manually. Failing to type `.cpp` can result in compilation errors.

Tip

This adds a `.cpp` source file. To add a header file, simply type `.h` instead of `.cpp` in the Source File box.

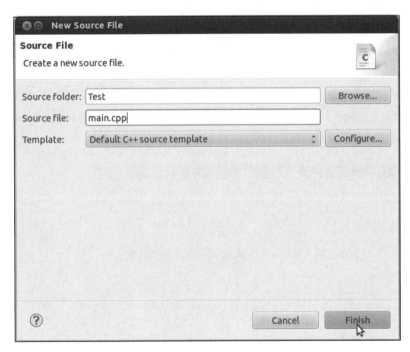

Figure 1.41
Creating a source file named `main.cpp`.
Source: Eclipse, © The Eclipse Foundation.

Listing 1.2: A Test Application for Linux

```
#include <SDL/SDL.h>

int main(int arc, char* args[])
{
    SDL_Init( SDL_INIT_EVERYTHING );
    printf("Linux FTW!!!");
    SDL_Quit();

    return 0;
}
```

Tip

You don't have to type the code in Listing 1.2 by hand. You can get the `main.cpp` file from `BAMGP\`. It is located under the directory `Source\Chapter_01\1_1_Test\`. Copy the file into your project's directory and you're all set to build the project and run it.

Save the file and click on Project → Build Project. Then click on Run → Run. The program should compile and print out `Linux FTW!!!` in the Console tab of the bottom panel (see Figure 1.42).

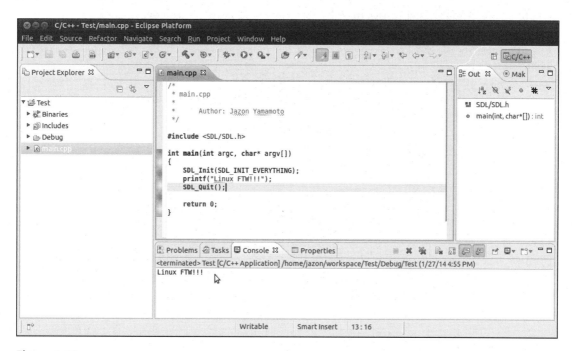

Figure 1.42
The code and a successful compilation.
Source: Eclipse, © The Eclipse Foundation.

Tip

You can also run the program by entering the `debug` folder in the project's directory and opening the file with the same name as the project. This file doesn't have an extension because they are not necessary for executable files in Linux. Since this is a console application, it won't do anything unless you open it with the terminal.

If you didn't get this far, go back and make sure that all the steps were performed correctly. When it comes to setting up compilers, there are thousands of things that can go wrong.

Summary

 At this point, you should have a workstation set up and should also be able to compile SDL projects. If you couldn't get the SDL to compile, go back and try again. Compilers are quite picky, and one wrong setting can be the difference between a successful build and a few hours trying to get the compiler to work. Just make sure you did everything right. Keep in mind that when using SDL, the source code of programs written for Windows should also compile on Linux without modification. Also remember to watch the video tutorial for this chapter, which is located in BAMGP\ under the Videos directory. Enough with the boring setup; let's make some video games!

CHAPTER 2

ENTERING THE DIGITAL DOMAIN

Now that your environment is ready for coding, you are ready to embark on the adventure of creating video games with SDL! There are many things that must be learned, but they will be learned along the way. To create a video game, first you need a window to run the game on. Creating this window is actually pretty simple, but there are a few things that should be covered before plunging deeper into game creation. In this chapter, expect to learn:

- How to create a window.
- How to start SDL in fullscreen mode.
- How draw an image on the screen.
- How to make a game loop.

Tip

Before getting started, you can check out the video tutorial for this chapter, which is located in BAMGP\ under the Videos directory. The video contains extra material and insights, and reviews the chapter from a high level, so be sure to watch it.

THE ANATOMY OF A WINDOW

In terms of computing, a window is typically a rectangular portion of the screen used to display graphical elements to the user. Windows can range in sizes, and it is up to the programmer to determine a window's purpose. For the purpose of this book, windows will be used to provide a surface to display game graphics on. A basic window can be composed of the following elements: a title bar, borders, and a client area. The title bar typically rests at the top of a window and displays the title of the window. Some windows with title bars also have buttons used for closing, minimizing, and maximizing the window. The borders of a window are at the very edges, and they can sometimes be used to resize the window. Other than that, the borders are mainly there to make it easy to differentiate between stacked windows. The client area is the area on a window used for drawing. This is the area you'll be most concerned with since it is the area most commonly used for displaying games. Figure 2.1 demonstrates a diagram of a window.

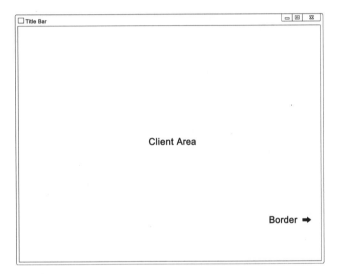

Figure 2.1
A diagram of a basic window.
© Jazon Yamamoto.

Tip

Windows may look very different across different OSs. Some of the platforms that SDL supports don't even use windows and run only in fullscreen mode!

CREATING A WINDOW

To create a window, go ahead and make a new project. After that, add a file called main.cpp and enter the code in Listing 2.1.

Listing 2.1: A Blank Window

```
#include <SDL/SDL.h>

int main(int argc, char* args[])
{
    if(SDL_Init( SDL_INIT_EVERYTHING) < 0)
    {
        printf("SDL failed to initialize!");
        SDL_Quit();
        return 0;
    }

    SDL_SetVideoMode(800, 600, 32, SDL_SWSURFACE);
    SDL_WM_SetCaption("SDL!!!", NULL);
    SDL_Delay(3000);
    SDL_Quit();

    return 1;
}
```

Building the App

You can find the files necessary to build this app in BAMGP\. They are located in Source\Chapter_02\ 2_1_Window\. You need to create an SDL project and copy main.cpp into to your project's directory. If you're using Windows, make sure to include the .dll files in the project's directory. Also make sure your project is configured properly, as shown in Chapter 1, and that all the files were properly included. When all is set, you'll be able to build the program and run it on your own. Additionally, a precompiled version is in the Source directory named 2_1_Window.exe.

This program creates a window that has SDL!!! as a title and a client area that is 800 pixels by 600 pixels in size. For now, you can think of a pixel as a unit for measuring a window's size, but they will be covered in deeper detail in Chapter 3. See Figure 2.2 for a screenshot of the program and refer to Table 2.1 for a brief description of all the SDL functions used in this program.

Figure 2.2
A screenshot of the demo.
© Jazon Yamamoto.

Table 2.1   SDL Functions Used in This Demo

SDL Function	Description
`int SDL_Init(Uint32 flags);`	This function initializes SDL, and it must be called before calling any other SDL functions. It only takes one argument. You're only going to use `SDL_INIT_EVERYTHING` because it initializes every aspect of SDL you are going to be working with. Bear in mind that there are other arguments that you can use, such as `SDL_INIT_VIDEO`, which only initializes the video subsystem, and `SDL_INIT_AUDIO`, which only initializes the audio subsystem. This program returns 0 if it succeeded and −1 otherwise.

`SDL_Surface* SDL_SetVideoMode(`
`    int width,`
`    int height,`
`    int bitsperpixel,`
`    Uint32 flags);`
	This function is responsible for creating the window. The arguments `width` and `height` designate the width and height of the window in pixels. The argument `bitsperpixel` defines the bits per pixel. The *bits per pixel* (or bpp) defines the color resolution of every pixel on the screen.

	More bpp gives you more colors to work with, but 32 bpp is more than enough for most applications. The argument `flags` defines the video mode. You use `SDL_SWSURFACE` because it is the easiest to use and the most stable. Using `SDL_SWSURFACE` creates a surface in system memory. You will learn more about surfaces later on in this chapter. Using `SDL_HWSURFACE` creates a surface in video memory that may be faster but less stable. This program returns a pointer to the surface created.

`void SDL_WM_SetCaption(`
`  const char *title,`
`  const char *icon);`
	This function is simple, and it takes only two arguments. The first argument takes a string and sets it as the title of the window. The second argument also takes a string, which will act as the title for the window when it is minimized. For the sake of simplicity, you can just set it to `NULL`.

`void SDL_Delay(Uint32 ms);`	This function is used to pause the program, and it takes only one argument. This argument is an integer, and it determines how long the program will be paused in milliseconds.
`void SDL_Quit();`	This function is responsible for gracefully releasing all the resources acquired by SDL. It must always be called before exiting the program. This is most often the last SDL function called in every SDL program.

© Jazon Yamamoto.

GOING FULLSCREEN

An alternative to using a window as a means of displaying graphics is using the entire screen. This is the standard for most video games, and it makes for a more immersive gaming experience. Going fullscreen is actually very easy to do. To go fullscreen, just replace the following code:

```
SDL_SetVideoMode(800, 600, 32, SDL_SWSURFACE);
```

in the previous demo with:

```
SDL_SetVideoMode(800, 600, 32, SDL_FULLSCREEN | SDL_SWSURFACE);
```

Doing so will render the application in fullscreen mode. This program will make the entire screen black for three seconds. Providing a screenshot of it is unnecessary since it would just look like a black rectangle.

DRAWING AN IMAGE

Okay, this demo should be a bit more interesting. Instead of seeing a plain black screen, this time there will be a screen with an image on it. To work with images, they must first be loaded into memory and, after the program is done using them, released from memory. Images are stored in so-called *surfaces*. In SDL, surfaces are rectangular grids of pixels. These grids and the pixels they hold create two-dimensional images. Surfaces have many uses, but you'll use them for two main purposes. One is to hold images you load, meaning you can use them in games for things such as sprites and backgrounds. The other is to hold the backbuffer. A *backbuffer* is a surface on which you draw images and other graphical elements that you want to display on the screen. You can think of a backbuffer as a canvas on which to draw images. You must also "flip" the backbuffer to draw its content to the screen.

Tip

It's possible to draw directly to the screen, but that causes flickering. It's better to draw to the backbuffer and then draw the entire backbuffer to the screen.

SDL Surfaces

SDL stores surfaces in the SDL_Surface structure. For simple image operations, you do not need to look deep into this structure. Listing 2.2 demonstrates the code for the next demo. You might notice that you'll use pointers to SDL_Surface as opposed to the actual surface itself. This is because SDL takes care of all the surface-related operations, and you just need pointers to tell SDL what to do with these surfaces.

Listing 2.2: Displaying an Image

```
#include <SDL/SDL.h>

SDL_Surface* image = NULL;
SDL_Surface* backbuffer = NULL;

int main(int argc, char* args[])
{
    //Init SDL
    if(SDL_Init(SDL_INIT_EVERYTHING) < 0)
    {
        printf("SDL failed to initialize!");
        SDL_Quit();
        return 0;
    }
```

```
backbuffer = SDL_SetVideoMode(800, 600, 32, SDL_SWSURFACE);
SDL_WM_SetCaption("SDL!!!", NULL);

//Load the image
image = SDL_LoadBMP("graphics/image.bmp");

if(image == NULL)
{
    printf("Image failed to load!\n");
    SDL_Quit();
    return 0;
}

//Draw the image
SDL_BlitSurface(image, NULL, backbuffer, NULL);
SDL_Flip(backbuffer);

//Wait
SDL_Delay(3000);

//Finish
SDL_FreeSurface(image);
SDL_Quit();

return 1;
}
```

Building the App

You can find the files necessary to build this app in `BAMGP\`. They are located in `Source\Chapter_02\ 2_2_image\`. You need to create an SDL project and copy `main.cpp` and the `graphics` folder into your project's directory. If you're using Windows, make sure to include the `.dll` files in the project's directory. Also make sure your project is configured properly, as shown in Chapter 1, and that all the files were properly included. When all is set, you'll be able to build the program and run it on your own. Additionally, a precompiled version is in the `Source` directory named `2_2_Image.exe`.

This demo creates a window with an image on it. Refer to Figure 2.3 for a screenshot of the program. First, you create pointers to surfaces that will hold the image and the backbuffer. After initializing SDL, you create your window using `SDL_SetVideoMode`. This function returns a pointer to the backbuffer. After that, you load the image using `SDL_LoadBMP` and draw it onto the backbuffer using `SDL_BlitSurface`. You then use `SDL_Flip` to draw the backbuffer onto the screen. You use `SDL_Delay` to pause the program for three seconds so that you can see the screen before it closes. After the pause, `SDL_FreeSurface` is used to release the image data acquired by the program. This must be done for every image that was loaded. At the end, `SDL_Quit` is called to kill SDL. Refer to Table 2.2 for a brief description of all the functions used in this program.

Figure 2.3
A screenshot of the image demo.
© Jazon Yamamoto.

Table 2.2 SDL Functions Used in This Demo

SDL Function	Description
SDL_Surface *SDL_LoadBMP(const char *file);	This function takes only one argument, and it is a string. It will load an image with the same name as the string provided. Note that the location of the image is relative to the location of the program, and it only loads BMP image formats. This function returns a pointer to the surface in which the image was stored and NULL if the function failed.
int SDL_BlitSurface(SDL_Surface *src, SDL_Rect *srcrect, SDL_Surface *dst, SDL_Rect *dstrect);	This function takes four arguments and copies the contents of one surface onto the other. The first argument is a pointer to the source surface. The second argument defines the area of the source surface that will be copied. Setting this argument to NULL selects the entire surface. The third argument is a pointer to the destination surface. The selected contents of the source surface will be copied into the

	destination surface. The final argument defines the destination of the data that will be copied. Setting it to NULL copies the entire surface. If successful, this function will return 0 and −1 otherwise.
`int SDL_Flip(SDL_Surface* screen);`	This function takes one parameter, which is a pointer to a surface. This surface is drawn on the screen. It returns 0 upon success and −1 upon failure.

CREATING THE GAME LOOP

So far, all of the example programs close after three seconds, and the user has no influence on their behavior. A game loop is a system that allows the game to run with or without user input. There is a game loop at the heart of every single real-time video game. Listing 2.3 is a pseudo-code example of a game loop.

Listing 2.3: A Sample Game Loop in Pseudo-Code

```
While(Game Still Running)
    Update Artificial Intelligence
    Update Physics
    Update and Process Input
    Move the Player and all the other objects in the game
    Draw all the graphics on the screen
    Regulate frame rate
End While
```

A game loop will be at the core of all the games that you'll create in this book. A game loop will enable the program to keep running with or without user input, and it will give the user the ability to exit the program at any given point. The demos presented so far only run for a predetermined amount of time, and trying to close them by clicking on the X icon at the corner of the window does not work. To create a solid game loop, let's learn a little bit more about the SDL Event subsystem.

THE SDL EVENT SUBSYSTEM

The SDL Event subsystem handles "events" that occur during the execution of a program. Some events that it tracks are mouse movements and keyboard buttons being pressed. For now, the only event you are concerned with is the SDL_QUIT event.

Whenever an event occurs, SDL stores information regarding this event in a queue. You use SDL_PollEvent to look through the records of events that have occurred so far. SDL_PollEvent returns descriptions of these events, one at a time, in the form of an SDL_Event structure. After returning the description of the event, it's removed from the queue. Not all events received have to be processed, only the necessary ones do. For now, your programs are only going to process the SDL_QUIT event, which is triggered when the user clicks on the X button at the corner of the window. The Event subsystem is covered with greater detail in later chapters.

Tip

Note that SDL_QUIT refers to the event, and SDL_Quit refers to the function that closes SDL in programs. Do *not* get them mixed up.

MOVING ON TO THE DEMO...

The following program will demonstrate a simple game loop. Note that this program will close only if the user presses the X button, and it should *not* be run in fullscreen since the X button is inaccessible in fullscreen mode! All the event-related business was wrapped into a function called ProgramIsRunning. This makes the code easier to understand and much more convenient to work with. Listing 2.4 demonstrates a simple game loop.

Listing 2.4: A Basic Game Loop

```
#include <SDL/SDL.h>

SDL_Surface* background = NULL;
SDL_Surface* sprite = NULL;
SDL_Surface* backbuffer = NULL;

bool ProgramIsRunning();
bool LoadImages();
void FreeImages();

int main(int argc, char* args[])
{
    if(SDL_Init(SDL_INIT_EVERYTHING) < 0)
    {
        printf("SDL failed to initialize!\n");
        SDL_Quit();
        return 0;
    }
```

```
    backbuffer = SDL_SetVideoMode(800, 600, 32, SDL_SWSURFACE);
    SDL_WM_SetCaption("SDL!!!", NULL);

    if(!LoadImages())
    {
        printf("Images failed to load!\n");
        FreeImages();
        SDL_Quit();

        return 0;
    }

    SDL_BlitSurface(background, NULL, backbuffer, NULL );

    while(ProgramIsRunning())
    {
        SDL_Rect spritePos;
        spritePos.x = rand()%800;
        spritePos.y = rand()%600;

        SDL_BlitSurface(sprite, NULL, backbuffer, &spritePos);

        SDL_Flip(backbuffer);

        SDL_Delay(100);
    }

    SDL_Quit();

    return 1;
}

bool ProgramIsRunning()
{
    SDL_Event event;

    bool running = true;

    while(SDL_PollEvent(&event))
    {
        if(event.type == SDL_QUIT)
            running = false;
    }

    return running;
}

bool LoadImages()
{
    background = SDL_LoadBMP("graphics/background.bmp");

    if(background == NULL)
        return false;
```

```
    sprite = SDL_LoadBMP("graphics/sprite.bmp");

    if(sprite == NULL)
        return false;

    return true;
}
void FreeImages()
{
    if(background != NULL)
    {
        SDL_FreeSurface(background);
        background = NULL;
    }

    if(sprite != NULL)
    {
        SDL_FreeSurface(sprite);
        sprite = NULL;
    }
}
```

Building the App

You can find the files necessary to build this app in BAMGP\. They are located in Source\Chapter_02\ 2_3_GameLoop\. You need to create an SDL project and copy main.cpp and the graphics directory into your project's directory. If you're using Windows, make sure to include the .dll files in the project's directory. Also make sure your project is configured properly, as shown in Chapter 1, and that all the files were properly included. When all is set, you'll be able to build the program and run it on your own. Additionally, there is a precompiled version in the Source directory named 2_3_GameLoop.exe.

This program loads two images. One is the background, and the other is a sprite. A *sprite* is a two-dimensional graphical element that is integrated into a scene on a computer display. In this program, a sprite is repeatedly drawn on top of a static background at a random location. Note that the screen is never cleared, and the sprites drawn in previous cycles of the game loop remain on the screen. Table 2.3 shows the new functions used in this demo, and Figure 2.4 shows the demo in action.

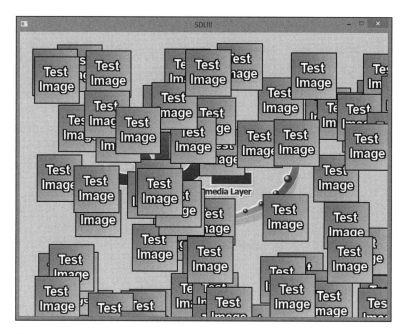

Figure 2.4
A screenshot of the game loop demo.
© Jazon Yamamoto.

Table 2.3   New Functions Used in This Demo

Function	Description
`bool ProgramIsRunning();`	This is the function you created to make the code cleaner. It returns `false` if the user clicked on the X button.
`bool LoadImages();`	This function loads the images used in this program. It will return `true` if it succeeds and `false` if it fails.
`void FreeImages();`	This function frees the images that were loaded.
`int SDL_PollEvent( SDL_Event *event);`	This function is used to obtain the event information about the next event stored in the queue. It takes one argument, which is a pointer to an `SDL_Event` structure. The description of the event is stored in the instance of `SDL_Event` to which the pointer points. This function returns `1` if there are any events pending and `0` if all events were cleared.

© Jazon Yamamoto.

Summary

This chapter covered window creation and basic image drawing. Additionally, game loops were introduced and explained with sufficient detail to make a multitude of different video games. If you haven't done so already, check out the video tutorial for this chapter for a quick recap. You can find it in BAMGP\ under the Videos directory. Before continuing, try completing some of the following exercises to test your mastery of the subject.

Exercises

- Try changing the title of the windows you created to your name.

- Try loading your own images and drawing them on the screen. Remember that the images must be in BMP format.

- Lastly, try loading and drawing multiple sprites on the screen.

CHAPTER 3

TAPPING INTO THE WORLD OF GRAPHICS

Graphics are essential to video games since video games are pretty much impossible to make without them. The previous chapter covered how to draw simple images on the screen. While this may be sufficient to create simple games, it is not enough to create a game that is visually astounding. In this chapter, you'll take a closer look at graphics and learn new tricks that can be used when dealing with them. This chapter covers:

- How to draw individual pixels.
- How to draw primitive graphics.
- How to incorporate simple transparency in images.
- How to animate an image.
- How to draw raster fonts.
- How to draw outline fonts.

Tip

Before getting started, you can check out the video tutorial for this chapter, located in BAMGP\ under the Videos directory. The video contains extra material and insights, and reviews the chapter from a high level, so be sure to watch it.

THE BASICS OF COMPUTER GRAPHICS

Images on a computer screen can be thought of as a grid of squares, each holding an individual color. When these squares become small enough in size and large enough in

47

quantity, they create the illusion of a smooth image. This is why zooming into images on computers makes them look "pixelated." Figure 3.1 demonstrates a computer image represented as a grid of squares. Every square in this grid is known as a pixel. A *pixel* (picture element) is the smallest manipulable graphical unit when it comes to computer graphics. Pixels can be seen as the building blocks for two-dimensional digital imagery because every complicated image on a computer screen is composed of a multitude of pixels strung together. A computer screen itself can be thought of as a canvas on which programmers can plot pixels. Before actually working with computer graphics, let's take a look at the coordinate system and data structures that SDL uses for working with graphics.

Figure 3.1
A computer image as a grid of squares.
© Jazon Yamamoto. Source: 3DRT.com.

Understanding the Coordinate System

When drawing pixels on a computer screen, the programmer has to specify the color of every individual pixel as well as the corresponding position of each pixel. Specifying the color of the pixel will be covered later on in this chapter. The position of a pixel can be represented by a two-dimensional point. This point is defined by two values commonly known as the X and the Y coordinates. The X coordinate represents the point's horizontal position, and the Y coordinate represents the point's vertical position. This system of plotting points is known as the *Cartesian coordinate system*. In this system, X ascends from left to right, and Y ascends from down to up. The line at which Y is equal to zero is known as the *x-axis*, and the line at which X is equal to zero is known as the *y-axis*. The point in which X and Y are both equal to zero is known as the *origin*. Figure 3.2 depicts the Cartesian coordinate system.

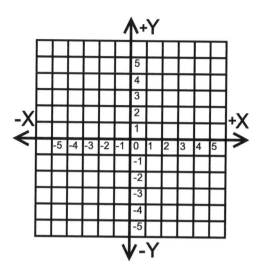

Figure 3.2
The Cartesian coordinate system.
© Jazon Yamamoto.

In the field of computer graphics, the y-axis is usually flipped such that Y ascends in the downward direction, and the x-axis remains unchanged. The origin of the graph is placed at the top-left corner of the window's client area (or computer screen when in fullscreen mode). Figure 3.3 displays a diagram of a window and its coordinate system.

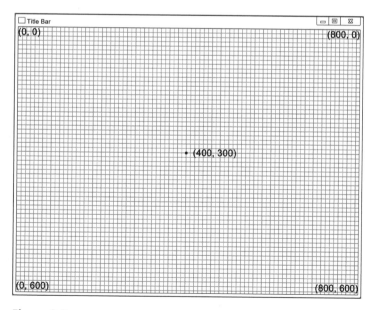

Figure 3.3
The computer's coordinate system.
© Jazon Yamamoto.

SDL Surfaces

Surfaces in SDL are used to store and manipulate arrays of pixels. This effectively provides you with the means to work with graphics at a low level. They are stored in the SDL_Surface structure, which is defined in the SDL.h header file. SDL surfaces are composed of pixels arranged in an axis-aligned rectangle. An *axis-aligned rectangle* is a rectangle with its sides aligned parallel to the x-axis and y-axis of the screen. Figure 3.4 demonstrates the difference between an axis-aligned rectangle and a non-axis-aligned rectangle. These surfaces are important because they can be used to hold graphical data, such as images, that will eventually be drawn to the screen. The backbuffer itself is stored in a surface and can be treated as such. SDL provides many functions to manipulate surfaces. These functions give programmers the ability to manipulate images with relative ease.

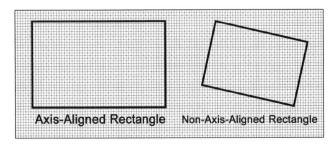

Figure 3.4
An axis-aligned rectangle and a non-axis-aligned rectangle.
© Jazon Yamamoto.

Setting Individual Pixels

Being able to set individual pixels in a surface ultimately gives you complete control over the images stored in it. With this control, you can draw on a surface every image that can possibly be displayed on a computer screen. To plot a pixel onto a surface, you must directly access the surface's memory and modify the desired pixel data.

Preparing to Access a Surface

To access the data on a surface, you might have to "lock" it first. Locking surfaces gives you access to modify them, but not all surfaces must be locked. To check if a surface must be locked, call SDL_MUSTLOCK and pass a pointer to the surface. If this returns true, you call SDL_LockSurface and pass a pointer to the surface to lock it. After locking the surface, you can modify its contents. If the surface was locked before any modifications, you must unlock it. You do so by calling SDL_UnlockSurface and passing a pointer to the surface. Note that this can be done for any surface, including surfaces holding images that were loaded.

Modifying a Surface

Since only individual pixels will be set, only the location and color of the pixel are necessary. Color values in SDL are stored in RGB format. The *RGB* format is a format for storing colors using three numerical values that represent the red, green, and blue intensities of the color. Every color in SDL can be represented by these values, and each of them ranges from 0 to 255. There are over 16 million possible combinations of colors possible with these values. Color information in SDL is stored in Uint32 variables. These variables are 32-bit unsigned ints. You use SDL_MapRGB and pass in a pointer to the surface you are going to modify and three values for the desired color in RGB format. This function will return the desired format in Uint32 format. The following line of code demonstrates the creation of a Uint32 color value:

```
Uint32 color = SDL_MapRGB(surface->format, red, green, blue);
```

To set the pixel in the desired location, first create a pointer of type Uint32 and assign it to the individual pixel you wish to modify. Next, assign the color value to the pixel. It is done by accessing the data in the pixels property of the surface. This is a complicated process, but all the main points were covered.

Table 3.1 displays a description of the new functions used in this program, and Listing 3.1 demonstrates the source code for a pixel-plotting program.

Listing 3.1: The Pixel Plotting Demo

```
#include <SDL/SDL.h>
#include <cstdlib>

SDL_Surface* Backbuffer = NULL;

bool ProgramIsRunning();
void DrawPixel(SDL_Surface *surface,           //Target Surface
    int x, int y,                    //Position
    Uint8 r, Uint8 g, Uint8 b);    //Color

int main(int argc, char* args[])
{
    if(SDL_Init(SDL_INIT_EVERYTHING) < 0)
    {
        printf("Failed to initialize SDL!\n");
        return 0;
    }
```

```
    Backbuffer = SDL_SetVideoMode(800, 600, 32, SDL_SWSURFACE);

    SDL_WM_SetCaption("Pixel Plot", NULL);

    while(ProgramIsRunning())
    {

        for(int i = 0; i < 100; i++)
        {
            DrawPixel(Backbuffer,
                rand()%800, rand()%600,                 //Random Location
                rand()%255, rand()%255, rand()%255);//Random Color
        }

        SDL_Delay(20);
        SDL_Flip(Backbuffer);
    }

    SDL_Quit();

    return 0;
}
bool ProgramIsRunning()
{

    SDL_Event event;
    bool running = true;

    while(SDL_PollEvent(&event))
    {
        if(event.type == SDL_QUIT)
            running = false;
    }

    return running;
}

void DrawPixel(SDL_Surface *surface, int x, int y, Uint8 r, Uint8 g, Uint8 b)
{
    if(SDL_MUSTLOCK(surface))
    {
        if(SDL_LockSurface(surface) < 0)
            return;
    }
    if(x >= surface->w || x < 0 || y >= surface->h || y < 0)
        return;

    Uint32 *buffer;
    Uint32 color;

    color = SDL_MapRGB(surface->format, r, g, b);
```

```
buffer = (Uint32*)surface->pixels + y*surface->pitch/4 + x;
(*buffer) = color;

if(SDL_MUSTLOCK(surface))
    SDL_UnlockSurface(surface);
}
```

Building the App

You can find the files necessary to build this app in BAMGP\. They are located in Source\Chapter_03\ 3_1_PixelPlot\. You need to create an SDL project and copy main.cpp into your project's directory. If you're using Windows, make sure to include the .dll files in the project's directory. Also make sure your project is configured properly, as shown in Chapter 1, and that all the files were properly included. When all is set, you'll be able to build the program and run it on your own. Additionally, a precompiled version is in the Source directory named 3_1_PixelPlot.exe.

Table 3.1   New Functions Used in This Demo

Function	Description
SDL_bool SDL_MUSTLOCK(SDL_Surface* surface)	This function takes one argument, and it is the pointer to a surface. If this function returns true, the surface must be locked before it can be modified.
int SDL_LockSurface(SDL_Surface *surface)	This function takes one argument, and it is the pointer to a surface. This function locks the desired surface. Note that surfaces must be unlocked after being locked.
void SDL_UnlockSurface(SDL_Surface *surface)	This function takes one argument, and it is the pointer to a surface. This function unlocks the desired surface.
int rand()	This function takes no arguments, and it returns a pseudo-random number that can range from 0 to at least 32767. You use the % operator to give a number from a desired range (e.g. rand() % 100 will return a number ranging from 0 to 100, and rand() % 256 will return a number ranging from 0 to 255). This function is part of cstdlib, and it must be included in the file.
Uint32 SDL_MapRGB(SDL_PixelFormat *fmt, Uint8 r, Uint8 g, Uint8 b);	This function takes four arguments. The first is the desired pixel format. The latter three are the RGB values of the desired color. This function returns pixel information in the form of a Uint32 with the desired pixel format and color.

(Continued)

Table 3.1   New Functions Used in This Demo (*Continued*)

Function	Description
| ```
void DrawPixel(
  SDL_Surface *surface,
  int x,
  int y,
  Uint8 r,
  Uint8 g,
  Uint8 b)
``` | This is the function that was created to draw pixels, and it takes six arguments. The first is a pointer to the surface. The second and third are the X and Y values of the pixel, and the last three arguments are the RGB values. This function makes it possible to plot a single pixel in a single line of code. This function can be used to draw directly to the screen. |

© Jazon Yamamoto.

This program plots pixels in pseudo-random positions and pseudo-random colors in the window. Note that much of the program structure is the same as the structure used in the game loop demo. Also notice that the ProgramIsRunning function that was created in the previous demo was reused. Figure 3.5 displays the demo after running for a few seconds.

Figure 3.5
The pixel demo.
© Jazon Yamamoto.
```

DRAWING SIMPLE AXIS-ALIGNED RECTANGLES

Drawing axis-aligned rectangles is very easy to accomplish by writing a loop that draws several horizontal lines of pixels. Even though this approach is viable, the designers of SDL provided a function, SDL_FillRect, that is highly optimized to draw rectangles. The two types of rectangles you should be concerned with are solid and hollow rectangles.

Drawing Solid Rectangles

Drawing solid rectangles is pretty straightforward. To do so, call SDL_FillRect and specify a surface, an area of the surface, and the color of the rectangle. Listing 3.2 shows a wrapper function for SDL_FillRect.

Listing 3.2: The FillRect Function

```
void FillRect(SDL_Surface* surface, int x, int y,
    int width, int height,
    Uint8 r, Uint8 g, Uint8 b)
{
    Uint32 color;

    color = SDL_MapRGB(surface->format, r, g, b );

    SDL_Rect rect;
    rect.x = x;
    rect.y = y;
    rect.w = width;
    rect.h = height;

    SDL_FillRect(surface, &rect, color);
}
```

This code uses SDL_Rect, which is a data structure that stores the information of an axis-aligned rectangle. It has four fields. The x and y fields hold the X and Y coordinates of the rectangle, and the w and h fields hold the width and height of the rectangle, respectively.

Drawing Hollow Rectangles

There isn't a native SDL function to draw a hollow rectangle, but this can be accomplished by drawing four lines: two vertical and two horizontal. These four lines connect to form the edges of the rectangle. Listing 3.3 is shows the hollow-rectangle-drawing algorithm.

Listing 3.3: The DrawRect Function

```
void DrawRect(SDL_Surface* surface, int x, int y,
    int width, int height,
    Uint8 r, Uint8 g, Uint8 b)
{
    FillRect(surface, x, y, width, 1, r, g, b);
    FillRect(surface, x, y+height-1, width, 1, r, g, b);
    FillRect(surface, x, y, 1, height, r, g, b);
    FillRect(surface, x+width-1, y, 1, height, r, g, b);
}
```

On to the Demo

With the two new functions at hand, you can draw a world of rectangles! Listing 3.4 demonstrates a game loop much like the one in the previous demo, but drawing rectangles instead.

Listing 3.4: The Rectangle Drawing Demo

```
while(ProgramIsRunning())
{
    DrawRect(Backbuffer,
        rand()%800, rand()%600,              //Random Position
        rand()%200, rand()%200,              //Random Size
        rand()%255, rand()%255, rand()%255); //Random Color

    FillRect(Backbuffer,
        rand()%800, rand()%600,              //Random Position
        rand()%200, rand()%200,              //Random Size
        rand()%255, rand()%255, rand()%255); //Random Color

    SDL_Delay(20);
    SDL_Flip(Backbuffer);
}
```

Building the App

You can find the files necessary to build this app in BAMGP\. They are located in Source\Chapter_03\ 3_2_Rectangles\. You need to create an SDL project and copy main.cpp into your project's directory. If you're using Windows, make sure to include the .dll files in the project's directory. Also make sure your project is configured properly, as shown in Chapter 1, and that all the files were properly included. When all is set, you'll be able to build the program and run it on your own. Additionally, a precompiled version is in the Source directory named 3_2_Rectangles.exe.

This program draws solid and hollow rectangles on the screen at random positions and with random colors. Refer to Table 3.2 for a description of the functions used in this demo, and Figure 3.6 for a screenshot of the demo.

Table 3.2   New Functions Used in This Demo

Function	Description

int SDL_FillRect(
  SDL_Surface *dst,
  SDL_Rect *dstrect,
  Uint32 color)
	This function takes three parameters and draws a filled rectangle on a surface. The first parameter is a pointer to the surface. The second parameter is a pointer to a variable of type SDL_Rect, and it describes the size and position of the rectangle. The last parameter is of type Uint32, and it specifies the color of the rectangle.

void DrawRect(
  SDL_Surface* surface,
  int x,
  int y,
  int width,
  int height,
  Uint8 r,
  Uint8 g,
  Uint8 b)
	This function takes six arguments and draws a hollow rectangle on a surface. The first is a pointer to the surface in which you want to draw your rectangle. The second and third are the X and Y values of the location where you want to draw your rectangle. The last three represent the color of the rectangle in RGB format.

void FillRect(
  SDL_Surface* surface,
  int x,
  int y,
  int width,
  int height, .
  Uint8 r,
  Uint8 g,
  Uint8 b)
	This function takes six arguments and draws a solid rectangle on a surface. The first is a pointer to the surface in which you want to draw your rectangle. The second and third are the X and Y values of the location where you want to draw your rectangle. The last three represent the color of the rectangle in RGB format.

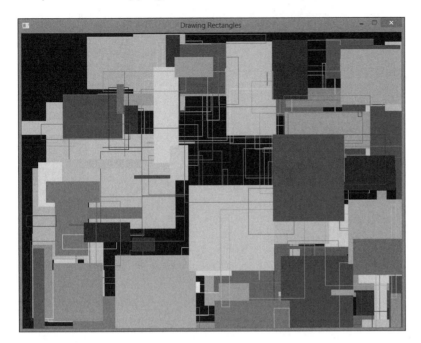

Figure 3.6
The rectangle demo.
© Jazon Yamamoto.

Drawing a Moving Sprite

Drawing single pixels and rectangles can get kind of boring after a while, but there are other techniques that can be used for rendering graphics. Drawing sprites that move smoothly is a huge leap forward to making a more interesting game. Remember that a sprite is a graphical element on the screen that is usually loaded from an image file. To draw a moving sprite, simply change the X or Y value of the sprite every frame and clear the screen before drawing it to erase the sprite's previous position. This creates the illusion of motion. Listing 3.5 demonstrates the heart of a program that draws a background with a moving sprite on top of it.

Listing 3.5: The Moving Sprite Demo

```
#include <SDL/SDL.h>

SDL_Surface* Background = NULL;
SDL_Surface* SpriteImage = NULL;
SDL_Surface* Backbuffer = NULL;

SDL_Rect SpritePos;
```

```
bool LoadFiles();
void FreeFiles();
bool ProgramIsRunning();

int main(int argc, char* args[])
{
    if(SDL_Init(SDL_INIT_EVERYTHING) < 0)
    {
        printf("Failed to initialize SDL!\n");
        return 0;
    }

    Backbuffer = SDL_SetVideoMode(800, 600, 32, SDL_SWSURFACE);

    SDL_WM_SetCaption("Moving Image", NULL);

    if(!LoadFiles())
    {
        printf("Failed to load files!\n");
        FreeFiles();
        SDL_Quit();

        return 0;
    }

    SpritePos.x = 0;
    SpritePos.y = 250;

    while(ProgramIsRunning())
    {
        SpritePos.x+=5;

        if(SpritePos.x > 800)
            SpritePos.x = -200;

        SDL_BlitSurface(Background, NULL, Backbuffer, NULL);
        SDL_BlitSurface(SpriteImage, NULL, Backbuffer, &SpritePos);

        SDL_Delay(20);
        SDL_Flip(Backbuffer);
    }

    FreeFiles();

    SDL_Quit();

    return 0;
}
```

Building the App

You can find the files necessary to build this app in BAMGP\. They are located in Source\Chapter_03\ 3_3_MovingImage\. You need to create an SDL project and copy main.cpp and the graphics directory into your project's directory. If you're using Windows, make sure to include the .dll files in the project's directory. Also make sure your project is configured properly, as shown in Chapter 1, and that all the files were properly included. When all is set, you'll be able to build the program and run it on your own. Additionally, a precompiled version is in the Source directory named 3_3_MovingImage.exe.

Moving sprites are much more interesting than static ones. They help to bring life into the screen. There is one more step you must take to make them blend in more naturally with the scene. This is covered in the following section. Figure 3.7 shows a screenshot of the demo.

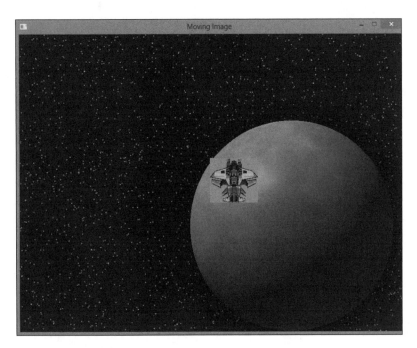

Figure 3.7
A screenshot of the moving image demo.
© Jazon Yamamoto. Source: 3DRT.com.

Alpha Masking

In the previous example, notice that the sprite was enclosed in a rectangle and didn't blend well into the scene. To get rid of that rectangle, an alpha mask must be applied. *Alpha masking* is a technique used in video game graphics that allows programmers to select a color (sometimes known as the *color key*) in an image that will not be drawn when the image is rendered on the screen. This is also known as *color keying*. Figure 3.8 displays an early look at the demo for this section.

Tip

This example uses the color (255, 0, 255) for the color key. This color is very common for alpha masking when it comes to video games.

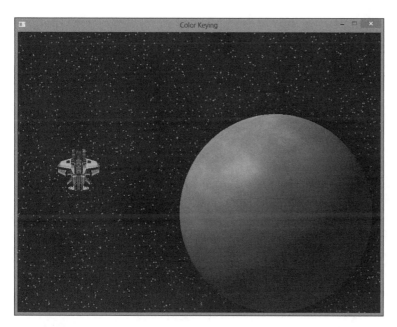

Figure 3.8
An alpha masked image running in the demo.
© Jazon Yamamoto. Source: 3DRT.com.

Alpha Masking Images

The `SDL_SetColorKey` function is used to apply an alpha mask. Since typing the code to mask every image that was loaded can be tedious, `SDL_LoadBMP` can be replaced with a wrapper image-loading function that will take care of all the dirty work. Listing 3.6 demonstrates the new and improved image-loading function.

Listing 3.6: The `LoadImage` Function with Color Keying

```
SDL_Surface* LoadImage(char* fileName)
{
    SDL_Surface* imageLoaded = NULL;
    SDL_Surface* processedImage = NULL;
```

```
    imageLoaded = SDL_LoadBMP(fileName);

    //Ensure the image was loaded correctly before proceeding
    if(imageLoaded != NULL)
    {
        processedImage = SDL_DisplayFormat(imageLoaded);
        SDL_FreeSurface(imageLoaded);

        //Ensure the image was processed correctly before proceeding
        if( processedImage != NULL )
        {
            Uint32 colorKey = SDL_MapRGB(processedImage->format,
                255, 0, 255 );
            SDL_SetColorKey(processedImage, SDL_SRCCOLORKEY, colorKey);
        }

    }

    //return the processed image
    return processedImage;
}
```

Building the App

You can find the files necessary to build this app in BAMGP\. They are located in Source\Chapter_03\ 3_4_ColorKey\. You need to create an SDL project and copy main.cpp and the graphics directory into your project's directory. If you're using Windows, make sure to include the .dll files in the project's directory. Also make sure your project is configured properly, as shown in Chapter 1, and that all the files were properly included. When all is set, you'll be able to build the program and run it on your own. Additionally, a precompiled version is in the Source directory named 3_4_ColorKey.exe.

To draw color-keyed images, simply substitute SDL_LoadBMP with this function and continue drawing the images as usual. This function actually does two things. First, it loads an image as usual, and then it converts the image to the program's display format (in terms of bpp) to optimize drawing.

Tip

The term *bpp* stands for bits per pixel. This value represents the number of bits that describe a pixel's color. The more bits there are, the more variety of colors there is. All of the demos in this book work in 32bpp mode, but some image formats may store images with only 24bpp or even less. If a program has to convert from 24bpp to 32bpp on the fly while drawing images, it will affect performance. Preconverting the images that are not in the same format as the screen will speed up the image-drawing procedures. After an image is obtained with the same bpp as the program, the original image is freed, and the new image is used. In this demo, the color with an RGB value of (255, 0, 255) will be transparent in the image. SDL_SetColorKey is used to apply the color key and return the masked image.

Table 3.3 displays all the new functions used in this demo.

Table 3.3 New Functions Used in This Demo

Function	Description
SDL_Surface *SDL_DisplayFormat(SDL_Surface *surface)	This function takes one parameter, and it is a pointer to a surface. It returns a copy of the specified surface using the display's pixel format (in terms of bpp). The returned surface will be optimized for drawing onto the screen. This will make drawing these surfaces much faster in some cases.

int SDL_SetColorKey(
    SDL_Surface *surface,
    Uint32 flag,
    Uint32 key)
	This function takes three parameters, and it sets the color key of a surface. The first parameter is a pointer to the surface. The second is a flag. For this flag, SDL_SRCCOLORKEY is used to make the desired pixels transparent. The last parameter specifies the color that will be masked. This function returns 0 or -1 upon failure.

© Jazon Yamamoto.

Since the alpha masking demo is much like the previous demo, let's focus on the LoadFiles function. Listing 3.7 demonstrates the LoadFiles function.

Listing 3.7: The LoadFiles Function for the Color Key Demo

```
bool LoadFiles()
{
    Background = LoadImage("graphics/background.bmp");
    if(Background == NULL)
        return false;

    SpriteImage = LoadImage("graphics/spaceship.bmp");
    if(SpriteImage == NULL)
        return false;

    return true;
}
```

This demo is almost identical to the previous one, but the spaceship actually blends in with the background. With this novel technique at your disposal, you can now seamlessly populate digital worlds with sprites!

ANIMATING IMAGES

Populating a world with static images and blending them into a scene is a milestone, but using only static images can make a game dull. This is where animated images come in. Animated images are extremely useful for making a game look alive. Animation makes gameplay more exciting by allowing for more elaborate visuals. To animate an image, an animation strip is necessary. An *animation strip* is an image that contains all the frames of an animation. Drawing one frame at a time in rapid succession will create the illusion of the image being animated. Figure 3.9 illustrates an animation strip. The entire animation strip can be loaded into a surface from bitmap files using the image-loading function created earlier. Portions of the composite image can be drawn frame by frame.

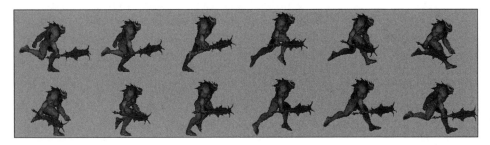

Figure 3.9
An animation strip.
© Jazon Yamamoto. Source: 3Dmodels-textures.

To draw single frames from an image, the second argument in SDL_BlitSurface comes into play. This argument denotes the source portion of the image that is to be rendered, which is defined with a pointer to an SDL_Rect structure.

To make the drawing of images much cleaner, wrap the whole thing in a single function that will draw a specific frame from an animation strip. The image can be animated by changing the frame every time it is drawn. Listing 3.8 demonstrates the new image-drawing function.

Listing 3.8: The DrawImageFrame Function

```
void DrawImageFrame(SDL_Surface* image,
    SDL_Surface* destSurface,
    int x, int y,
    int width, int height, int frame)
{
    SDL_Rect destRect;
    destRect.x = x;
    destRect.y = y;
```

```
    int columns = image->w/width;

    SDL_Rect sourceRect;
    sourceRect.y = (frame/columns)*height;
    sourceRect.x = (frame%columns)*width;
    sourceRect.w = width;
    sourceRect.h = height;

    SDL_BlitSurface(image, &sourceRect, destSurface, &destRect);
}
```

This is a lengthy function, but it is very powerful. The first argument is the source image (in this case, the animation strip). The second argument is the destination image (in this case, the backbuffer). The third and fourth arguments represent the location where the image will be drawn. The fifth and sixth arguments represent the frame width and height, respectively. The last parameter represents the frame number. 0 is passed as the frame number to draw the first frame, 1 to draw the second frame, and so on.

The first part of this function creates the destRect variable, which will be passed into SDL_BlitSurface to define the position where the frame will be drawn on the screen. The second part creates sourceRect, which describes which portion of the source image will be drawn. The source's Y coordinate is computed by dividing the frame number by the columns of frames in the animation strip. This yields the row of the desired frame. Multiply that by the frame height to get the exact value. The X value is computed by obtaining the remainder of dividing the frame number by the columns of frames and multiplying it by the frame width. It may seem a bit complicated, but it's actually quite simple once you begin to visualize the logic involved.

The code in Listing 3.9 demonstrates the variables used in this demo.

Listing 3.9: Some Variables Used in the Animation Demo

```
SDL_Surface* Background = NULL;
SDL_Surface* SpriteImage = NULL;
SDL_Surface* Backbuffer = NULL;

int SpriteFrame = 0;
int FrameCounter = 0;

const int MaxSpriteFrame = 11;
const int FrameDelay = 2;

int BackgroundX = 0;
```

These variables are necessary to store the images, and they create a simple mechanism to regulate the rate at which the frame is updated. The code from Listing 3.10 defines a more convenient function for drawing images.

Listing 3.10: The `DrawImage` Function

```
void DrawImage(SDL_Surface* image, SDL_Surface* destSurface, int x, int y)
{
    SDL_Rect destRect;
    destRect.x = x;
    destRect.y = y;

    SDL_BlitSurface(image, NULL, destSurface, &destRect);
}
```

This function is just a wrapper of `SDL_BlitSurface`, but with limited functionality. It is easier to use since it doesn't require as many parameters. Listing 3.11 demonstrates the heart of the program's code.

Listing 3.11: The Animation Demo's Game Loop

```
while(ProgramIsRunning())
{
    //Updates the sprite's frame
    FrameCounter++;

    if(FrameCounter > FrameDelay)
    {
        FrameCounter = 0;
        SpriteFrame++;
    }

    if(SpriteFrame > MaxSpriteFrame)
        SpriteFrame = 0;

    //Updates Background scrolling
    BackgroundX-=6;
    if(BackgroundX <= -800)
        BackgroundX = 0;

    //Render the scene
    DrawImage(Background,Backbuffer, BackgroundX, 0);
    DrawImage(Background,Backbuffer, BackgroundX+800, 0);

     DrawImageFrame(SpriteImage, Backbuffer,
        350,250,        //Position of the image
        150, 120,       //Frame Width/Height
        SpriteFrame); //Frame Number

    SDL_Delay(20);
    SDL_Flip(Backbuffer);
}
```

Building the App

You can find the files necessary to build this app in BAMGP\. They are located in Source\Chapter_03\ 3_5_Animation\. You need to create an SDL project and copy main.cpp and the graphics directory into your project's directory. If you're using Windows, make sure to include the .dll files in the project's directory. Also make sure your project is configured properly, as shown in Chapter 1, and that all the files were properly included. When all is set, you'll be able to build the program and run it on your own. Additionally, a precompiled version is in the Source directory named 3_5_Animation.exe.

This is the main loop of the demo. It updates the animated image's frame and keeps the background moving to make it appear as if the character is actually running to the right. The first part of the code updates the frame every few cycles and resets the frame when the maximum frame is reached to create a walk cycle. The second part updates the background's X coordinate. The final part draws all the elements into the scene. Since the background is scrolling indefinitely, it must be drawn twice to cover the whole screen. BackgroundX is set to 0 every time it's about to scroll off the screen to keep it scrolling forever. Figure 3.10 shows a screenshot of the animated image demo.

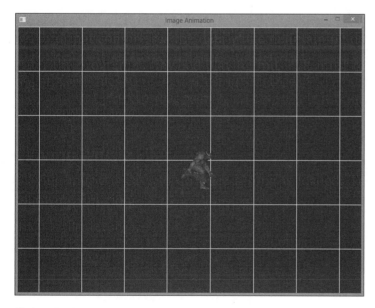

Figure 3.10
A monster running in the animation demo.
© Jazon Yamamoto. Source: 3Dmodels-textures.

Loading Alternate Image Formats

So far, BMP files were loaded using SDL_LoadBMP. While this approach works, this function only loads BMP files, which aren't always the most appropriate files to use in a game. Other image file formats that may be more suitable for many cases are the Portable Network Graphics (PNG) format and the Joint Photographic Experts Group (JPEG) format. The PNG format has advantages such as support for transparency and lossless compression. PNG files are usually much smaller than BMP files that contain the same information. These files are actually very nice to use in video games for sprites. JPEG files are stored using a lossy compression algorithm. JPEG files take even less space than a PNG file, but are unsuitable for transparency. JPEG files are best used when the image won't have any transparency and quality isn't a high priority (backgrounds maybe?).

Algorithms to load these files are very complicated, too, but fortunately, there is an SDL extension that can do all the dirty work. The SDL Image extension provides the function `IMG_Load`. This function is powerful enough to load images of different formats, and using it is as easy as including the `SDL_image.h` file. `IMG_Load` is simply a more versatile version of `BMP_Load` and behaves in an almost identical way. The code in Listing 3.12 shows the new function for loading images.

Listing 3.12: The New LoadImage Function

```
#include <SDL/SDL.h>
#include <SDL/SDL_image.h>

SDL_Surface* LoadImage(char* fileName)
{
    SDL_Surface* imageLoaded = NULL;
    SDL_Surface* processedImage = NULL;

    imageLoaded = IMG_Load(fileName);

    if(imageLoaded != NULL)
    {
        processedImage = SDL_DisplayFormat(imageLoaded);
        SDL_FreeSurface(imageLoaded);

        if(processedImage != NULL)
        {
            Uint32 colorKey = SDL_MapRGB(
                processedImage->format, 255, 0, 255);

            SDL_SetColorKey(processedImage,
                SDL_SRCCOLORKEY, colorKey);
        }
    }

    return processedImage;
}
```

Building the App

You can find the files necessary to build this app in BAMGP\. They are located in Source\Chapter_03\ 3_6_ImageFormats\. You need to create an SDL project and copy main.cpp and the graphics directory into to your project's directory. If you're using Windows, make sure to include the .dll files in the project's directory. Also make sure your project is configured properly, as shown in Chapter 1, and that all the files were properly included. When all is set, you'll be able to build the program and run it on your own. Additionally, a precompiled version is in the Source directory named 3_6_ImageFormats.exe.

Remember that to use the IMG_Load function, you must include the SDL_image.h file at the top of the program. Figure 3.11 displays a screenshot of the demo for this section.

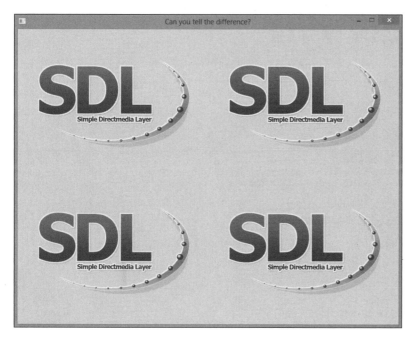

Figure 3.11
The image-loading demo. Can you tell the difference?
© Jazon Yamamoto.

Drawing Raster Fonts

Drawing text is another important requirement for making games. The easiest way to go about this is by using raster fonts. A *raster font* is a font stored in an image file. It is easy to use and is a fast way to draw text on the screen. In this method, an image file holds all the characters of a font. Figure 3.12 shows an example of a font stored in an image file. To draw a string, take each character in the string and draw the appropriate portion of the image for that character. Note that all the characters stored in the image are evenly spaced from each other. This is because every character in the image is like a frame of an animation strip. This makes it possible to draw any character you want by calling the DrawImageFrame function and specifying the appropriate frame.

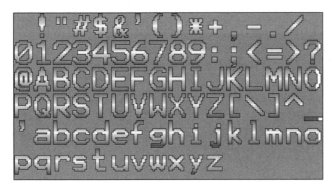

Figure 3.12
A font stored in an image file.
© Jazon Yamamoto.

The Text-Drawing Function

The code in Listing 3.13 implements the text-drawing function.

Listing 3.13: The Raster Font Text-Drawing Function

```
void DrawRasterText(SDL_Surface* surface, SDL_Surface* destSurface,
    char string[], int x, int y, int charSize)
{
    for(int i = 0; i < strlen(string); i++)
        DrawImageFrame(surface, destSurface,
        x+i*charSize, y, charSize, charSize, string[i]-32);
}
```

This function iterates through every character in the string, and it draws the appropriate frame. The frame is determined by the character's ASCII value. *ASCII* stands for American Standard Code for Information Interchange, and it is a numerical value assigned to different text characters. The "space" character is the first character in the image, and it happens to have an ASCII code of 32. To get the correct frame for each character, take its ASCII code and subtract 32 from it. Failing to do so will result in the screen displaying gibberish.

Listing 3.14 exhibits the text-drawing function in action.

Listing 3.14: Drawing Text with Raster Fonts

```
while(ProgramIsRunning())
{
    DrawImage(Background,Backbuffer, 0, 0);

    DrawRasterText(FontImage, Backbuffer, "All Systems Go!",
        100, 100, charSize);

     DrawRasterText(FontImage, Backbuffer, "Drawing Fonts is Fun!",
        100, 116, charSize);

    SDL_Delay(20);
    SDL_Flip(Backbuffer);
}
```

Building the App

You can find the files necessary to build this app in BAMGP\. They are located in Source\Chapter_03\ 3_7_RasterFonts\. You need to create an SDL project and copy main.cpp and the graphics directory into your project's directory. If you're using Windows, make sure to include the .dll files in the project's directory. Also make sure your project is configured properly, as shown in Chapter 1, and that all the files were properly included. When all is set, you'll be able to build the program and run it on your own. Additionally, a precompiled version is in the Source directory named 3_7_RasterFonts.exe.

Figure 3.13 shows the compiled application.

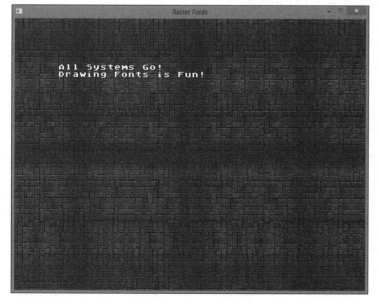

Figure 3.13
The raster font demo.
© Jazon Yamamoto.

This wraps up raster fonts. Remember that they are very fast and easy to work with, but may not be the best solution for drawing text all the time. There are limitations to this approach, but there are ways to get around them.

Drawing Outline Fonts

Outline fonts are a great alternative to raster fonts. Whereas raster fonts are stored in general-purpose image files, outline fonts are stored in file formats, such as TTF, that are specifically tailored for font files. Unlike raster fonts, outline font files store the information about a font in mathematical formulae in order to be able to reproduce text in any size and without pixelation. This is achieved by representing the font in a format that allows scaling and rotation, such as spline or Bezier curves.

Figure 3.14 depicts a raster font and an outline font being scaled up side-to-side. Notice that the text on the left is much smoother as it gets larger than the text on the right.

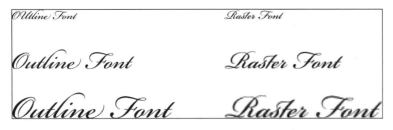

Figure 3.14
A comparison of scaled raster and outline fonts.
© Jazon Yamamoto.

Since outline font files only store the font information, text can be drawn in any color. Outline fonts don't need to be monospaced, which makes text look more natural. It's nice to build up an arsenal of fonts for use with video games, and free font files can be found on the Internet with a simple search. The tradeoff is that outline text rendering is not nearly as fast as raster rendering in most cases.

Much like images, fonts must be loaded before being used and released when the program is done with them. These fonts are stored in TTF_Font structures. Since SDL doesn't support loading and drawing outline fonts out of the box, the SDL_ttf extension is necessary. Before using any SDL_ttf functions, remember that the appropriate header file must be included as shown:

```
#include <SDL/SDL.h>
#include <SDL/SDL_ttf.h>
```

Because SDL_ttf is an extension of SDL and not a core part of it, it must be initialized and released much like SDL. The following code initializes the TTF system, and it must be called after initializing SDL:

```
TTF_Init();
```

Before closing SDL, TTF must be closed. This is accomplished with the following piece of code:

```
TTF_Quit();
```

A variable is necessary to store the font information. The following code creates a pointer to the TTF_Font structure, which will be used to store the font:

```
TTF_Font* Font = NULL;
```

That should look very similar to the pointers created to store images. The following code loads the font files into memory:

```
Font = TTF_OpenFont( "fonts/Alfphabet.ttf", 24 );
```

The first parameter indicates the font's filename. The font must be stored in the same directory as the project file. The second parameter designates the font size. Once the program is done with the font, it must be released like so:

```
TTF_CloseFont(Font);
```

The function in Listing 3.15 prints text using the font that was loaded.

Listing 3.15: The Outline Font Text-Drawing Function

```
void DrawOutlineText(SDL_Surface* surface, char* string, int x, int y,
    TTF_Font* font, Uint8 r, Uint8 g, Uint8 b)
{
    SDL_Surface* renderedText = NULL;

    SDL_Color color;

    color.r = r;
    color.g = g;
    color.b = b;

    renderedText = TTF_RenderText_Solid(font, string, color);

    SDL_Rect pos;

    pos.x = x;
    pos.y = y;

    SDL_BlitSurface(renderedText, NULL, surface, &pos);
    SDL_FreeSurface(renderedText);
}
```

This function was created to draw text with outline fonts. It uses the function `TTF_RenderText_Solid` to draw the fonts. This function requires a pointer to the font, the string, and the color information. The color information is stored in an `SDL_Color` structure. This function generates a surface with the rendered text. The surface is drawn on the screen and released afterwards.

Listing 3.16 demonstrates the outline font text-drawing function in action.

Listing 3.16: Drawing Text with Outline Fonts

```
while(ProgramIsRunning())
{
    SDL_FillRect(Backbuffer, NULL, 0);

    counter++;
    if(counter > 1000)
        counter = 0;

    char buffer[64];
    sprintf(buffer, "I can count to 1000 really fast: %d", counter);

    DrawOutlineText(Backbuffer, "I am the king of Drawing Text!",
        100, 100, Font, 255, 0, 0);

    DrawOutlineText(Backbuffer, "I can draw text in any color I want!",
        100,150, Font, 0, 255, 0);

    DrawOutlineText(Backbuffer, buffer, 100, 200,
        Font, 0, 0, 255);

    SDL_Delay(20);
    SDL_Flip(Backbuffer);
}
```

Building the App

You can find the files necessary to build this app in `BAMGP\`. They are located in `Source\Chapter_03\ 3_8_OutlineFonts\`. You need to create an SDL project and copy `main.cpp` and the `fonts` directory into your project's directory. If you're using Windows, make sure to include the `.dll` files in the project's directory. Also make sure your project is configured properly, as shown in Chapter 1, and that all the files were properly included. When all is set, you'll be able to build the program and run it on your own. Additionally, a precompiled version is in the `Source` directory named `3_8_OutlineFonts.exe`.

This program renders three different strings with three different colors, and one part even draws the variable `counter` and constantly updates it. Figure 3.15 demonstrates the outline font demo running, and Table 3.4 details the new functions used in this section.

Figure 3.15
A screenshot of the outline font demo.
© Jazon Yamamoto.

Table 3.4   New Functions Used in This Demo

Function	Description
`int TTF_Init()`	This function initiates the TTF system, and it must be called after initializing SDL, but before calling any TTF functions.
`void TTF_Quit()`	This function gracefully closes the TTF system. It must be called before closing SDL.

`TTF_Font *TTF_OpenFont(`
`const char *file,`
`int ptsize)`
	This function loads a font, and it only requires two arguments. The first is the filename of the font that is to be loaded, and the second is the desired font size. This function returns a pointer to the loaded font.

`void TTF_CloseFont(` `TTF_Font *font)`	This function releases a font, and it takes only one parameter, which is a pointer to the font that is no longer necessary.

(Continued)

Table 3.4 New Functions Used in This Demo (*Continued*)

Function	Description

`SDL_Surface *TTF_RenderText_Solid(`
`TTF_Font *font,`
`const char *text,`
`SDL_Color fg)`
	This function takes four parameters, and it returns a pointer to a surface. The first parameter is a pointer to the font that will be used. The second parameter is the string that is to be drawn. The last parameter is the color of the text. It returns a surface of the text that was generated.

`void DrawOutlineText(`
`SDL_Surface* surface,`
`char* string,`
`int x, int y,`
`TTF_Font* font,`
`Uint8 r, Uint8 g, Uint8 b)`
	This function was created to make drawing text easier. It requires eight parameters. The first indicates the surface for the text to be drawn on. The second is a string of the text that is to be drawn. The third and fifth are the X and Y coordinates of the text. The last three indicate the RGB values of the color of the text.

© Jazon Yamamoto.

Regulating Frame Rate

The last aspect that needs to be covered is frame rate regulation. In the previous examples, the game loop consisted of updating the game, drawing the graphics, and waiting 20 milliseconds before repeating the cycle. This resulted in a little less than 50 frames per second. The disadvantage of this is that the more processing the game does in the game loop, the slower the frame rate, and slower frame rates mean sluggish games. To be able to add more processing to the game loop without slowing it down, the program should make an intelligent delay based on the time that has elapsed since the last frame was drawn, and not a static 20 millisecond delay. To do this, take note of the time before drawing the graphics and the time after drawing them. Compare these two values to get the time that was required to draw the frame. Finally, make a delay with this time subtracted. Two common frame rates are 30Hz and 60Hz. These are very widely used in videogames and have become a standard. Faster frame rates make for smoother animation, but 30Hz will be used for these examples because 30Hz is more widely supported. Remember that SDL also runs on various portable devices that might not support 60Hz frame rates.

The code in Listing 3.17 shows a modified version of the animation demo's game loop and the definition of new constants used to regulate frame rates.

Listing 3.17: The Frame Rate Regulation Demo's Game Loop

```
const int FPS = 30;
const int FRAME_DELAY = 1000/FPS;

while(ProgramIsRunning())
{
    int frameStart = SDL_GetTicks();

    //Updates the sprites frame
    FrameCounter++;

    if(FrameCounter > FrameDelay)
    {
        FrameCounter = 0;
        SpriteFrame++;
    }

    if(SpriteFrame > MaxSpriteFrame)
        SpriteFrame = 0;

    //Updates Background scrolling
    BackgroundX-=6;
    if(BackgroundX <= -800)
        BackgroundX = 0;

    //Render the scene
    DrawImage(Background,Backbuffer, BackgroundX, 0);
    DrawImage(Background,Backbuffer, BackgroundX+800, 0);
    DrawImageFrame(SpriteImage, Backbuffer, 350,250, 150, 120, SpriteFrame);

    int frameTime = SDL_GetTicks() - frameStart;

    if(frameTime < FRAME_DELAY)
        SDL_Delay(FRAME_DELAY - frameTime);

    SDL_Flip(Backbuffer);
}
```

Building the App

You can find the files necessary to build this app in BAMGP\. They are located in Source\Chapter_03\ 3_9_FrameRate\. You need to create an SDL project and copy main.cpp and the graphics directory into your project's directory. If you're using Windows, make sure to include the .dll files in the project's directory. Also make sure your project is configured properly, as shown in Chapter 1, and that all the files were properly included. When all is set, you'll be able to build the program and run it on your own. Additionally, a precompiled version is in the Source directory named 3_9_FrameRate.exe.

This concludes frame rate regulation. This is important, and it ensures that games run at a fixed speed. Lack of frame rate regulation may result in games running extremely fast on some computers and painfully slow on others.

SUMMARY

 This chapter was quite intense, but it provided the tools to make a game look more visually appealing. Many topics were covered, including working with low-level graphics, drawing animated images, drawing text, and even regulating frame rate. This is one of the chapters that you might want to look back on multiple times for reference, so set a bookmark somewhere along these pages. Don't forget to check out the video tutorial for this chapter since it summarizes everything that was covered, with additional commentary. Before making the next hit indie game, try completing some of the following exercises to ensure you mastered all the topics covered in this chapter.

Exercises

- Try drawing a line of horizontal pixels that is 256 pixels long and fades from green to black (a gradient).

- Try drawing 10 green rectangles that are 50 pixels wide and 100 pixels tall anywhere in the screen. Just make sure they don't overlap each other.

- Draw multiple images on the screen with transparency and make them overlap each other.

- In the animation demo, try making the animation slower or faster. See how smooth it looks when it's faster and how choppy it gets the slower it is.

- Try drawing your name on the screen using raster fonts.

- Try drawing your name on the screen using outline fonts, and do it multiple times in different colors.

CHAPTER 4

INTERACTING WITH THE MATRIX

Now that you have the ability to draw anything on the screen, the next step in game programming is processing user input. Input is what allows the users to tell a computer program what to do. This is what makes interactive applications interactive. This chapter covers topics such as interacting with programs by using the mouse and keyboard. This chapter covers how to:

- Work with event-based mouse input.
- Work with event-based keyboard input.
- Work with buffered mouse input.
- Work with buffered keyboard input.

Tip

Before getting started, you can check out the video tutorial for this chapter, which is located in BAMGP\ under the Videos directory. The video contains extra material and insights, and reviews the chapter from a high level, so be sure to watch it.

THE BASICS OF INPUT

A computer can be seen as a system of inputs and outputs. Without input, you really have no control over your computer. To interface with the computer, engineers created devices, such as keyboard and the mouse, that allow users to send electric signals to a computer processor. These devices turn physical motions into electrical signals that the computer can understand. Programmers don't usually have direct access to these devices, and an extra layer of software is used for dealing with these devices. In this case, SDL will provide the tools to interact with input devices. Input in SDL can be processed as an event (which is covered next) or as a state (which is covered later in this chapter).

The Event System

SDL comes packed with a system to handle "events." These events describe actions, such as a mouse button being pressed, the window being closed, or a key being pressed. Every event that occurs is stored in a queue until the program processes it. The SDL event system was used earlier in this book to check if the user presses the X button to close the program. Another potential use for the event system is to check if the user interacted with the mouse or the keyboard.

When an event occurs, the description of the event is stored in the SDL_Event structure, and it is sent to a queue. This queue will process the first event stored in it first and the last event stored last. This is known as *first in, first out* order (commonly abbreviated as FIFO).

Event-Based Mouse Input

You can access the event queue using SDL_PollEvent. This function returns the next event in the queue and then removes it to make sure that every event is only processed once. To help identify the type of event that was received, the SDL_Event structure has a variable called type. This variable holds the type of event that occurred. It was used earlier to check if the type was SDL_QUIT, which indicates that the X button at the top of the window was clicked. SDL_PollEvent can also be used to process the mouse's input.

The code in Listing 4.1 demonstrates the modified ProgramIsRunning function for this demo.

Listing 4.1: Processing Event-Based Mouse Input

```
bool ProgramIsRunning()
{
    SDL_Event event;
    bool running = true;
    while(SDL_PollEvent(&event))
    {
        if(event.type == SDL_QUIT)
            running = false;
```

```
    if( event.type == SDL_MOUSEBUTTONDOWN)
    {
        if(event.button.button == SDL_BUTTON_LEFT)
        {
            Cross1X = event.button.x;
            Cross1Y = event.button.y;
        }
        if(event.button.button == SDL_BUTTON_RIGHT)
        {
            Cross2X = event.button.x;
            Cross2Y = event.button.y;
        }
    }
    if( event.type == SDL_MOUSEMOTION)
    {
        int mouseX = event.motion.x;
        int mouseY = event.motion.y;

        char buffer[64];
        sprintf(buffer, "Mouse X: %d, Mouse Y: %d",
            mouseX, mouseY);
        SDL_WM_SetCaption(buffer, NULL);
    }
    }

    return running;
}
```

This function processes mouse events as well as the SDL_QUIT event. The SDL_MOUSEBUTTONDOWN event occurs when mouse buttons are pressed. The program identifies which button was pressed by looking into the *(SDL_Event)*.button.button variable of the SDL_Event object. SDL_BUTTON_RIGHT indicates the right button was pressed, SDL_BUTTON_LEFT indicates the left button was pressed, and SDL_BUTTON_MIDDLE indicates the middle button was pressed, if there is one. The coordinates of location of the cursor can be obtained when a button is pressed. They are stored in the *(SDL_Event)*.button.x, and the *(SDL_Event)*.button.y variables. Another type of event sent by SDL is the SDL_MOUSEMOTION event. This event occurs whenever the mouse is moved, and the X and Y coordinates of the mouse are stored in *(SDL_Event)*.motion.x and *(SDL_Event)*. motion.y. The code in Listing 4.2 demonstrates the declaration of the variables used in this demo.

Listing 4.2: The Variables for the Event-Based Mouse Input Demo

```
int Cross1X = -100;     //Give the sprites an off-screen
int Cross1Y = -100;     //initial location

int Cross2X = -100;
int Cross2Y = -100;

SDL_Surface* Cross1 = NULL;
SDL_Surface* Cross2 = NULL;
SDL_Surface* Background = NULL;
SDL_Surface* Backbuffer = NULL;
```

The first four variables hold the X and Y coordinates of two cursors that will be drawn. They are set to –100 in order to draw them off the screen when the program first starts and are updated when the left and right mouse buttons are pressed. The rest of the variables store images of the cursors, the background, and the backbuffer. Listing 4.3 exhibits the game loop for the program.

Listing 4.3: The Game Loop for the Event-Based Mouse Input Demo

```
while(ProgramIsRunning())
{
    SDL_FillRect(Backbuffer,NULL, 0);

    DrawImage(Background, Backbuffer, 0, 0);
    DrawImage(Cross1, Backbuffer, Cross1X - 50, Cross1Y - 50);
    DrawImage(Cross2, Backbuffer, Cross2X - 50, Cross2Y - 50);

    SDL_Delay(20);
    SDL_Flip(Backbuffer);
}
```

Building the App

You can find the files necessary to build this app in BAMGP\. They are located in Source\Chapter_04\ 4_1_EventMouse\. You need to create an SDL project and copy main.cpp and the graphics folder into your project's directory. If you're using Windows, make sure to include the .dll files in the project's directory. Also make sure your project is configured properly, as shown in Chapter 1, and that all the files were properly included. When all is set, you'll be able to build the program and run it on your own. Additionally, a precompiled version is in the Source directory named 4_1_EventMouse.exe.

This demo draws the cursors in the indicated locations. Refer to Table 4.1 for a description of the functions used in this demo and Figure 4.1 for a screenshot of the demo.

Table 4.1 New Functions Used in This Demo

Function	Description
int SDL_PollEvent(SDL_Event *event)	This function takes one parameter, and it is a pointer to an SDL_Event structure. It stores the information about the next event on the queue in the variable provided and then removes it from the event queue. It returns 1 if there was an event in the queue and 0 otherwise.
bool ProgramIsRunning()	This function was modified from the previous examples to also analyze mouse events. It still returns false when the SDL_QUIT event occurs.

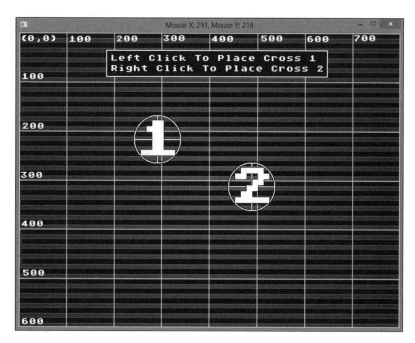

Figure 4.1
A screenshot of the demo.

Event-Based Keyboard Input

Keyboard events are handled in a similar fashion. There are events of type SDL_KEYDOWN when a key is pressed down (and SDL_KEYUP when a key is released), and you can tell which key was pressed by looking into the (SDL_Event).key.keysm.sym variable. The code in Listing 4.4 checks when the arrow keys are pressed and changes a sprite's position accordingly.

Listing 4.4: Processing Event-Based Keyboard Input

```
bool ProgramIsRunning()
{
    SDL_Event event;
    bool running = true;
    while(SDL_PollEvent(&event))
    {
        if(event.type == SDL_QUIT)
            running = false;
        if( event.type == SDL_KEYDOWN )
        {
            switch( event.key.keysym.sym )
            {
                case SDLK_ESCAPE:
                    running = false;
                    break;
                case SDLK_LEFT:
                    SpriteX-=50;
                    break;
                case SDLK_RIGHT:
                    SpriteX+=50;
                    break;
                case SDLK_UP:
                    SpriteY-=50;
                    break;
                case SDLK_DOWN:
                    SpriteY+=50;
                    break;
                default:
                    break;
            }
        }
    }
    return running;
}
```

Building the App

Take note of how the `ProgramIsRunning` function now checks if the Escape key was pressed and closes the application if it was. Listing 4.5 displays the game loop for the demo.

Listing 4.5: The Game Loop for the Event-Based Keyboard Input Demo

```
while(ProgramIsRunning())
{
    DrawImage(Background,Backbuffer, 0, 0);
    DrawImage(SpriteImage, Backbuffer, SpriteX, SpriteY);

    SDL_Delay(20);
    SDL_Flip(Backbuffer);
}
```

The game loop is very simple since the program only draws images and processes events. In this demo, an image is drawn at (spriteX, spriteY), and it is moved when an arrow key is pressed. Refer to Table 4.2 for a list of SDL key codes for keys commonly used in video games and Figure 4.2 for a screenshot of the demo.

Table 4.2 Common Keys Used In Video Games

Key	Description
SDLK_BACKSPACE	Backspace
SDLK_RETURN	Return or Enter
SDLK_ESCAPE	Escape
SDLK_SPACE	Space
SDLK_0 - SDLK_9	0 – 9 on the keyboard
SDLK_a - SDLK_z	The keys A - Z
SDLK_KP0 - SDLK_KP9	Keypad 0 – 9
SDLK_KP_PERIOD	Keypad period
SDLK_KP_DIVIDE	Keypad divide
SDLK_KP_MULTIPLY	Keypad multiply
SDLK_KP_MINUS	Keypad minus
SDLK_KP_PLUS	Keypad plus
SDLK_KP_ENTER	Keypad enter
SDLK_KP_EQUALS	Keypad equals
SDLK_UP	Up Arrow
SDLK_DOWN	Down Arrow
SDLK_RIGHT	Right Arrow
SDLK_LEFT	Left Arrow
SDLK_F1 - SDLK_F15	F1 - F15
SDLK_RSHIFT	Right Shift
SDLK_LSHIFT	Left Shift
SDLK_RCTRL	Right Ctrl
SDLK_LCTRL	Left Ctrl

Figure 4.2
The keyboard demo.
© Jazon Yamamoto. Source: 3DRT.com.

Notice that in this example, the sprite only moves once when the key is pressed down. This is because the event that moves the sprite is processed only once. The advantage of event-based input is that it produces simple game loops, but it can be a bit intrusive since it forces programs to process all input in one place, along with other events that are not input related.

Buffered Input

Buffered input is a second alternative to receiving input, and it is better suited in most cases for making video games. This approach can be easier to work with since it is possible to process buffered input from anywhere in the code, and you're not forced to process all the input in one loop. With buffered input, SDL stores the entire state of the keyboard and mouse in a place in memory, which can be accessed to see which keys are currently being pressed or where the mouse is currently positioned. This is very useful because the program accesses this data from anywhere in the code and not just from the event processing loop.

Buffered Mouse Input

To handle buffered mouse input, you can use the SDL_GetMouseState function to retrieve the entire state of the mouse. The code in Listing 4.6 implements the game loop for the buffered mouse event demo.

Listing 4.6: Processing Buffered Mouse Input

```
while(ProgramIsRunning())
{
    int mouseX;
    int mouseY;

    SDL_GetMouseState(&mouseX, &mouseY);

    char buffer[64];
    sprintf(buffer, "Mouse X: %d, Mouse Y: %d", mouseX, mouseY);
    SDL_WM_SetCaption(buffer, NULL);

    //Process Buttons;
    if(SDL_GetMouseState(NULL,NULL) & SDL_BUTTON(1))
    {
        Cross1X = mouseX;
        Cross1Y = mouseY;
    }

    if(SDL_GetMouseState(NULL,NULL) & SDL_BUTTON(3))
    {
        Cross2X = mouseX;
        Cross2Y = mouseY;
    }

    DrawImage(Background, Backbuffer, 0, 0);
    DrawImage(Cross1, Backbuffer, Cross1X - 50, Cross1Y - 50);
    DrawImage(Cross2, Backbuffer, Cross2X - 50, Cross2Y - 50);

    SDL_Delay(20);
    SDL_Flip(Backbuffer);
}
```

Building the App

You can find the files necessary to build this app in BAMGP\. They are located in Source\Chapter_04\ 4_3_BufferedMouse\. You need to create an SDL project and copy main.cpp and the graphics folder into your project's directory. If you're using Windows, make sure to include the .dll files in the project's directory. Also make sure your project is configured properly, as shown in Chapter 1, and that all the files were properly included. When all is set, you'll be able to build the program and run it on your own. Additionally, a precompiled version is in the Source directory named 4_3_BufferedMouse.exe.

The function SDL_GetMouseState takes two parameters, and they are both pointers to integers. This function stores the X and Y values of the position of the mouse in these integers. It returns a bitmasked number containing the button information, and that's why retrieving the mouse states looks sort of strange. Just know that using SDL_GetMouseState(NULL,NULL) & SDL_BUTTON(1) returns true if the left key is being pressed, SDL_GetMouseState(NULL,NULL) & SDL_BUTTON(2) returns true if the middle key is being pressed, and SDL_GetMouseState(NULL,NULL) & SDL_BUTTON(3) returns true if the right key is being pressed.

Figure 4.3 demonstrates the updated demo with buffer mouse input.

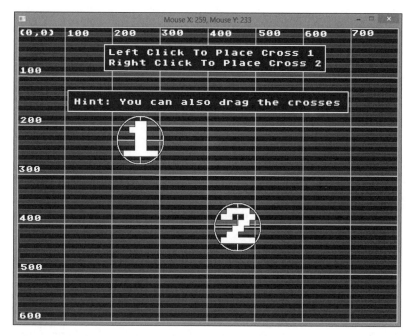

Figure 4.3
The new mouse input demo.
© Jazon Yamamoto.

Tip

This program checks for input every single frame and processes it immediately. This is why the cross hairs can be dragged in real time.

Buffered Keyboard Input

Buffered keyboard input is much easier to use than event-based input. All you need to do is create a pointer of type Uint8 and assign it to the array returned by

`SDL_GetKeyState`. This will produce an array with all the keystates. To figure out whether a key is down or not, a program can check if the key's code value in the array is `true` or `false`. Listing 4.7 demonstrates the code for this demo's game loop.

Listing 4.7: Processing Buffered Keyboard Input

```
while(ProgramIsRunning())
{
    //Handle Input
    Uint8* keys = SDL_GetKeyState(NULL);

    if(keys[SDLK_ESCAPE])
        break;

    if(keys[SDLK_LEFT])
        SpriteX-=8;

    if(keys[SDLK_RIGHT])
        SpriteX+=8;

    if(keys[SDLK_UP])
        SpriteY-=8;

    if(keys[SDLK_DOWN])
        SpriteY+=8;

    DrawImage(Background,Backbuffer, 0, 0);
    DrawImage(SpriteImage, Backbuffer, SpriteX, SpriteY);

    SDL_Delay(20);
    SDL_Flip(Backbuffer);
}
```

Building the App

You can find the files necessary to build this app in `BAMGP\`. They are located in `Source\Chapter_04\` `4_4_BufferedKeyboard\`. You need to create an SDL project and copy `main.cpp` and the `graphics` folder into your project's directory. If you're using Windows, make sure to include the `.dll` files in the project's directory. Also make sure your project is configured properly, as shown in Chapter 1, and that all the files were properly included. When all is set, you'll be able to build the program and run it on your own. Additionally, a precompiled version is in the `Source` directory named `4_4_BufferedKeyboard.exe`.

This way of checking for keyboard input is much cleaner than event-based input since it doesn't have to all be processed in one giant nasty loop. The argument `NULL` is passed into `SDL_GetKeyState`, but it is possible to pass in a pointer to an integer to get the size of the array. Refer to Table 4.3 for a list of new functions used in the last two demos and Figure 4.4 for an illustration of the last demo.

Table 4.3 New Functions Used in This Demo

Function	Description

`Uint8 SDL_GetMouseState(`
  `int *x,`
  `int *y)`
	This function takes two parameters, and they are pointers to two `int` variables. These variables are assigned the mouse's X and Y screen coordinates, respectively. They may also be `NULL`. It returns a bit-masked number detailing the mouse button's state.

`Uint8 *SDL_GetKeyState(` `int *numkeys)`	This function returns an array filled with the current state of every key SDL works with. It takes one parameter, and it is a pointer of type `int`. The variable the pointer points to will be filled with the number of keys on the keyboard. This may be useful in programs that use a `for` loop to run through every single key.

© Jazon Yamamoto.

Figure 4.4
The buffered keyboard demo.
© Jazon Yamamoto. Source: 3DRT.com.

SUMMARY

This is it! This chapter is over! Feel welcome to interact with your computer programs. In theory, this is enough to create a video game, but there's something missing. There is one more ingredient that needs to be added. The next chapter covers sound in detail. Sound helps bring life into video games and can take a great experience to amazing! If you haven't done it already, check out the video tutorial for this chapter. It contains some extra commentary on all the topics that were covered. Before continuing on your journey, try completing a few of the following exercises.

Exercises

- Using event-based input or buffered input, try drawing two sprites and using different keys to move each of them independently.

- Try moving one of the sprites with the mouse and the other with the keyboard.

- Try writing a program that draws pixels at the current mouse position when the user holds the right mouse button down. Then don't clear the screen every frame, and you should have a primitive drawing program!

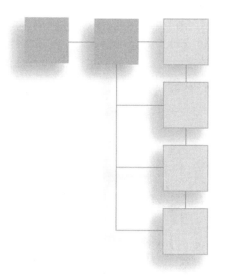

CHAPTER 5

BLASTING MUSIC AND SOUND EFFECTS

Imagine playing a fast-paced first-person shooter with soldiers screaming, bombs exploding, and bullets blazing all around, but your television is muted. This wouldn't be nearly as exciting as hearing amazing sound effects as you make your way through a virtual battlefield. Audio can make or break a game, and that's why it's covered before you learn to make a game. All the secrets of SDL are covered in this chapter, and this book will move on to topics like actual game programming, game engine development, and software design. For now, let's focus on these topics:

- The theory behind digital audio.
- How to play/stop sound effects.
- How to play/stop songs.

Tip

Before getting started, you can check out the video tutorial for this chapter, which is located in BAMGP\ under the Videos directory. The video contains extra material and insights, and reviews the chapter from a high level, so be sure to watch it.

THE BASICS OF AUDIO

A *sound wave* is a series of mechanical vibrations through an air medium that the ear can detect as the pressure waves impinge on the eardrum. For a graphical representation of a simple sound wave, see Figure 5.1. In this model, the straight line is used as a reference with time flowing forward to the right, but the wavy line describes the amplitude, volume, and frequency of a sound wave. Sounds can be captured by a recording device (such as a microphone), stored in a memory device (such as a hard drive or a CD), and reproduced on a playback device (such as a CD player or a computer). Sounds can also be synthesized in computers and electronic instruments. Sounds have three main properties that characterize them. These are pitch, volume, and timbre.

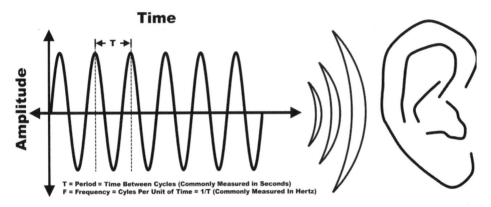

Figure 5.1
A simple sound wave.
© Jazon Yamamoto.

Pitch

Pitch, or *frequency*, is the rate at which sound vibrations oscillate. In the realm of sound, lower pitches correspond to lower frequencies, and higher pitches correspond to higher frequencies. The frequency is the rate at which a cycle is completed, and it is measured in Hertz (Hz). The human ear can hear frequencies as low as 20Hz and as high as 20,000Hz (or 20kHz).

Volume

Volume is the strength of the sound. Higher volumes produce louder sounds, while lower ones produce softer sounds. Volume is measured in decibels (dB). A soft whisper is usually about 30dB, and a heavy metal concert can be as loud as 120dB.

Timbre

Timbre is the waveform of the sound. This is what gives sounds their personality. A note played on an electric guitar can have the same pitch and volume as a note played on the piano, but one can easily distinguish the source instrument by listening to the timbre alone.

UNDERSTANDING DIGITAL AUDIO

Since computers can't capture audio waves with infinite precision, the audio waves stored in a computer are close approximations of the real audio waves. This is done by taking a sound wave and "cutting" it into a series of finite numerical values. A digitized sound has two properties that define its quality. These are the sample rate and bit size. The *sample rate* is the rate at which a sound is "cut." A sound is cut into a bunch of samples, and each of these samples represents the volume of the sound at a particular time. Higher sample rates lead to higher sound quality. A CD stores sound using a sample rate of 44.1kHz. This is higher than what the human ear can hear, so the engineers that created CDs went overboard to ensure great quality.

The *bit size* is the precision of each sample. Higher bit sizes lead to more precision in the volume of a sample. A CD uses 16-bit precision, but it's not uncommon to have 24-bit audio precision in computers. It's also important to acknowledge stereo sound. A stereo sound file usually has two channels of sound. One is for the right ear, and one is for the left. This makes it possible to have sounds that seem to be emanating from multiple directions.

USING THE SDL MIXER SYSTEM

While creating custom sounds is beyond the scope of this book, loading sound files and playing them using SDL Mixer is more than good enough for most purposes. SDL Mixer is an extension library that can be used to simplify the process of playing sounds. To use it, a program must include the library as shown:

```
#include <SDL/SDL_mixer.h>
```

SDL Mixer system should be initialized before using any of the Mixer's functions, as shown:

```
Mix_OpenAudio(22050, MIX_DEFAULT_FORMAT, 2, 2048);
```

For now, just use the parameters above because they should be suitable for your purposes. There are other options, but these parameters are optimized for quality and performance. After the program is finished using the sound system, you must close it gracefully with the following function:

```
Mix_CloseAudio();
```

Table 5.1 explains the functions presented so far in more detail.

Table 5.1 New Functions Used in This Demo

Function	Description

`int Mix_OpenAudio(`
    `int frequency,`
    `Uint16 format,`
    `int channels,`
    `int chunksize)`
	This function initiates SDL Mixer and takes four parameters. The first parameter signifies the sample rate. The second parameter designates the sound format. `MIX_DEFAULT_FORMAT` is used to pick a format that is compatible with the system. The third parameter indicates the number of channels that will be used, and it is set to 2 for stereo sound. The fourth parameter indicates the chunk size, and it will be set to 2048 so that the sounds don't have a short delay before playing but still retain decent quality. This function returns −1 if it fails and 0 otherwise.

`void Mix_CloseAudio()`	This function is used to close SDL Mixer. It must be called when the SDL Mixer is no longer in use.

© Jazon Yamamoto.

Using Sound Effects

Sound effects are short pieces of sound as opposed to a musical arrangement that plays for an extended period of time. Using both together can generate a rich gameplay experience. Sound effects can occur when a player is hit, a ball is bounced, a missile is fired, and so on. In order to use sound effects in your program, they must be loaded from a sound file and released before the program closes.

Loading Sound Effects

Before playing sound effects, the program must load them. To load a sound effect, create a pointer to `Mix_Chunk` to store the sound as shown:

`Mix_Chunk* sound = NULL;`

After that, load the sound from a file and store it as shown:

`sound = Mix_LoadWAV(filename);`

Keep in mind that `filename` is a placeholder for the file's name, which would be a string. `Mix_LoadWAV` can load sound file formats including WAV, WAVE, OGG, MIDI, and MP3. After the program is finished playing sounds, it must release them as so:

`Mix_FreeChunk(sound);`

The variable *sound* is a placeholder for a `Mix_Chunk` pointer of the sound that will be freed.

Playing Sound Effects

Now that the sounds are loaded, the program can play them. Programs play sounds across different channels. A channel can be thought of as a stream of sound. There are eight streams of sound that SDL Mixer provides. This means only eight sounds can play simultaneously. This is enough in most cases. Don't confuse these with the left and right channels that produce stereo. These eight channels are mixed down to two that are eventually played on the computer speakers as stereo. To play a sound, use `Mix_PlayChannel` as shown in the following code:

```
int channel = Mix_PlayChannel(-1, sound, 0);
```

The first parameter specifies the channel in which the sound effect will be played. There are eight channels to choose from, but passing –1 as the first parameter will choose the most appropriate channel to play the sound. The second parameter will be a pointer to the sound effect, and the third indicates how many times the sound will loop. Passing 0 plays the sound once, passing 1 plays it twice, and so on. It's also interesting to know that passing –1 will loop the sound indefinitely. This function returns the number of the channel in which the sound will be played. This value can be useful since it lets you pause, resume, and stop the sound. The code in Listing 5.1 plays a sound, then pauses it, resumes it, and finally stops it.

Listing 5.1: Conducting Channel Operations

```
int channel = Mix_PlayChannel(-1, sound, 0);
SDL_Delay(1000);
Mix_Pause(channel);
SDL_Delay(1000);
Mix_Resume(channel);
SDL_Delay(1000);
Mix_Halt(channel);
```

Building the App

You can find the files necessary to build this app in `BAMGP\`. They are located in `Source\Chapter_05\` `5_1_SoundEffects\`. You need to create an SDL project and copy `main.cpp` as well as the `graphics` and `notes` folders into your project's directory. If you're using Windows, make sure to include the `.dll` files in the project's directory. This project requires additional `.dll` files that are specifically used for sound, so make sure to include those as well. Your project should be configured properly, as shown in Chapter 1, and all the files should also be properly included. When all is set, you'll be able to build the program and run it on your own. Additionally, a precompiled version is in the `Source` directory named `5_1_SoundEffects.exe`.

Figure 5.2 exhibits a screenshot of the sound demo. This demo loads digitized piano notes as individual sounds and plays them when certain keys on the keyboard are pressed (much like a piano). Table 5.2 describes the functions necessary to load sounds.

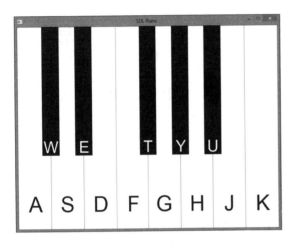

Figure 5.2
The sound demo.
© Jazon Yamamoto.

Table 5.2 New Functions Used in This Demo

Function	Description
`Mix_Chunk *Mix_LoadWAV( const char *fname);`	This function takes one parameter, and it is the string of the filename of a sound file. It loads the sound as an instance of `Mix_Chunk` and returns a pointer to it.
`void Mix_FreeChunk( Mix_Chunk *chunk)`	This function gracefully releases a sound file. It takes one parameter, and it is a pointer to an instance of `Mix_Chunk` that is to be released.
`int Mix_PlayChannel ( int channel, Mix_Chunk *chunk, int loops)`	This function plays the channel. The first parameter indicates the channel in which you want to play the sound. Passing −1 will play the sound on any channel that is available. The second parameter is a pointer to the instance of `Mix_Chunk` that will be played. The third parameter indicates the number of times the sound should loop. Passing 0 plays the sound one time, passing 1 plays the sound two times, and so on. It also returns an `int` holding the channel in which the sound will be played.
`void Mix_Pause( int channel)`	This function pauses a channel, and it takes only one parameter. This parameter is an `int` indicating the channel that is to be paused. Passing −1 pauses all the channels.

`void Mix_Resume(` `int channel)`	This function resumes a paused channel and takes one parameter. This parameter is an `int` indicating the paused channel that is to be resumed. Passing −1 resumes all the paused channels.
`int Mix_HaltChannel(` `int channel)`	This function stops a channel, and it takes one parameter. This parameter is an `int` indicating the channel that is to be stopped. Passing −1 stops all the channels.

© Jazon Yamamoto.

PLAYING MUSIC

Playing music is much like playing sounds, but SDL Mixer can only play one song at a time. Technically, it is possible to load a music file as if it were a simple sound, but SDL has a data structure that is specifically optimized for playing music. Just like with sounds, you must load them before they are used and free them before the program closes.

Loading Music Files

Music is stored in instances of `Mix_Music`. `Mix_LoadMUS` can be used to create an instance of `Mix_Music` and populate it with music loaded from a file as shown:

```
Mix_Music* song = NULL;
song = Mix_LoadMUS(filename);
```

This function can load different file formats, such as WAV, OGG, and MIDI. MP3 is probably the most fitting format because music files can take up a lot of space, and the MP3 format compresses the data while maintaining decent quality.

After the program is finished playing music, it must release it as shown in the following code:

```
Mix_FreeMusic(song);
```

Playing Music Files

Playing music is easy to do once a song is loaded. To play the song, simply use the following function:

```
Mix_PlayMusic(song, -1);
```

The first parameter is a pointer to the loaded song, and the second parameter designates the amount of times that the song will be looped. Passing −1 will loop it indefinitely. It is also possible to pause the music by calling:

```
Mix_PauseMusic();
```

If the music is paused, you can resume it by calling:

```
Mix_ResumeMusic();
```

To stop the music, use the following code:

```
Mix_HaltMusic();
```

To check if the music is playing, use the following code:

```
if(Mix_PlayingMusic())
{
    //Music is playing
}
else
{
    //Music is not playing
}
```

Building the App

You can find the files necessary to build this app in BAMGP\. They are located in Source\Chapter_05\ 5_2_MusicFiles\. You need to create an SDL project and copy main.cpp as well as the graphics and audio folders into your project's directory. If you're using Windows, make sure to include the .dll files in the project's directory. This project requires additional .dll files that are specifically used for sound, so make sure to include those as well. Your project should be configured properly, as shown in Chapter 1, and all the files should also be properly included. When all is set, you'll be able to build the program and run it on your own. Additionally, a precompiled version is in the Source directory named 5_2_MusicFiles.exe.

Figure 5.3 shows a screenshot of the demo for playing music. This demo plays/pauses a song when the spacebar key is pressed and stops when the Esc key is pressed. Table 5.3 details the functions used for playing music.

Figure 5.3
The music demo.
© Jazon Yamamoto.

Table 5.3 New Functions Used in This Demo

Function	Description
Mix_Music *Mix_LoadMUS(const char *file)	This function takes one parameter, and it is the filename to a sound file that you want to load. It returns a pointer to an instance of Mix_Music with the sound stored in it.
void Mix_FreeMusic(Mix_Music *music)	This function takes one parameter, and it is a pointer to an instance of Mix_Music that will be released.
int Mix_PlayMusic(Mix_Music *music, int loops)	This function takes two parameters. The first is a pointer to an instance of Mix_Music that is to be played, and the second is the number of times it will loop. Passing −1 loops it indefinitely. Passing 0 plays the song once, passing 1 plays it twice, and so on.
void Mix_PauseMusic()	This function takes no parameters, and it pauses the music if it's playing.
void Mix_ResumeMusic()	This function takes no parameters, and it resumes the music if it's paused.

(Continued)

Table 5.3   New Functions Used in This Demo (*Continued*)

Function	Description
int Mix_HaltMusic()	This function takes no parameters, and it stops the music. It always returns 0.
int Mix_PlayingMusic()	This function takes no parameters, and it returns true if the music is playing and false otherwise.

© Jazon Yamamoto.

SUMMARY

By now, you should be able to play sound effects and music with ease. This also marks the point at which this book transitions into greater challenges, since all the basic aspects of SDL have been covered. You have all the skills you need to start making some interactive masterpieces! Remember to watch the video tutorial for this chapter since it contains some extra information and commentary related to the topics covered. Also make sure that you are ready to continue by completing some of the following exercises.

Exercises

- Load your own custom sounds and play them. If you have a microphone, try recording your name, exporting it to a WAV file, and playing it whenever the spacebar is pressed.

- If you can find an MP3 file of your favorite song on your computer (any song will do), blast that song using SDL Mixer.

CHAPTER 6

YOUR FIRST PLAYABLE VIDEO GAME

With SDL out of the way, this book will go into hardcore mode in the next few chapters. Creating games is a rather complicated process, and the complexity only grows with the complexity of gameplay. Before you create the next jaw-dropping first-person shooter, take a minute to create a few simple games. The first project is a paddle game with a simple objective. This chapter is a milestone in this book, and it covers:

- The design and implementation of a video game.
- Incorporating a player into the game.
- Basic artificial intelligence.
- Basic resource management.

Tip

Before getting started, you can check out the video tutorial for this chapter, which is located in BAMGP\ under the Videos directory. The video contains extra material and insights, and reviews the chapter from a high level, so be sure to watch it.

UNDERSTANDING THE GAME DESIGN

Before you start coding, it's important to have an idea of what the final game might look like. Having a design helps clear up what needs to be done before you start creating your game. This game will be a simple paddle game in which the players control paddles that move along the y-axis. There will be two paddles. One paddle will be located near the right edge of the screen, and the other near the left edge of the screen. The left paddle is controlled by the player, and the right paddle is controlled by the computer. A ball will spawn in the center of the screen moving in a random direction, and the player's goal is to score on the computer by bouncing a ball into the edge of the screen. The ball will bounce when it hits the top or bottom border of the screen or when it hits a paddle. When a player scores, that player's score is incremented by one, both paddles will be repositioned at the center of the y-axis, and the ball will reappear in the center of the screen. Figure 6.1 illustrates the layout of the game mechanics. Before you continue, play the game. It is located in `BAMGP\` under `Source\Chapter_06\` `6_1_PaddleGame\`, and it is called `6_1_PaddleGame.exe`.

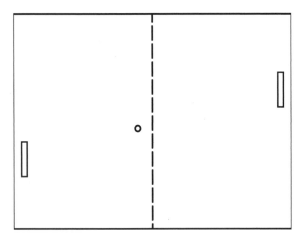

Figure 6.1
The layout of the paddle ball game.
© Jazon Yamamoto.

Tip

This design should look very similar to *Pong* by Atari.

Adding the Program Variables

In this game, there are a few types of variables that do a number of things. Variables can be constant variables, game variables, and resource variables. All of these need to work in conjunction to make gameplay possible.

Constant Variables

Constant variables hold properties of static elements in the game. These properties will not change as gameplay progresses, and constant variables are an ideal form of storage for them. Table 6.1 displays the constant variables in the game, along with a brief description of their roles.

Table 6.1 Constant Variables Used in This Game

Variable	Description
const int SCREEN_WIDTH	This constant holds the width of the screen in pixels.
const int SCREEN_HEIGHT	This constant holds the height of the screen in pixels.
const int PADDLE_WIDTH	This constant holds the width of both players' paddles in pixels.
const int PADDLE_HEIGHT	This constant holds the height of both players' paddles in pixels.
const int BALL_WIDTH	This constant holds the width of the ball in pixels.
const int BALL_HEIGHT	This constant holds the height of the ball in pixels.
const int BALL_MAX_SPEED	This constant holds the maximum speed the ball can reach.
const int PLAYER_PADDLE_X	This constant holds the X coordinate of the player's paddle. This coordinate won't change since the paddle can only move along the y-axis.
const int ENEMY_PADDLE_X	This constant holds the X coordinate of the computer's paddle. This coordinate won't change since the paddle can only move along the y-axis.
const int PLAYER_SPEED	This constant holds the speed at which the player moves.
const int ENEMY_SPEED	This constant holds the speed at which the computer moves.

(Continued)

Table 6.1 Constant Variables Used in This Game (*Continued*)

Variable	Description
const int FPS	This constant holds the number of frames the program will draw per second.
const int FRAME_DELAY	This constant holds the delay between frames in milliseconds, and it will be used for frame-rate regulation.

© Jazon Yamamoto.

Game Variables

These variables are in charge of holding the different possible states of the program. They will change often as gameplay progresses, and they are vital to having a dynamic game. Table 6.2 holds a list of all the game variables and their functions.

Table 6.2 Game Variables Used in This Game

Variable	Description
int PlayerScore	This variable holds the current score of the player.
int EnemyScore	This variable holds the current score of the computer.
int BallXVel	This variable holds the X velocity of the ball.
int BallYVel	This variable holds the Y velocity of the ball.
SDL_Rect PlayerPaddleRect	This variable holds the dimensions and coordinates of the player's paddle.
SDL_Rect EnemyPaddleRect	This variable holds the dimensions and coordinates of the computer's paddle.
SDL_Rect BallRect	This variable holds the dimensions and coordinates of the ball.

© Jazon Yamamoto.

Resource Variables

Resource variables will hold the game's resources. These are images, sounds, songs, or fonts. Table 6.3 holds all the resource variables and brief describes their contents.

Table 6.3   Resource Variables Used in This Game

Variable	Description
SDL_Surface *Backbuffer	This variable holds the pointer to the backbuffer.
SDL_Surface *BackgroundImage	This variable holds the pointer to the background image.
SDL_Surface *BallImage	This variable holds the pointer to the ball's image.
SDL_Surface *PlayerPaddleImage	This variable holds the pointer to the image of the player's paddle.
SDL_Surface *EnemyPaddleImage	This variable holds the pointer to the image of the computer's paddle.
TTF_Font *GameFont	This variable holds the pointer to the font that will be used to draw the game scores in the game.
Mix_Chunk *BallBounceSound	This variable holds the pointer to the sound that will play when the ball bounces off the walls or paddles.
Mix_Chunk *BallSpawnSound	This variable holds the pointer to the sound that will play when the ball is spawned.
Mix_Chunk *PlayerScoreSound	This variable holds the pointer to the sound that will be played when the player scores.
Mix_Chunk *EnemyScoreSound	This variable holds the pointer to the sound that will be played when the computer scores.
Mix_Music *GameMusic	This variable holds the pointer to the music that will be played when the game is running.

UNDERSTANDING THE CODE STRUCTURE

The structure for this game will consist of core game functions, game-specific functions, and a few auxiliary functions. There will also be functions created in the previous chapters to avoid rewriting code. Core game functions are responsible for initializing the game, updating the game running, drawing the screen, and cleaning up after the program is finished. The four core game functions are InitGame, RunGame, DrawGame, and FreeGame. All of these functions consist of other game-specific functions, but packing all of the game-specific code in these functions will create a very general-looking main function, like the one shown in Listing 6.1.

Listing 6.1: The main Function

```
int main(int argc, char *argv[])
{
    if(!InitGame())
    {
        FreeGame();      //If InitGame failed, kill the program
        return 0;
    }
    while(ProgramIsRunning())
    {
        long int oldTime = SDL_GetTicks();
        SDL_FillRect(Backbuffer, NULL, 0);
        RunGame();
        DrawGame();

        int frameTime = SDL_GetTicks() - oldTime;

        if(frameTime < FRAME_DELAY)
            SDL_Delay(FRAME_DELAY - frameTime);
        SDL_Flip(Backbuffer);
    }
    FreeGame();

    return 0;
}
```

The first line in the main function attempts to initialize the game by calling InitGame. If it fails, it will call FreeGame to free any resources it might have loaded and return 0 to exit the program. If the game initializes successfully, it enters the game loop. At the beginning of the game loop, the variable called oldTime is set to SDL_GetTicks(). SDL_GetTicks() returns the number of milliseconds that have elapsed since SDL was initialized. Afterward, the program clears the screen and calls RunGame. This function updates all the game variables. DrawGame is called to draw all the sprites onto the backbuffer. After that, a variable called frameTime is assigned to the arithmetic differ-ence between SDL_GetTicks() and oldTime to get the amount of time that it took to update and render the game. Next, a delay is made based on this value to regulate the frame rate, and the backbuffer is drawn onto the screen. When the game loop exits, FreeGame is called to free all the resources that were acquired. None of the code in the main function is game-specific and can be reused with relative ease.

The InitGame Function

The InitGame function is responsible for setting up the initial state of the game. It will initialize SDL, load resources (images, fonts, and sounds), and set up the game vari-ables. If the function fails to initialize SDL or load the resources, it will return false. This function is called before any other core game functions. The code for the InitGame function is demonstrated in Listing 6.2.

Listing 6.2: The InitGame Function

```
bool InitGame()
{
    //Init SDL
    if(!InitSDL())
        return false;

    //Load Files
    if(!LoadFiles())
        return false;

    //Initialize game variables

    //Set the title
    SDL_WM_SetCaption("Paddle Game!",NULL);

    //Set scores to 0
    PlayerScore = 0;
    EnemyScore = 0;

    //This can also set the initial variables
    ResetGame();

    //Play Music
    Mix_PlayMusic(GameMusic, -1);

    return true;
}
```

The first part of this function initializes SDL by calling InitSDL. If it fails, it returns false, but if it succeeds, it will attempt to load the game's resources by calling LoadFiles. If LoadFiles returns false, InitGame will also return false. If everything goes right, this function will set the window's title and initialize the scores to 0. After that, it will call ResetGame to initialize the paddles' positions, the ball's position, and the ball's velocity. Finally, it will play the game's music and return true.

The InitSDL Function

This function simplifies the initialization of SDL by packing it into one simple and convenient function that returns false if SDL fails to be initialized, as shown in Listing 6.3.

Listing 6.3: The InitSDL Function

```
bool InitSDL()
{
    if(SDL_Init(SDL_INIT_EVERYTHING) == -1)
        return false;

    //Init audio subsystem
    if(Mix_OpenAudio( 22050, MIX_DEFAULT_FORMAT, 2, 2048 ) == -1)
    {
        return false;
    }

    //Init TTF subsystem
    if(TTF_Init() == -1)
    {
        return false;
    }

    //Generate screen
    Backbuffer = SDL_SetVideoMode(SCREEN_WIDTH, SCREEN_HEIGHT,
        32, SDL_SWSURFACE );

    //Error check Backbuffer
    if(Backbuffer == NULL)
        return false;

    return true;
}
```

Tip

This function is very reusable when initializing SDL. It only handles SDL, and it can simply be copied and pasted into new projects.

This function initializes SDL, the audio system, the TTF system, and the backbuffer. It will return false if anything fails and true otherwise.

The LoadFiles Function

This function loads all the images, sounds, fonts, and music. If any of them fails to load, it will return `false`. Otherwise, it will return `true`. After execution of this function, all resource variables must be successfully loaded.

The ResetGame Function

This function resets the paddles and the ball to prepare them for a new round. It is called when initializing the game and after either player scores. The code in Listing 6.4 shows the `ResetGame` function.

Listing 6.4: The `ResetGame` Function

```
void ResetGame()
{
    //Position the player's paddle
    PlayerPaddleRect.x = PLAYER_PADDLE_X;
    PlayerPaddleRect.y = SCREEN_HEIGHT/2 - PADDLE_HEIGHT/2;
    PlayerPaddleRect.w = PADDLE_WIDTH;
    PlayerPaddleRect.h = PADDLE_HEIGHT;

    //Position the enemy's paddle
    EnemyPaddleRect.x = ENEMY_PADDLE_X;
    EnemyPaddleRect.y = SCREEN_HEIGHT/2 - PADDLE_HEIGHT/2;
    EnemyPaddleRect.w = PADDLE_WIDTH;
    EnemyPaddleRect.h = PADDLE_HEIGHT;

    //Position the ball
    BallRect.x = SCREEN_WIDTH/2 - BALL_WIDTH/2;
    BallRect.y = SCREEN_HEIGHT/2 - BALL_HEIGHT/2;
    BallRect.w = BALL_WIDTH;
    BallRect.h = BALL_HEIGHT;

    //Make the ball X velocity a random value from 1 to BALL_MAX_SPEED
    BallXVel = rand()%BALL_MAX_SPEED + 1;

    //Make the ball Y velocity a random value
    //from - BALL_MAX_SPEED to BALL_MAX_SPEED
    BallYVel = (rand()%BALL_MAX_SPEED*2 + 1) - BALL_MAX_SPEED;

    //Give it a 50% probability of going toward the player
    if(rand()%2 == 0)
        BallXVel *= -1;


    //Play the spawn sound
    Mix_PlayChannel(-1, BallSpawnSound, 0);
}
```

This function centers the paddles on the y-axis and sets their width/height and X positions. It also places the ball at the center of the screen and gives it random velocities. After that, it plays the ball spawn sound and sets the game up for a new round.

The RunGame Function

This function updates the paddles and the ball every frame. It consists of the code in Listing 6.5.

Listing 6.5: The RunGame Function

```
void RunGame()
{
    UpdatePlayer();
    UpdateAI();
    UpdateBall();
}
```

The function itself is not complicated, but the complexity lies in the sub-functions. Breaking up this function into three separate functions makes the code easier to read and debug.

Updating the Player

The function in Listing 6.6 is used to update the player's paddle.

Listing 6.6: The UpdatePlayer Function

```
void UpdatePlayer()
{
    Uint8 *keys = SDL_GetKeyState(NULL);

    //Move the paddle when the up/down key is pressed
    if(keys[SDLK_UP])
        PlayerPaddleRect.y -= PLAYER_SPEED;

    if(keys[SDLK_DOWN])
        PlayerPaddleRect.y += PLAYER_SPEED;

    //Make sure the paddle doesn't leave the screen
    if(PlayerPaddleRect.y < 0)
        PlayerPaddleRect.y = 0;

    if(PlayerPaddleRect.y > SCREEN_HEIGHT-PlayerPaddleRect.h)
        PlayerPaddleRect.y = SCREEN_HEIGHT-PlayerPaddleRect.h;
}
```

The first half of this function acquires the key states and moves the player up when the up arrow key is pressed or down when the down arrow key is pressed. The second half of the function makes sure the player's paddle doesn't exit the screen and fade into oblivion.

Updating the Computer

The function in Listing 6.7 updates the computer's paddle.

Listing 6.7: The `UpdateAI` Function

```
void UpdateAI()
{
    //If the paddle's center is higher than the ball's center then
    //move the paddle up
    if((EnemyPaddleRect.y + EnemyPaddleRect.h/2) > (BallRect.y+BallRect.h/2))
        EnemyPaddleRect.y -= ENEMY_SPEED;

    //If the paddle's center is lower than the ball's center then
    //move the paddle down
    if((EnemyPaddleRect.y + EnemyPaddleRect.h/2) < (BallRect.y+BallRect.h/2))
        EnemyPaddleRect.y += ENEMY_SPEED;

    //Make sure the paddle doesn't leave the screen
    if(EnemyPaddleRect.y < 0)
        EnemyPaddleRect.y = 0;

    if(EnemyPaddleRect.y > SCREEN_HEIGHT-EnemyPaddleRect.h)
        EnemyPaddleRect.y = SCREEN_HEIGHT-EnemyPaddleRect.h;
}
```

The first half of this function is a primitive form of artificial intelligence. If the paddle's center is higher than the ball's center along the y-axis, it will lower the paddle's y variable, but if the paddle's center is lower than the ball's center along the y-axis, it will raise the paddle's y variable. The second half of the function makes sure the paddle doesn't leave the screen.

Updating the Ball

Updating the ball is a bit more complicated than updating the paddles because you need to update the ball's position, as well as direction, and adjust the score if the ball makes it to either side of the screen. The code in Listing 6.8 updates the ball.

Listing 6.8: The UpdateBall Function

```
void UpdateBall()
{
    BallRect.x += BallXVel;
    BallRect.y += BallYVel;

    //If the ball hits the player, make it bounce
    if(RectsOverlap(BallRect, PlayerPaddleRect))
    {
        BallXVel = rand()%BALL_MAX_SPEED + 1;
        Mix_PlayChannel(-1, BallBounceSound, 0);
    }

    //If the ball hits the enemy, make it bounce
    if(RectsOverlap(BallRect, EnemyPaddleRect))
    {
        BallXVel = (rand()%BALL_MAX_SPEED +1) * -1;
        Mix_PlayChannel(-1, BallBounceSound, 0);
    }

    //Make sure the ball doesn't leave the screen and make it
    //bounce randomly
    if(BallRect.y < 0)
    {
        BallRect.y = 0;
        BallYVel = rand()%BALL_MAX_SPEED + 1;
        Mix_PlayChannel(-1, BallBounceSound, 0);
    }

    if(BallRect.y > SCREEN_HEIGHT - BallRect.h)
    {
        BallRect.y = SCREEN_HEIGHT - BallRect.h;
        BallYVel = (rand()%BALL_MAX_SPEED + 1)* -1;
        Mix_PlayChannel(-1, BallBounceSound, 0);
    }

    //If player scores
    if(BallRect.x > SCREEN_WIDTH)
    {
        PlayerScore++;
        Mix_PlayChannel(-1, PlayerScoreSound, 0);
        ResetGame();
    }

    //If enemy scores
    if(BallRect.x < 0-BallRect.h)
    {
```

```
        EnemyScore++;
        Mix_PlayChannel(-1, EnemyScoreSound, 0);
        ResetGame();
    }
}
```

This function can be divided into four sections. The first section updates the ball's position according to its velocity. The second section uses the function RectsOverlap to check if the ball collided with either paddle and makes it bounce if it did. The third part bounces the ball off of the top and bottom edges of the screen. The last part checks if the ball scored on either player. If a player scores, the scores are updated accordingly, the appropriate sound is played, and the game is reset. The code in Listing 6.9 displays the RectsOverlap function.

Listing 6.9: The RectsOverlap Function

```
bool RectsOverlap(SDL_Rect rect1, SDL_Rect rect2)
{
    if(rect1.x >= rect2.x+rect2.w)
        return false;
    if(rect1.y >= rect2.y+rect2.h)
        return false;
    if(rect2.x >= rect1.x+rect1.w)
        return false;
    if(rect2.y >= rect1.y+rect1.h)
        return false;
    return true;
}
```

This function checks if two axis-aligned rectangles overlap.

Tip

This function is very fast at checking for collisions, and it can be reused for any game that doesn't need perfect collision detection.

Drawing the Game

This core game function draws all the images on the screen. The code in Listing 6.10 shows the DrawGame function.

Listing 6.10: The `DrawGame` Function

```
void DrawGame()
{
    DrawImage(BackgroundImage, Backbuffer, 0, 0);
    DrawImage(BallImage, Backbuffer, BallRect.x, BallRect.y);

    DrawImage(PlayerPaddleImage, Backbuffer,
        PlayerPaddleRect.x, PlayerPaddleRect.y);
    DrawImage(EnemyPaddleImage, Backbuffer,
        EnemyPaddleRect.x, EnemyPaddleRect.y);

    char playerHUD[64];
    char enemyHUD[64];

    sprintf(playerHUD, "Player Score: %d", PlayerScore);
    sprintf(enemyHUD, "Enemy Score: %d", EnemyScore);

    DrawText(Backbuffer, playerHUD, 0, 1, GameFont, 64, 64, 64);
    DrawText(Backbuffer, enemyHUD, 0, 30, GameFont, 64, 64, 64);
}
```

This function first draws the background, then the ball, and finally the paddles. After that, it creates two strings to hold both players' scores and draws them onto the screen.

Freeing the Resources

The resources are released using `FreeGame`. This will close all of the SDL systems and free all the files that were loaded. The code in Listing 6.11 shows the `FreeGame` function.

Listing 6.11: The `FreeGame` Function

```
void FreeGame()
{
    Mix_HaltMusic();        //Stop the music
    FreeFiles();            //Release the files that were loaded
    Mix_CloseAudio();       //Close the audio system
    TTF_Quit();             //Close the font system
    SDL_Quit();             //Close SDL
}
```

This function stops the music, calls `FreeFiles` to free the files that were loaded with `LoadFiles`, and finally closes the SDL systems that were opened.

The `FreeFiles` Function

This function is in charge of freeing all the files that were loaded with `LoadFiles`. It is very simple, and there is nothing new in it. All of the code in this function is simple and repetitive, so it isn't listed here.

PUTTING IT ALL TOGETHER

Now that all the functions have been defined, you can compile the game. If you made your own project and typed the code by hand, make sure you write the LoadFiles and FreeFiles functions since they are essential parts of the game. Also make sure that the images load and are the appropriate sizes. When all is set and done, compile the application. If all the code was entered correctly, the output should resemble Figure 6.2.

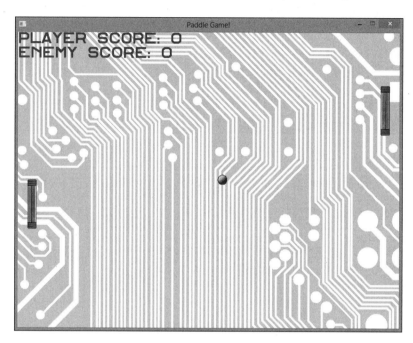

Figure 6.2
A screenshot of the paddle game.
© Jazon Yamamoto.

Building the App

You can find the files necessary to build this app in the BAMGP\. They are located in Source\ Chapter_06\6_1_PaddleGame\. You need to create an SDL project and copy main.cpp as well as the graphics and audio folders into your project's directory. If you're using Windows, make sure to include the .dll files in the project's directory. This project requires additional .dll files that are specifically used for sound and images, so make sure to include those as well. Your project should be configured properly, as shown in Chapter 1, and all the files should be properly included. When all is set, you'll be able to build the program and run it on your own. Additionally, a precompiled version is in the Source directory named 6_1_PaddleGame.exe.

SUMMARY

This chapter was quite intense, but it was also quite exciting. While the game that you created may not be much, it has all the basics of a video game. The mechanics of this game are simple, but there are many improvements that could be done to improve the gameplay. Also make sure you check out this chapter's video tutorial for additional commentary. Before continuing on to the next chapter, complete some of the following exercises to improve the gameplay and to refine your game-development skills.

Exercises

- Sometimes the ball moves at an excruciatingly slow speed. Try setting a minimum speed at which the ball must travel.

- Modify the UpdateAI function to make a second player control the enemy's paddle instead of the computer (a multiplayer game). Keep in mind that the enemy's paddle moves slower than the player's paddle, so if no modifications are made to the enemy's paddle's speed, the second player will always have a disadvantage.

- The ball bounces off the paddles in a random direction, thus giving the player little control over the ball's trajectory. Make the paddle's direction affect the velocity of the ball when the ball bounces to give the players more control over the ball. This adds skill-based offensive potential to the game.

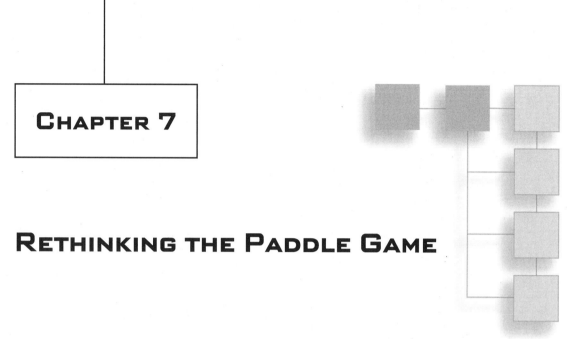

CHAPTER 7

RETHINKING THE PADDLE GAME

In the previous chapter, you created a simple program that had all the basic functionality of a primitive video game. It had simple physics, collision detection, and artificial intelligence. To establish a firmer grasp on video game development, this chapter will kick things up a notch. In this chapter, you learn to transform the simple paddle game into a completely different beast. Doing so, you will learn about:

- More advanced object collision detection and response.

- Game states.

- Handling more objects on the screen.

- Structuring your game for more complicated gameplay.

Tip

Before you get started, you can check out the video tutorial for this chapter, which is located in BAMGP\ under the Videos directory. The video contains extra material and insights, and reviews the chapter from a high level, so be sure to watch it.

IMPLEMENTING THE NEW DESIGN

In the new paddle game, there will be only one player playing against the computer. The player will use the arrow keys to move a horizontal paddle at the bottom of the screen left and right. A ball will spawn on the paddle, and the player will be able to fire the ball upon pressing the spacebar. After firing the ball, the player will have to bounce the ball against blocks that will be positioned on the upper side of the screen. If the ball hits a block, it will bounce off, and the block will disappear. If the ball hits the left, upper, or right side of the screen, it will simply bounce. If the ball hits the bottom side of the screen, the player will lose a life, and the ball will be respawned on the player's paddle. The player will start out with three lives and will lose the game if all the lives are lost. If all the blocks are destroyed, the player will win another round of the game. Figure 7.1 demonstrates a mockup of the game.

Before you continue, it's a good idea to play the prebuilt game to get a general feel for it. It is located in BAMGP\ under Source\Chapter_07\7_1_PaddleGame2\, and it is named 7_1_PaddleGame2.exe.

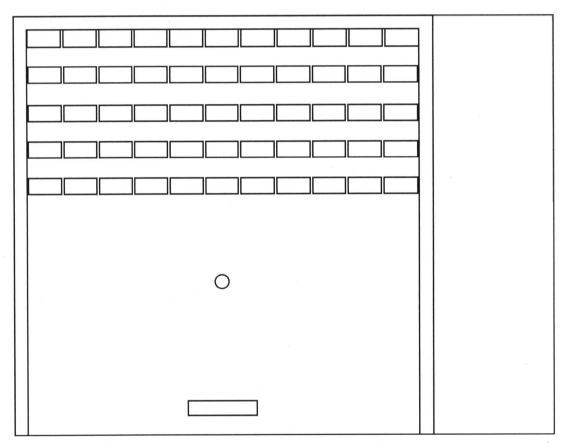

Figure 7.1
A mockup of the game.
© Jazon Yamamoto.

The Player

The player will control a paddle at the bottom of the screen. This paddle will have several behaviors. First, it will have a restricted area of movement. It won't be able to move up, down, too far to the right, or to the left. If the top side of the player's paddle collides with the ball, the ball will bounce according to how close it was to the center of the paddle. If the ball hits the left side of the paddle, it will bounce toward the left, and if it hits the right side, it will bounce toward the right. If the ball hits the exact center of the paddle, it will bounce straight up. Figure 7.2 demonstrates the different directions a ball can go upon colliding with the paddle, depending on the point of collision.

Figure 7.2
The ball's post-collision directions.
© Jazon Yamamoto.

The Game Area

The game area is the space in which the game will take place. In the previous game, the entire screen was dedicated to the game. In this game, however, you will restrict the game to a portion of the screen. The rest of the screen will be used to display other information. Restricting the game area to a small portion of the screen to make room for displaying scores, lives, and other game elements is common practice in many arcade games. Figure 7.3 demonstrates the restricted game area.

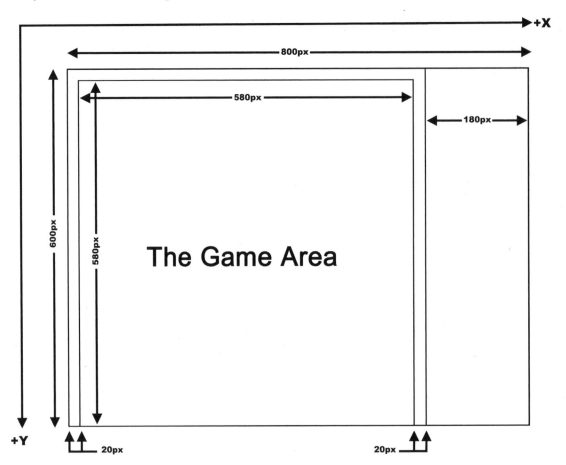

Figure 7.3
The game area.
© Jazon Yamamoto.

The Blocks

The objective of the game is to destroy every block on the screen. A block will be destroyed when a ball collides with it. Upon collision, the ball will bounce, and the velocity of the ball after the collision will be determined by the side of the block that the ball hit. Hitting the block on the top or bottom side will invert the ball's Y velocity, and hitting the block on the left or right side will invert the ball's X velocity. Figure 7.4 demonstrates the ball's collision detection and response. When all the blocks are destroyed, the game will reset.

Figure 7.4
A brick disintegrating after a collision.
© Jazon Yamamoto.

Game States

Using game states will make the game more complete and professional. A game state is, for the lack of a better description, the state the game is in. In the previous game, there was one game state. The game could not be paused and didn't have a nice splash screen to greet the player. This game will support different game states. This will not affect how the game is played, but it'll make a nicer experience for the players. This game will have four game states. The game will be able to go from one game state or another, depending on the player's actions. Figure 7.5 shows the network of game states this game will have.

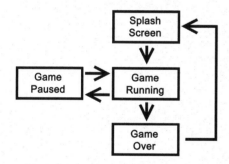

Figure 7.5
The game state network.
© Jazon Yamamoto.

The Splash Screen State

After the game has finished loading its resources, it will enter the splash screen state. In this state, an image will be displayed on the screen to greet the player, and the game will wait for the player to press a key to kick the game into the game running state. Figure 7.6 demonstrates a screenshot of the splash screen state.

Figure 7.6
The splash screen.
© Jazon Yamamoto.

The Game Running State

The game running state is the main state of the game. In this state, the player will actually play the game. Figure 7.7 demonstrates the game running state. There are two ways to exit this game state. The first is by pressing the Esc key. This will change the game's state to paused. Losing all three lives will also change the running state by putting the game in the game over state.

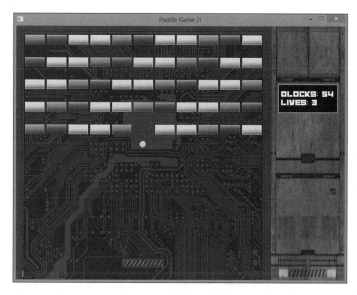

Figure 7.7
The game is running.
© Jazon Yamamoto.

The Game Paused State

The game paused state occurs when the player presses the Esc key during gameplay. In this state, the game will be paused. The game will resume when the player presses the Esc key again. Figure 7.8 displays the game in the paused state.

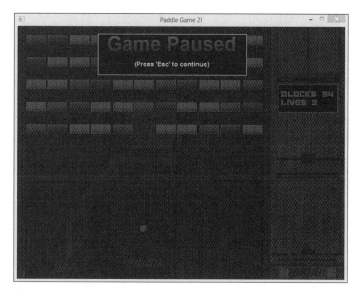

Figure 7.8
The game paused screen.
© Jazon Yamamoto.

The Game Over State

The game enters this state when the player loses all of his lives. In this state, the player will be informed that the game is over. The player can exit this state and return to the splash screen state by pressing the spacebar. Figure 7.9 demonstrates this state.

Figure 7.9
The game over screen.
© Jazon Yamamoto.

CREATING GAME DATA STRUCTURES

To keep things simple, data structures weren't created in the previous game. This time, doing so will make the code more organized and easier to read. Creating three structures to hold some variables for the game will result in a much cleaner code base.

The Player Structure

This structure holds the player's information. It contains the player's bounding rectangle and the player's lives. Listing 7.1 contains the code for the player's structure.

Listing 7.1: The Player Structure

```
struct Player
{
    SDL_Rect rect;
    int lives;
};
```

The Ball Structure

This structure contains the ball's bounding rectangle, X velocity, Y velocity, and a variable called isLocked. isLocked determines if the ball is locked on the player's paddle. When the ball is locked on the player's paddle, its position will be relative to the paddle, and the ball will not move unless the paddle moves. When the ball is not locked, it will move around the screen according to its velocity. Listing 7.2 exhibits the code for the ball's structure.

Listing 7.2: The Ball Structure

```
struct Ball
{
    SDL_Rect rect;
    int xVel;
    int yVel;
    bool isLocked;
};
```

The Block Structure

The Block structure will hold a block's bounding rectangle and frame. There will be four different blocks. Instead of storing them in different images, they will be stored in the same image, and each will be drawn from different frames of the image of each block. There is also a variable called alive, which determines if the block has been destroyed. Destroyed blocks will not be drawn, and the ball will no longer collide with them. Listing 7.3 demonstrates the code for the block's structure.

Listing 7.3: The Block Structure

```
struct Block
{
    SDL_Rect rect;
    bool alive;
    int frame;
};
```

CREATING THE GAME VARIABLES

Much like the previous game, this one will consist of many variables working together to keep the game running. There are still only three types of variables: constant variables, game variables, and resource variables.

The Constant Variables

Table 7.1 lists the game's constant variables and their values.

Table 7.1   The Constant Variables and Their Values

Variable	Value
const int SCREEN_WIDTH	The game's screen width.
const int SCREEN_HEIGHT	The game's screen height.
const int PADDLE_WIDTH	The paddle's width.
const int PADDLE_HEIGHT	The paddle's height.
const int PADDLE_Y	The paddle's Y coordinate.
const int BALL_WIDTH	The ball's width.
const int BALL_HEIGHT	The ball's height.
const int BALL_SPEED	The ball's speed.
const int PLAYER_SPEED	The player's speed.
const int FP	The frames per second.
const int FRAME_DELAY	The frame delay according to the frames per second.
const int GAMEAREA_X1	The game area's X1 coordinate.
const int GAMEAREA_Y1	The game area's Y1 coordinate.
const int GAMEAREA_X2	The game area's X2 coordinate.
const int GAMEAREA_Y2	The game area's Y2 coordinate.
const int BLOCK_COLUMNS	The number of block columns in the game.
const int BLOCK_ROWS	The number of block rows in the game.
const int BLOCK_WIDTH	The width of every block in the game.
const int BLOCK_HEIGHT	The height of every block in the game.
const int GS_SPLASH	The arbitrary value assigned to the splash screen state.

`const int GS_RUNNING`	The arbitrary value assigned to the game running state.
`const int GS_GAMEOVER`	The arbitrary value assigned to the game over state.
`const int GS_PAUSED`	The arbitrary value assigned to the game paused state.

© Jazon Yamamoto.

The Game Variables

This game will consist of a few game variables because you used structures to keep all the data together. Table 7.2 shows the game variables and descriptions of what they hold.

Table 7.2   The Game Variables

Variable	Description
`Block blocks[BLOCK_COLUMNS * BLOCK_ROWS];`	This array holds every block's data.
`Player player;`	The player's data.
`Ball ball;`	The ball's data.
`int gameState;`	The current game state.

© Jazon Yamamoto.

The Resource Variables

This game will have more resource variables than the previous one. Table 7.3 shows the game's resource variables and their values.

Table 7.3   The Resource Variables

Variable	Description
`SDL_Surface *Backbuffer = NULL;`	The backbuffer.
`SDL_Surface *BackgroundImage = NULL;`	The background image for the game while it's running.
`SDL_Surface *BallImage = NULL;`	The ball's image.
`SDL_Surface *PlayerPaddleImage = NULL;`	The paddle's image.

(Continued)

Table 7.3 The Resource Variables (*Continued*)

Variable	Description
`SDL_Surface *BlockImage = NULL;`	The block images.
`SDL_Surface *SplashImage = NULL;`	The splash screen image.
`SDL_Surface *GameoverImage = NULL;`	The game over image.
`SDL_Surface *GamepausedImage = NULL;`	The game paused image.
`TTF_Font *GameFont = NULL;`	The game's font.
`Mix_Chunk *BallBounceSound = NULL;`	The sound played when the ball bounces.
`Mix_Chunk *BallSpawnSound = NULL;`	The sound played when the ball is spawned.
`Mix_Chunk *ExplosionSound = NULL;`	The sound played when a block is destroyed.
`Mix_Music *GameMusic = NULL;`	The background music.

© Jazon Yamamoto.

UNDERSTANDING THE PROGRAM STRUCTURE

The new `main` function will look slightly different. The only difference is that the function named `DrawGame` is replaced by `DrawScreen`. The code in Listing 7.4 shows the new `main` function.

Listing 7.4: The `main` Function

```
int main(int argc, char *argv[])
{
    if(!InitGame())
    {
        FreeGame();   //If InitGame failed, kill the program
        return 0;
    }
    while(ProgramIsRunning())
    {
        long int oldTime = SDL_GetTicks();
        SDL_FillRect(Backbuffer, NULL, 0);
        RunGame();
        DrawScreen();

        int frameTime = SDL_GetTicks() - oldTime;

        if(frameTime < FRAME_DELAY)
            SDL_Delay(FRAME_DELAY - frameTime);
        SDL_Flip(Backbuffer);
    }
```

```
    FreeGame();

    return 0;
}
```

Initializing the Game

The function to initialize the game has not changed too much. The only difference is that the game state is set to GS_SPLASH to make the game enter the splash screen state. The code in Listing 7.5 demonstrates the new InitGame function.

Listing 7.5: The InitGame Function

```
bool InitGame()
{
    //Init SDL
    if(!InitSDL())
        return false;

    //Load Files
    if(!LoadFiles())
        return false;

    //Initialize game variables

    //Set the title
    SDL_WM_SetCaption("Paddle Game 2!",NULL);

    //Play Music
    Mix_PlayMusic(GameMusic, -1);

    //Set the game state
    gameState = GS_SPLASH;

    return true;
}
```

Updating the Current Game State

Since a new game state system was implemented, the game will update according to its current game state. The switch statement is used to select the appropriate action, depending on the game state. The code in Listing 7.6 shows the RunGame function.

Listing 7.6: The RunGame Function

```
void RunGame()
{
    switch(gameState)
    {
    case GS_SPLASH:
        UpdateSplash();
```

```
        break;
    case GS_RUNNING:
        UpdateGame();
        break;
    case GS_GAMEOVER:
        UpdateGameOver();
        break;
    default:
        break;
    }
}
```

Drawing the Screen

Drawing the game is similar to updating it since the game will be drawn according to the current game state. The code in Listing 7.7 displays the DrawScreen function.

Listing 7.7: The DrawScreen Function

```
void DrawScreen()
{
    switch(gameState)
    {
    case GS_SPLASH:
        DrawSplash();
        break;
    case GS_RUNNING:
        DrawGame();
        break;
    case GS_GAMEOVER:
        DrawGameOver();
        break;
    case GS_PAUSED:
        DrawGamePaused();
        break;
    default:
        break;
    }
}
```

CREATING THE SPLASH SCREEN

The purpose of the splash screen is to greet the player. This is not necessary in a video game, but it makes the game look and feel more professional.

Updating the Splash Screen

The `UpdateSplash` function updates the splash screen when the game is in the splash screen state. In this function, the game will be reset, and the game state will be changed to the running state. The code in Listing 7.8 updates the splash screen.

Listing 7.8: The `UpdateSplash` Function

```
void UpdateSplash()
{
    Uint8 *keys = SDL_GetKeyState(NULL);
    if(keys[SDLK_RETURN])
    {
        //This will start a new game
        ResetGame();
        gameState = GS_RUNNING;
    }
}
```

Resetting the Game

The `ResetGame` function sets the initial state of the ball, the player, and the blocks. The code in Listing 7.9 shows the guts of the `ResetGame` function.

Listing 7.9: The `ResetGame` Function

```
void ResetGame()
{
    //Position the player's paddle
    player.rect.x = (GAMEAREA_X2-GAMEAREA_X1)/2 -
                        PADDLE_WIDTH/2 + GAMEAREA_X1;
    player.rect.y = PADDLE_Y;
    player.rect.w = PADDLE_WIDTH;
    player.rect.h = PADDLE_HEIGHT;

    //Position the ball
    ball.rect.x = SCREEN_WIDTH/2 - BALL_WIDTH/2;
    ball.rect.y = SCREEN_HEIGHT/2 - BALL_HEIGHT/2;
    ball.rect.w = BALL_WIDTH;
    ball.rect.h = BALL_HEIGHT;

    //Play the spawn sound
    Mix_PlayChannel(-1, BallSpawnSound, 0);

    //Set blocks
    SetBlocks();
    ball.isLocked = true;
    player.lives = 3;
}
```

Drawing the Splash Screen

When drawing the splash screen, a single image will be drawn to greet the player. The code in Listing 7.10 shows the DrawSplash function.

Listing 7.10: The DrawSplash Function

```
void DrawSplash()
{
    DrawImage(SplashImage, Backbuffer, 0, 0);
}
```

CREATING THE GAME RUNNING STATE

The game running state is the most important state since it's the state in which the player will play the game. This state is also the most complex. It consists of a few functions that wrap up the complexity of updating the game.

Updating the Game

The game is updated with the UpdateGame function. This function updates the player and the ball. Additionally, this function determines if the game is over. It also resets the game if all the blocks are destroyed. The code in Listing 7.11 demonstrates this function.

Listing 7.11: The UpdateGame Function

```
void UpdateGame()
{
    UpdatePlayer();
    UpdateBall();

    if(player.lives <= 0)
        gameState = GS_GAMEOVER;

    if(NumBlocksLeft() <= 0)
        ResetGame();
}
```

Calculating the Number of Blocks Left

To calculate the number of blocks left, simply traverse through the block list and count the blocks that have not been destroyed. The code in Listing 7.12 demonstrates the NumBlocksLeft function, which is used to count the number of blocks left.

Listing 7.12: The `NumBlocksLeft` Function

```
int NumBlocksLeft()
{
    int result = 0;
    for(int i = 0; i < BLOCK_COLUMNS*BLOCK_ROWS; i++)
    {
        if(blocks[i].alive)
        {
            result++;
        }
    }
    return result;
}
```

Updating the Player

The UpdatePlayer function moves the players when they press the left/right arrow keys and releases the ball when the spacebar is pressed. This function also makes sure the paddle can't leave the game area. Listing 7.13 demonstrates the code for this function.

Listing 7.13: The `UpdatePlayer` Function

```
void UpdatePlayer()
{
    Uint8 *keys = SDL_GetKeyState(NULL);
    //Move the paddle when the left/right key is pressed
    if(keys[SDLK_LEFT])
        player.rect.x -= PLAYER_SPEED;
    if(keys[SDLK_RIGHT])
        player.rect.x += PLAYER_SPEED;
    if(keys[SDLK_SPACE] && ball.isLocked)
    {
        ball.isLocked = false;
        ball.xVel = rand()%3 - 1;
        ball.yVel = BALL_SPEED;
    }
    //Make sure the paddle doesn't leave the screen
    if(player.rect.x < GAMEAREA_X1)
        player.rect.x = GAMEAREA_X1;
    if(player.rect.x > GAMEAREA_X2-player.rect.w)
        player.rect.x = GAMEAREA_X2-player.rect.w;
}
```

Updating the Ball

The code to update the ball is by far the most complicated since the ball handles most of the interaction between the game objects. The code is broken into three sections to make the explanation clearer.

Handling Ball Collision

The first part of the `UpdateBall` function updates the ball if it's locked. It centers the ball on the paddle's X coordinate and places the ball right on top of the paddle. The code in Listing 7.14 demonstrates the first part of this function.

Listing 7.14: The `UpdateBall` Function (Part 1)

```
void UpdateBall()
{
    if(ball.isLocked)
    {
        int PaddleCenterX = player.rect.x + player.rect.w/2;
        ball.rect.x = PaddleCenterX - ball.rect.w/2;
        ball.rect.y = player.rect.y - ball.rect.h;
    }
    else
    {
```

If the ball is not locked, it is most likely bouncing around the game area and colliding with other objects. This part of the code shows the ball's collision detection and response. To update the ball's position, first move the ball in the X coordinate and check if it collided with a block or with the player. If it does collide, the ball will be moved back to its original X coordinate, and its X velocity will be inverted. The code in Listing 7.15 shows the ball's collision detection and response when moving on the x-axis.

Listing 7.15: The `UpdateBall` Function (Part 2)

```
ball.rect.x += ball.xVel;

if(RectsOverlap(ball.rect, player.rect))
{
    ball.rect.x -= ball.xVel;
    ball.xVel *= -1;
    Mix_PlayChannel(-1, BallBounceSound, 0);
}
else
{
```

```
        for(int i = 0; i < BLOCK_COLUMNS*BLOCK_ROWS; i++)
        {
            if(blocks[i].alive &&
                RectsOverlap(ball.rect, blocks[i].rect))
            {
                ball.rect.x -= ball.xVel;
                ball.xVel *= -1;
                blocks[i].alive = false;
                Mix_PlayChannel(-1, ExplosionSound, 0);
            }
        }
    }
}
```

After moving the ball on the x-axis, this function moves it on the y-axis. The collision detection and response algorithm for the y-axis looks almost identical to the x-axis one, with the exception of the player's collision response. When the collision is closer to the paddle's right edge, the ball will bounce toward the right. When the collision is closer to the left edge, it will bounce toward the left. When the ball collides with the paddle's center, it will bounce straight up. The ball's X velocity is divided by five to dampen this effect, which makes the ball's path more predictable. The code in Listing 7.16 shows the algorithms involved with moving the ball along the y-axis.

Listing 7.16: The UpdateBall Function (Part 3)

```
ball.rect.y += ball.yVel;

if(RectsOverlap(ball.rect, player.rect))
{
    ball.rect.y -= ball.yVel;
    ball.yVel *= -1;

    int ballCenterX = ball.rect.x+ball.rect.w/2;
    int paddleCenterX = player.rect.x+player.rect.w/2;

    ball.xVel = (ballCenterX - paddleCenterX)/5;
    Mix_PlayChannel(-1, BallBounceSound, 0);
}
else
{
    for(int i = 0; i < BLOCK_COLUMNS*BLOCK_ROWS; i++)
    {
        if(blocks[i].alive &&
            RectsOverlap(ball.rect, blocks[i].rect))
        {
            ball.rect.y -= ball.yVel;
            ball.yVel *= -1;
```

```
            blocks[i].alive = false;

            Mix_PlayChannel(-1, ExplosionSound, 0);
        }
    }
}
```

The final part of the UpdateBall function bounces the ball if it hits the top, left, and right edges of the game area. It also repositions the ball and decrements the player's lives if the ball left the screen. The code in Listing 7.17 shows the rest of the UpdateBall function.

Listing 7.17: The UpdateBall Function (Part 4)

```
//Make sure the ball doesn't leave the screen and make it
//bounce randomly
if(ball.rect.y < GAMEAREA_Y1)
{
    ball.rect.y = GAMEAREA_Y1;
    ball.yVel *= -1;
    Mix_PlayChannel(-1, BallBounceSound, 0);
}

if(ball.rect.x > GAMEAREA_X2 - ball.rect.w)
{
    ball.rect.x = GAMEAREA_X2 - ball.rect.w;
    ball.xVel *= -1;
    Mix_PlayChannel(-1, BallBounceSound, 0);
}

if(ball.rect.x < GAMEAREA_X1)
{
    ball.rect.x = GAMEAREA_X1;
    ball.xVel *= -1;
    Mix_PlayChannel(-1, BallBounceSound, 0);
}

//If the player loses the ball

if(ball.rect.y > GAMEAREA_Y2)
{
    ball.isLocked = true;

    //Reposition Ball
    int PaddleCenterX = player.rect.x + player.rect.w/2;
    ball.rect.x = PaddleCenterX - ball.rect.w/2;
    ball.rect.y = player.rect.y - ball.rect.h;

    player.lives--;
    Mix_PlayChannel(-1, BallSpawnSound, 0);
}
```

Drawing the Screen

Since a game state system was implemented, every game state will have its own drawing procedures. The code in Listing 7.18 demonstrates the function that will draw the game according to the current state.

Listing 7.18: The DrawScreen Function

```
void DrawScreen()
{
    switch(gameState)
    {
    case GS_SPLASH:
        DrawSplash();
        break;
    case GS_RUNNING:
        DrawGame();
        break;
    case GS_GAMEOVER:
        DrawGameOver();
        break;
    case GS_PAUSED:
        DrawGamePaused();
        break;
    default:
        break;
    }
}
```

Drawing the Game

The DrawGame function draws the game. It draws the background image, the ball's image, the player's image, and the blocks, and then it prints information about the number of lives left and the number of blocks left. The code in Listing 7.19 demonstrates this function.

Listing 7.19: The DrawGame Function

```
void DrawGame()
{
    DrawImage(BackgroundImage, Backbuffer, 0, 0);
    DrawImage(BallImage, Backbuffer, ball.rect.x, ball.rect.y);
    DrawImage(PlayerPaddleImage, Backbuffer, player.rect.x, player.rect.y);
    DrawBlocks();
```

```
    char blocksText[64];
    char livesText[64];

    sprintf(blocksText, "Blocks: %d", NumBlocksLeft());
    sprintf(livesText, "Lives: %d", player.lives);
    DrawText(Backbuffer, blocksText, 645, 150, GameFont, 255, 255, 255);
    DrawText(Backbuffer, livesText, 645, 170, GameFont, 255, 255, 255);
}
```

Drawing the Blocks

The DrawBlocks function traverses the block's array and draws all the blocks that are still alive. The code in Listing 7.20 demonstrates this function.

Listing 7.20: The DrawBlocks Function

```
void DrawBlocks()
{
    for(int i = 0; i < BLOCK_COLUMNS*BLOCK_ROWS; i++)
    {
        if(blocks[i].alive)
        {
            DrawImageFrame(BlockImage, Backbuffer,
                blocks[i].rect.x, blocks[i].rect.y,
                blocks[i].rect.w, blocks[i].rect.h,
                blocks[i].frame);
        }
    }
}
```

PAUSING THE GAME

The ProgramIsRunning function has been modified to pause and unpause the game when the player presses the Esc key. The code in Listing 7.21 demonstrates the modified function.

Listing 7.21: The ProgramIsRunning Function

```
bool ProgramIsRunning()
{
    SDL_Event event;

    bool running = true;

    while(SDL_PollEvent(&event))
    {
```

```
        if(event.type == SDL_QUIT)
            running = false;
        if( event.type == SDL_KEYDOWN )
        {
            if(event.key.keysym.sym == SDLK_ESCAPE)
            {
                if(gameState == GS_RUNNING)
                    gameState = GS_PAUSED;
                else if(gameState == GS_PAUSED)
                    gameState = GS_RUNNING;
            }
        }
    }
    return running;
}
```

Drawing the Game when It's Paused

Drawing the game when it's paused will draw the game as if it were running, but with an overlay on top of it to indicate that it's paused. The code in Listing 7.22 demonstrates the DrawGamePaused function.

Listing 7.22: The DrawGamePaused Function

```
void DrawGamePaused()
{
    DrawGame();
    DrawImage(GamepausedImage, Backbuffer, 0, 0);
}
```

CREATING THE GAME OVER STATE

The game over state occurs when a player loses all of his lives. This state is changed when the player presses the spacebar.

Updating the Game Over Screen

The UpdateGameOver function changes the game state to the splash screen state when the player presses the spacebar. The code in Listing 7.23 shows the implementation of this function.

Listing 7.23: The `UpdateGameOver` Function

```
void UpdateGameOver()
{
    Uint8 *keys = SDL_GetKeyState(NULL);

    if(keys[SDLK_SPACE])
    {
        gameState = GS_SPLASH;
    }
}
```

Drawing the Game Over Screen

Drawing the game over screen is almost exactly like drawing the game paused screen. The code in Listing 7.24 shows the `DrawGameOver` function.

Listing 7.24: The `DrawGameOver` Function

```
void DrawGameOver()
{
    DrawGame();
    DrawImage(GameoverImage, Backbuffer, 0, 0);
}
```

WRAPPING THINGS UP

When you put all this code together, you should have a functional game. Take a minute and play around with it. The mechanics aren't perfect, but they get the job done and leave a lot of room for improvement.

Building the App

You can find the files necessary to build this app in `BAMGP\`. They are located in `Source\Chapter_07\7_1_PaddleGame2\`. You need to create an SDL project and copy `main.cpp` as well as the `graphics` and `audio` folders into your project's directory. If you're using Windows, make sure to include the `.dll` files in the project's directory. This project requires additional `.dll` files that are specifically used for sound and images, so make sure to include those as well. Your project should be configured properly, as shown in Chapter 1, and all the files should also be properly included. When all is set, you'll be able to build the program and run it on your own. Additionally, a precompiled version is in the `Source` directory named `7_1_PaddleGame2.exe`.

In any case, Figure 7.10 displays the finished game after a few minutes of gameplay.

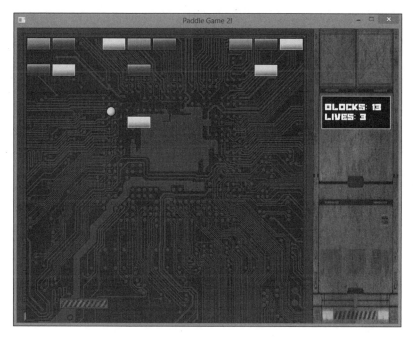

Figure 7.10
The new and improved paddle game during gameplay.
© Jazon Yamamoto.

SUMMARY

This chapter was a huge step toward game creation. The game created in this chapter actually feels like a real game. The previous programs were more like demos, while this one is much more complete than any of them. This game is also entertaining and functional. After completing it, you are ready to tackle new challenges and create more complicated games. Make sure you watch the video tutorial for this chapter since it contains additional information to complement your learning. Before you move on to the next chapter, try completing a few exercises.

Exercises

- Try adding a simple power-up that occurs when a player destroys a special block. This power-up could destroy additional blocks or maybe make the player move faster. Anything is possible at this point.

- Try adding a simple level system in which more blocks are created as the player progresses.

- Try adding animations to the ball, so when it collides with a brick or wall, the ball deforms and compresses, depending on which side it hits. Have the animation run a few frames very quickly.

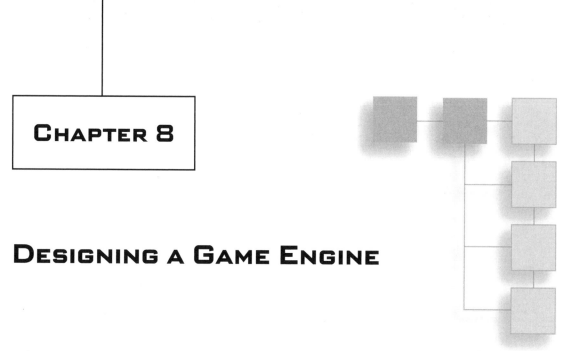

CHAPTER 8

DESIGNING A GAME ENGINE

When it comes to programming games, it is ideal to write code that you can reuse easily. This helps developers avoid reinventing the wheel. Code with general functionality, such as drawing images or playing sounds, can be reused on different game projects. To avoid rewriting general-purpose code, software developers invented game engines. In this chapter, expect to learn about:

- Designing game engines.
- Integrating graphics.
- Adding input support.
- Adding audio support.
- Extending functionality.

Tip

Before getting started, you can check out the video tutorial for this chapter, which is located in BAMGP\ under the Videos directory. The video contains extra material and insights, and reviews the chapter from a high level, so be sure to watch it.

GAME ENGINES EXPLAINED

A *game engine* is a system of reusable components that facilitates video game creation. Think of a game engine as a motor. It's possible to build a car around a motor, take the same motor, and build a motorcycle around it. Game engines are great tools since they have to be written only once, and countless games can be made with them. A game engine is a layer of software that is typically built on top of a library, such as SDL. Some famous game engines include Epic Games' Unreal, Unity, and id Software's line of id Tech engines. These are extremely powerful but not beginner friendly. Instead of using an existing engine, designing a simple one can be a great experience. This will ensure it contains lots of functionality but manages to stay beginner friendly.

Tip

Some developers are very generous and choose to release the source code of their engines to the public. id Software has released several world-class engines throughout the years. You can find some of these on their website, **www.idsoftware.com**.

DESIGNING A GAME ENGINE

When designing a game engine, you must take into consideration its requirements and limitations. First, you need to map out the basic requirements. These can be multimedia capabilities and possible game-related functionality. Second, you must map out some of the limitations. Mapping limitations may not seem beneficial, but it is important to know what the engine specifically targets. Engines tend to be tailored for specific purposes, and they have areas at which they greatly excel. A simple 2D engine may have blazing fast 2D drawing procedures but lack 3D drawing capabilities, while a state-of-the-art 3D engine could draw amazing 3D graphics but have slower 2D drawing procedures. The engine that will be created is simple but effective. It should be able to draw primitive graphics, work with loaded images, play sounds, and process input. It should also be flexible and easy to expand upon. That said, the game engine will use more advanced techniques of software development.

Modular Design

This engine will have a modular design. This means that different fields of functionality of the engine will be split into different sections. This is useful because if something is broken in the graphics section, it won't be necessary to mess with the audio section or the input section to fix it. The three main sections in the engine will be graphics, audio, and input.

Object-Oriented Approach

So far, only C-style coding techniques have been used in all the demos. This was done because C is easier to understand when coding simple applications. Since modular design will be incorporated and the goal is to have a reusable engine, C++ will be used to code the engine. C++ is more adequate than C since it allows programmers to take an object-oriented approach. The engine will make heavy use of objects. Using proper object-oriented code will make for an engine that is extremely powerful, easy to expand upon, and easy to use.

When coding in an object-oriented fashion, it is common to give classes their own header and source files. A header file has the declaration of the class, while the source file has the implementation. Look at Listing 8.1 for an example of what a header file for a class might look like and Listing 8.2 for an example of what the matching source file might look like.

Listing 8.1: A Sample Class Declaration

```
#ifndef CLASSNAME_H
#define CLASSNAME_H

#include <file>

class ClassName
{
private:
    int var;
public:
    ClassName();
    ~ClassName();
    bool method1(int x, int y);
};
#endif
```

Tip

This is a dummy class that's used only for demonstration purposes. ClassName would be a terrible name for a class!

Listing 8.2: A Sample Class Definition

```
#include "ClassName.h"

ClassName::ClassName()
{
    var = 1;
}

ClassName::~ClassName()
{

}
```

```
bool ClassName::method1(int x, int y)
{
    return 4 + x + y;
}
```

THE GRAPHICS CORE

The Graphics class will be created to handle graphics. An object instantiated from this class will have the ability to draw graphics on the screen. In practice, there will only be one instantiation of this class in a program, but in theory, the class can be instantiated multiple times. Remember that since modular design is a priority, this class will have its own header and source files. They will be named Graphics.cpp and Graphics.h. You can examine the header file by taking a look at Listing 8.3.

Listing 8.3: The Graphics Class

```
#ifndef GRAPHICS_H
#define GRAPHICS_H

#include <SDL/SDL.h>

class Graphics
{
private:
    SDL_Surface* backbuffer;
    int width;
    int height;
public:
    bool init(int aWidth, int aHeight, bool aFullscreen);
    void drawPixel(int x, int y, int r, int g, int b);
    void drawRect(int x, int y, int width, int height,
                  int r, int g, int b);

    void fillRect(int x, int y, int width, int height,
                  int r, int g, int b);

    void clear(int r, int g, int b);
    void flip();
    int getWidth();
    int getHeight();
    SDL_Surface* getBackbuffer();
};

#endif
```

Tip

Methods like `getWidth`, `getHeight`, and `getBackbuffer` are known as "getter" methods. Their only purpose is to grant access to their corresponding variables. Their definitions usually consist of a single line returning a variable.

Initializing the Graphics Core

Initializing video will now be easier than ever. All the functions of initializing video will be wrapped up in a single function that requires three parameters. Check out Listing 8.4 for the source code to the class's init function. This function should initialize all the variables with a small degree of error checking.

Listing 8.4: Initializing the Graphics Core

```
bool Graphics::init(int aWidth, int aHeight, bool aFullscreen)
{
    width = aWidth;
    height = aHeight;

    if(aFullscreen)
    {
        backbuffer = SDL_SetVideoMode(width, height, 32,
            SDL_SWSURFACE | SDL_FULLSCREEN);
    }
    else
    {
        backbuffer = SDL_SetVideoMode(width, height, 32,
            SDL_SWSURFACE);
    }

    if(backbuffer == NULL)
    {
        printf("Failed to initialize graphics!\n");
        return false;
    }

    return true;
}
```

Tip

Using `printf` as a means of obtaining rudimentary debug output is a viable option. There are different ways to go about this, but this one is the easiest to use.

Clearing and Updating the Screen

This class will also be in charge of clearing and updating the screen. The methods clear and flip will do just that. There shouldn't be anything complicated about this. You can examine the code to these functions in Listing 8.5.

Listing 8.5: Clearing and Flipping the Screen

```
void Graphics::clear(int r, int g, int b)
{
    if(backbuffer == NULL)
        return;

    Uint32 color;

    color = SDL_MapRGB(backbuffer->format, r, g, b );

    SDL_FillRect(backbuffer, NULL, color);
}
void Graphics::flip()
{
    SDL_Flip(backbuffer);
}
```

Drawing Primitives

Drawing primitives will be directly supported by the engine. Primitives are useful for rudimentary graphics. The two primitives that will be supported are single pixels and axis-aligned rectangles. Take a look at Listing 8.6 for the source code to the primitive functions.

Listing 8.6: Drawing Primitives

```
void Graphics::drawPixel(int x, int y, int r, int g, int b)
{
    if(backbuffer == NULL)
        return;

    if(SDL_MUSTLOCK(backbuffer))
    {
        if(SDL_LockSurface(backbuffer) < 0)
            return;
    }

    if(x >= backbuffer->w || x < 0 || y >= backbuffer->h || y < 0)
        return;

    Uint32 *buffer;
    Uint32 color;
```

```
    color = SDL_MapRGB( backbuffer->format, r, g, b );

    buffer = (Uint32*)backbuffer->pixels +
            y*backbuffer->pitch/4 + x;

    *buffer = color;

    if(SDL_MUSTLOCK(backbuffer))
            SDL_UnlockSurface(backbuffer);
}
void Graphics::drawRect(int x, int y, int width, int height,
        int r, int g, int b)
{
    fillRect(x, y, width, 1, r, g, b);
    fillRect(x, y+height-1, width, 1, r, g, b);
    fillRect(x, y, 1, height, r, g, b);
    fillRect(x+width-1, y, 1, height, r, g, b);
}
void Graphics::fillRect(int x, int y, int width, int height,
        int r, int g, int b)
{
    if(backbuffer == NULL)
        return;

    Uint32 color;

    color = SDL_MapRGB(backbuffer->format, r, g, b );

    SDL_Rect rect;
    rect.x = x;
    rect.y = y;
    rect.w = width;
    rect.h = height;

    SDL_FillRect(backbuffer, &rect, color);
}
```

Testing the Graphics Core

It is time to test the graphics core. Start out by calling the init function to initialize the graphics core, as shown in Listing 8.7.

Listing 8.7: Initializing a Graphics Object

```
if(!graphics.init(SCREEN_WIDTH, SCREEN_HEIGHT, FULLSCREEN))
        return false;
```

Notice how simple yet elegant that is. See Listing 8.8 for the game loop that draws rectangles and pixels and occasionally clears the screen.

Listing 8.8: The Sample Game Loop

```
while(ProgramRunning())
{
    int frameStart = SDL_GetTicks();

    counter++;

    if(counter > 90)
    {
        counter = 0;
        graphics.clear(rand()%255, rand()%255, rand()%255);
    }

    for(int i = 0; i < 100; i++)
    {
        graphics.drawPixel(rand()%SCREEN_WIDTH,
                           rand()%SCREEN_HEIGHT,
                           rand()%255, rand()%255, rand()%255);
    }

    graphics.drawRect(rand()%SCREEN_WIDTH, rand()%SCREEN_HEIGHT,
                      rand()%100, rand()%100,
                      rand()%255, rand()%255, rand()%255);

    graphics.fillRect(rand()%SCREEN_WIDTH, rand()%SCREEN_HEIGHT,
         rand()%100, rand()%100,
         rand()%255, rand()%255, rand()%255);

    graphics.flip();

    int frameTime = SDL_GetTicks()-frameStart;
    int delay = FRAME_TIME - frameTime;

    if(delay > 0)
        SDL_Delay(delay);
}
```

Building the App

You can find the files necessary to build this app in the BAMGP\. They are located in Source\
Chapter_08\8_1_Graphics\. You need to create an SDL project and copy these files

- main.cpp
- Graphics.h
- Graphics.cpp

into your project's directory. If you're using Windows, make sure to include the .dll files in the project's directory. This project requires additional .dll files that are specifically used for sound and images, so make sure to include those as well. Your project should be configured properly, as shown in Chapter 1, and all the files should be properly included. When all is set, you'll be able to build the program and run it on your own. Additionally, a precompiled version is in the Source directory named 8_1_Graphics.exe.

See Figure 8.1 for a screenshot of the demo in action.

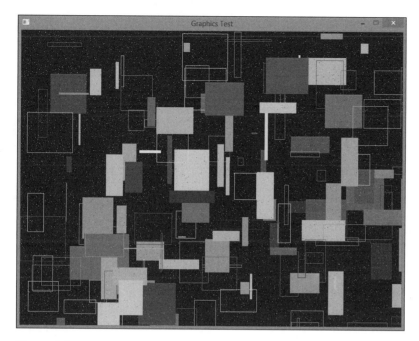

Figure 8.1
The graphics test.
© Jazon Yamamoto.

Handling Images

Images will be handled by the `Image` class. They will require access to the `Graphics` object when they are being drawn to the screen. Other than that, the `Image` class should be pretty straightforward. Take a look at the header file for the `Image` class in Listing 8.9.

Listing 8.9: The `Image` Class Declaration

```
class Image
{
private:
    SDL_Surface* surface;
    int width;
    int height;
    int frameWidth;
    int frameHeight;
```

```
public:
    Image();
    ~Image();
    bool load(char fileName[]);
    bool load(char fileName[], int aFrameWidth, int aFrameHeight);
    void draw(int x, int y, Graphics* g);
    void draw(int x, int y, int frame, Graphics* g);
    void free();

    int getWidth();
    int getHeight();
    int getFrameWidth();
    int getFrameHeight();
    void setFrameSize(int w, int h);
    bool isLoaded();
};
```

Tip

Notice how the function draw was declared two times, but with different sets of parameters. This is called *operator overloading*. Each declaration of the function will have its own definition. The program will execute the respective definition when the function is called, depending on the parameters that were provided.

This class provides the functionality to load and release an image. There are two options for loading. One requires a string to denote the filename, and the other requires two additional parameters. These parameters determine the image's frame width and height. They are necessary when drawing individual frames from an image. This class will also have a function to free the image. You can examine the source code for loading and freeing images in Listing 8.10.

Listing 8.10: Image Loading and Freeing Functions

```
bool Image::load(char fileName[])
{
    SDL_Surface* imageLoaded = NULL;
    imageLoaded = IMG_Load(fileName);

    if(imageLoaded != NULL)
    {
        surface = SDL_DisplayFormat(imageLoaded);
        SDL_FreeSurface(imageLoaded);

        if(surface != NULL)
        {
            Uint32 colorKey = SDL_MapRGB(surface->format,
                                         0xFF, 0, 0xFF );
            SDL_SetColorKey(surface, SDL_SRCCOLORKEY, colorKey );
```

```
                    width = surface->w;
                    height = surface->h;
                }
                else
                {
                    printf("Failed to load image: ");
                    printf(fileName);
                    printf("\n");
                    return false;
                }
        }
        else
        {
            printf("Failed to load image: ");
            printf(fileName);
            printf("\n");
            return false;
        }

        return true;
}
bool Image::load(char fileName[],
                 int aFrameWidth,
                 int aFrameHeight)
{
    if(load(fileName))
    {
        frameWidth = aFrameWidth;
        frameHeight = aFrameHeight;

        return true;
    }

    return false;
}
void Image::free()
{
    if(surface != NULL)
    {
        SDL_FreeSurface(surface);
        surface = NULL;
    }
}
```

This class provides a few options for drawing images. They can be drawn entirely or partially (as frames). You can see the implementation of these functions in Listing 8.11.

Listing 8.11: Drawing Images

```
void Image::draw(int x, int y, Graphics* g)
{
    if(surface == NULL)
        return;

    SDL_Rect destRect;
    destRect.x = x;
    destRect.y = y;

    SDL_BlitSurface(surface, NULL, g->getBackbuffer(), &destRect);
}
void Image::draw(int x, int y, int frame, Graphics* g)
{
    SDL_Rect destRect;
    destRect.x = x;
    destRect.y = y;

    int columns = width/frameWidth;

    SDL_Rect sourceRect;
    sourceRect.y = (frame/columns)*frameHeight;
    sourceRect.x = (frame%columns)*frameWidth;
    sourceRect.w = frameWidth;
    sourceRect.h = frameHeight;

    SDL_BlitSurface(surface, &sourceRect,
                    g->getBackbuffer(), &destRect);
}
```

Listing 8.12 exhibits the image-loading functions in action.

Listing 8.12: Loading Image Objects

```
if(!sprite.load("graphics/sprite.bmp",150,120))
    return false;

if(!background.load("graphics/background.bmp"))
        return false;
```

Keep in mind that drawing images requires access to a `Graphics` object. Listing 8.13 displays the implementation of the image-drawing functions.

Listing 8.13: The Body of a Sample Game Loop

```
graphics.clear(0,0,0);

background.draw(0,0, &graphics);

for(int x = 0; x < 800; x+=200)
    sprite.draw(x,300,imageFrame, &graphics);

graphics.flip();
```

Go ahead and free the images. Listing 8.14 shows the images being released.

Listing 8.14: Freeing Image Objects

```
sprite.free();
background.free();
```

Building the App

You can find the files necessary to build this app in the BAMGP\. They are located in Source\ Chapter_08\8_2_Image\. You need to create an SDL project and copy these files

- main.cpp
- Graphics.h
- Graphics.cpp
- Image.h
- Image.cpp

and the graphics folder into your project's directory. If you're using Windows, make sure to include the .dll files in the project's directory. This project requires additional .dll files that are specifically used for sound and images, so make sure to include those as well. Your project should be configured properly, as shown in Chapter 1, and all the files should also be properly included. When all is set, you'll be able to build the program and run it on your own. Additionally, a precompiled version is in the Source directory named 8_2_Image.exe.

Working with images should be a lot cleaner than with the new class that takes care of all the dirty work. See Figure 8.2 for a screenshot of the image demo.

Figure 8.2
The image test.
© Jazon Yamamoto. Source: 3Dmodels-textures.

Displaying Fonts

Like images, fonts will be handled separately from the Graphics class. There will even be two different classes for fonts. These will make drawing outline and raster fonts more convenient. Let's start with raster fonts. Listing 8.15 contains the code for the RasterFont header file.

Listing 8.15: The RasterFont Class Declaration

```
#ifndef RASTERFONT_H
#define RASTERFONT_H

#include "Image.h"

class RasterFont
{
private:
    static const int NUM_COLUMNS = 16;
    static const int START_CHAR = 32;

    Image image;
    int charSize;
public:
    bool load(char fileName[]);
    void draw(char text[], int x, int y, Graphics* g);
    void free();
};

#endif
```

This class only has three functions, but they prove the necessary functionality. Take a look at Listing 8.16 for the implementation of the class.

Listing 8.16: The RasterFont Class Definition

```
#include "RasterFont.h"

bool RasterFont::load(char fileName[])
{
    if(!image.load(fileName))
        return false;

    charSize = image.getWidth()/NUM_COLUMNS;

    image.setFrameSize(charSize, charSize);

    return true;
}
```

```
void RasterFont::draw(char text[], int x, int y, Graphics* g)
{
    if(!image.isLoaded())
        return;

    for(int i = 0; i < strlen(text); i++)
    {
        image.draw(x+i*charSize, y, text[i]-START_CHAR, g);
    }
}

void RasterFont::free()
{
    image.free();
}
```

Everything should be nice and easy to understand. Now, let's go on to outline fonts. Take a look at Listing 8.17 to examine the code for the OutlineFont header file.

Listing 8.17: The OutlineFont Class Declaration

```
#ifndef OUTLINEFONT_H
#define OUTLINEFONT_H

#include <SDL/SDL_ttf.h>
#include "Graphics.h"

class OutlineFont
{
private:
    TTF_Font* font;
public:
    OutlineFont();
    ~OutlineFont();

    bool load(char fileName[], int size);
    void free();

    void draw(char text[], int x, int y,
              int r, int g, int b, Graphics* gfx);
};

#endif
```

Aside from a few different parameters, this should look very similar to the RasterFont class. The implementation will be a bit different, but both classes will ultimately have very similar functionality. Listing 8.18 demonstrates the implementation of the OutlineFont class.

Listing 8.18: The OutlineFont Class Definition

```cpp
#include "OutlineFont.h"

OutlineFont::OutlineFont()
{
    font = NULL;
}

OutlineFont::~OutlineFont()
{
}

bool OutlineFont::load(char fileName[], int size)
{
    font = TTF_OpenFont(fileName, size);

    if(font == NULL)
        return false;

    return true;
}

void OutlineFont::free()
{
    if(font != NULL)
    {
        TTF_CloseFont(font);
    }
}

void OutlineFont::draw(char text[], int x, int y,
    int r, int g, int b, Graphics* gfx)
{
    if(font == NULL)
        return;

    SDL_Surface* renderedText = NULL;

    SDL_Color color;

    color.r = r;
    color.g = g;
    color.b = b;

    renderedText = TTF_RenderText_Solid(font, text, color);

    SDL_Rect pos;

    pos.x = x;
    pos.y = y;
```

```
        SDL_BlitSurface(renderedText, NULL,
                        gfx->getBackbuffer(), &pos );

        SDL_FreeSurface(renderedText);
}
```

This class is not as pretty as the previous one, but it does what it's intended to do. How about stepping things up a bit by using both classes in the same program? First, you load the fonts, as seen in Listing 8.19.

Listing 8.19: Loading Fonts

```
if(!rasterFont.load("graphics/blocky_font.bmp"))
    return false;

if(!outlineFont.load("graphics/bbrick.ttf", 25))
    return false;
```

Next, you draw the fonts, as seen in Listing 8.20.

Listing 8.20: Drawing Text

```
rasterFont.draw("Bitmap fonts are really cool!!!",
    100, 100, &graphics);

outlineFont.draw("Outline fonts are just as cool!!!",
    100, 150, 0, 0, 255, &graphics);
```

Finally, they can be released as seen in Listing 8.21.

Listing 8.21: Freeing Fonts

```
rasterFont.free();
outlineFont.free();
```

Building the App

You can find the files necessary to build this app in the BAMGP\. They are located in Source\
Chapter_08\8_3_Fonts\. You need to create an SDL project and copy these files

- main.cpp
- Graphics.h
- Graphics.cpp
- Image.h
- Image.cpp
- OutlineFont.h
- OutlineFont.cpp
- RasterFont.h
- RasterFont.cpp

as well as the `graphics` folder into your project's directory. If you're using Windows, make sure to include the `.dll` files in the project's directory. This project requires additional `.dll` files that are specifically used for sound and images, so make sure to include those as well. Your project should be configured properly, as shown in Chapter 1, and all the files should also be properly included. When all is set, you'll be able to build the program and run it on your own. Additionally, a precompiled version is in the `Source` directory named `8_3_Fonts.exe`.

With the current framework, it's easy to see just how much more convenient it is to draw fonts. Figure 8.3 displays the font demo.

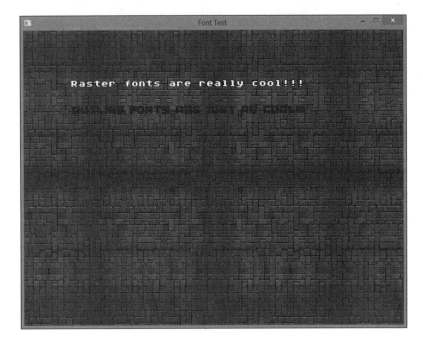

Figure 8.3
The font test.
© Jazon Yamamoto.

THE INPUT CORE

With the graphics core squared away, it's time to get started with input. It makes sense to handle mouse and keyboard input in separate classes, but for the sake of simplicity, there will be a general class for both of them. This class will have functions to fetch the mouse coordinates and let the program know if a key has been pressed, held down, or released. Without further ado, take a look at the header file for the `Input` class in Listing 8.22.

Listing 8.22: The Input Class Declaration

```cpp
#ifndef INPUT_H
#define INPUT_H

#include <SDL/SDL.h>

class Input
{
private:
    bool* keys;
    bool* prevKeys;

    bool mouseKeys[3];
    bool prevMouseKeys[3];

    int numKeys;
    int mouseX;
    int mouseY;
public:
    static const int MOUSE_LEFT = 1;
    static const int MOUSE_MIDDLE = 2;
    static const int MOUSE_RIGHT = 3;

    void init();
    void kill();

    void update();

    bool keyDown(int key);
    bool keyHit(int key);
    bool keyUp(int key);

    bool mouseDown(int key);
    bool mouseHit(int key);
    bool mouseUp(int key);

    int getMouseX();
    int getMouseY();

    void setMousePos(int x, int y);
    void hideCursor(bool hide = true);
};

#endif
```

Initializing the Input System

You may have noticed the functions in charge of initializing, updating, and killing the input system. The init function will be responsible for initializing all the variables in the Input class. These variables will keep track of the state of the mouse and keyboard. Examine the code for the init function in Listing 8.23 for a clearer understanding of its inner workings.

Listing 8.23: Initializing the Input Class

```
void Input::init()
{
    Uint8* keyboard = SDL_GetKeyState(&numKeys);

    keys = new bool[numKeys];
    prevKeys = new bool[numKeys];

    for(int i = 0; i < numKeys; i++)
    {
        keys[i] = keyboard[i];
        prevKeys[i] = false;
    }
    SDL_GetMouseState(&mouseX, &mouseY);

    for(int i = 1; i <= 3; i++)
    {
        mouseKeys[i] = SDL_GetMouseState(NULL,NULL)
            & SDL_BUTTON(i);
        prevMouseKeys[i] = false;
    }
}
```

The array keys will hold the current state of the keyboard. There is also an array called prevKeys. This will hold the keyboard's state prior to being updated. It will be useful when checking if a certain key has been pressed or released within the current cycle. The variable numKeys will hold the number of keys available on the keyboard. The mouse will have two variables, mouseX and mouseY, to hold its position. It will also have two arrays, mouseKeys and prevMouseKeys, to hold the mouse button states. The mouse buttons will be handled in a similar fashion to the keys.

Tip

The arrays keys and prevKeys were allocated dynamically. They should be released properly by using the delete command to avoid memory leaks.

Updating the System

The data in the input system must be updated every cycle if input is to be processed properly. This can be done with relative ease by calling the update function once during the game loop. The update function will sync the object's variables with the current state of the mouse/keyboard. See Listing 8.24 for the code implementing the update function.

Listing 8.24: Updating the Input Class

```
void Input::update()
{
    Uint8* keyboard = SDL_GetKeyState(&numKeys);

    for(int i = 0; i < numKeys; i++)
    {
        prevKeys[i] = keys[i];
        keys[i] = keyboard[i];
    }

    SDL_GetMouseState(&mouseX, &mouseY);

    for(int i = 1; i <= 3; i++)
    {
        prevMouseKeys[i] = mouseKeys[i];
        mouseKeys[i] = SDL_GetMouseState(NULL,NULL)
                    & SDL_BUTTON(i);
    }
}
```

The code should look similar to the `init` function with the exception of allocating memory for the `keys` and `prevKeys` variables and updating the `prevKeys` and `prevMouseKeys`.

Killing the Input System

When an input system is no longer being used, it should be disposed of properly, which is done by calling the `kill` function. This function is in charge of deallocating a few variables. You may examine the guts of this function in Listing 8.25.

Listing 8.25: Killing the Input Class

```
void Input::kill()
{
    delete[] keys;
    delete[] prevKeys;
}
```

Working with the Mouse

Working with the mouse is only a matter of accessing the mouse data. Look to Listing 8.26 to examine the inner workings of the mouse-related functions.

Listing 8.26: Checking the Mouse with the Input Class

```
bool Input::mouseDown(int key)
{
    if(key < 0 || key > 3)
        return false;

    return mouseKeys[key];
}

bool Input::mouseHit(int key)
{
    if(key < 0 || key > 3)
        return false;

    return (mouseKeys[key] && !prevMouseKeys[key]);
}

bool Input::mouseUp(int key)
{
    if(key < 0 || key > 3)
        return false;

    return (prevMouseKeys[key] && !mouseKeys[key]);
}

int Input::getMouseX()
{
    return mouseX;
}

int Input::getMouseY()
{
    return mouseY;
}

void Input::setMousePos(int x, int y)
{
    SDL_WarpMouse(x,y);
}

void Input::hideCursor(bool hide)
{
    if(hide)
        SDL_ShowCursor(SDL_DISABLE);
    else
        SDL_ShowCursor(SDL_ENABLE);
}
```

The first function, mouseDown, will return true if the specified key is currently being pressed down. The second function, mouseHit, will return true only if the key was pressed within the last cycle. The third function, mouseUp, will return true only if the cycle on which a pressed key was released. The next two functions, getMouseX and getMouseY, will grant access to the mouse's X and Y coordinates. The function setMousePos will warp the mouse to a new position, and the function hideCursor will hide/show the cursor.

Tip

The constant variables MOUSE_LEFT, MOUSE_MIDDLE, and MOUSE_RIGHT will be used to check which mouse key was pressed or released. Without these variables, it would be necessary to memorize the integer codes for each of these buttons.

Working with the Keyboard

Working with the keyboard will be easier than working with the mouse despite the fact that the keyboard is responsible for more buttons. You may study the code pertaining to keyboard input in Listing 8.27.

Listing 8.27: Checking the Keyboard with the Input Class

```
bool Input::keyDown(int key)
{
    if(key < 0 || key > numKeys)
        return false;

    return keys[key];
}
bool Input::keyHit(int key)
{
    if(key < 0 || key > numKeys)
        return false;

    return (keys[key] && !prevKeys[key]);
}
bool Input::keyUp(int key)
{
    if(key < 0 || key > numKeys)
        return false;

    return (prevKeys[key] && !keys[key]);
}
```

The functions keyDown, keyHit, and keyUp are parallels to the functions mouseDown, mouseHit, and mouseUp. They have the same functionality, but work with the keyboard keys instead.

Showing Off the Input Core

With a complete input system, the following demo will test some of its functionality. Remember that an Input object should be initialized before the game loop and killed after. See Listing 8.28 for the code to a game loop making use of an Input object.

Listing 8.28: A Sample Game Loop Using an Input Object

```
while(ProgramRunning())
{
    input.update();

    if(input.keyDown(SDLK_ESCAPE))
        break;

    int frameStart = SDL_GetTicks();

    if(input.mouseDown(Input::MOUSE_LEFT))
    {
        spriteX = input.getMouseX();
        spriteY = input.getMouseY();
    }

    if(input.mouseHit(Input::MOUSE_RIGHT))
    {
        spriteX = input.getMouseX();
        spriteY = input.getMouseY();
    }

    if(input.keyDown(SDLK_UP))
        spriteY -= SPRITE_SPEED;

    if(input.keyDown(SDLK_DOWN))
        spriteY += SPRITE_SPEED;

    if(input.keyDown(SDLK_LEFT))
        spriteX -= SPRITE_SPEED;

    if(input.keyDown(SDLK_RIGHT))
        spriteX += SPRITE_SPEED;

    graphics.clear(0,0,0);
    background.draw(0,0, &graphics);
    sprite.draw(spriteX,spriteY, &graphics);
    graphics.flip();

    int frameTime = SDL_GetTicks()-frameStart;
    int delay = FRAME_TIME - frameTime;

    if(delay > 0)
        SDL_Delay(delay);
}
```

Building the App

You can find the files necessary to build this app in the BAMGP\. They are located in Source\
Chapter_08\8_4_Input\. You need to create an SDL project and copy these files

- `main.cpp`
- `Graphics.h`
- `Graphics.cpp`
- `Image.h`
- `Image.cpp`
- `Input.h`
- `Input.cpp`

as well as the `graphics` folder into your project's directory. If you're using Windows, make sure to include the `.dll` files in the project's directory. This project requires additional `.dll` files that are specifically used for sound and images, so make sure to include those as well. Your project should be configured properly, as shown in Chapter 1, and all the files should also be properly included. When all is set, you'll be able to build the program and run it on your own. Additionally, a precompiled version is in the `Source` directory named `8_4_Input.exe`.

This demo allows the users to utilize the keyboard or mouse to position a sprite on the screen. It's not anything fancy, but it shows off all the main features of the engine. See Figure 8.4 for a screenshot of the demo.

Figure 8.4
The input test.
Source: Spaceship from 3DRT.com.

THE AUDIO CORE

The audio core is composed of three main classes. The main class is called `Audio`. This class is in charge of initializing the audio system, stopping channels, and pausing/stopping/resuming the music. You may examine the code for the header file of the `Audio` class in Listing 8.29.

Listing 8.29: The `Audio` Class Declaration

```
#ifndef AUDIO_H
#define AUDIO_H

#include <SDL/SDL.h>
#include <SDL/SDL_mixer.h>

class Audio
{
private:
public:
    bool init();
    void kill();

    bool musicPlaying();
    bool musicPaused();
    void pauseMusic();
    void resumeMusic();
    void stopMusic();

    void stopChannel(int channel);
};

#endif
```

Most of the functions in the `Audio` class are just wrappers of existing SDL functions. This might seem like a useless class, but it's nice to have a simple class that will take care of all this. Take a look at Listing 8.30 for the implementation of these functions.

Listing 8.30: The `Audio` Class Definition

```
bool Audio::init()
{
    if(Mix_OpenAudio( 22050, MIX_DEFAULT_FORMAT, 2, 2048 ) == -1 )
    {
        printf("Failed to initialize audio!\n");
        return false;
    }

    return true;
}
```

```
void Audio::kill()
{
    Mix_CloseAudio();
}
bool Audio::musicPlaying()
{
    return Mix_PlayingMusic();
}
bool Audio::musicPaused()
{
    return Mix_PausedMusic();
}
void Audio::pauseMusic()
{
    Mix_PauseMusic();
}
void Audio::resumeMusic()
{
    Mix_ResumeMusic();
}
void Audio::stopMusic()
{
    Mix_HaltMusic();
}
void Audio::stopChannel(int channel)
{
    Mix_HaltChannel(channel);
}
```

Working with Sound Effects

The class Sound will be in charge of loading/playing/freeing sound effects. It nicely wraps all the necessary steps of loading, playing, and releasing sound effects. Look at Listing 8.31 for the code of its header file.

Listing 8.31: The Sound Class Declaration

```
#ifndef SOUND_H
#define SOUND_H

#include "Audio.h"
```

```
class Sound
{
private:
    Mix_Chunk* sound;
public:
    Sound();
    ~Sound();
    bool load(char fileName[]);
    void free();

    int play(int loops = 0);
    bool isLoaded();
};

#endif
```

There are three main functions in this class. These can be studied in Listing 8.32.

Listing 8.32: The Sound Class Definition

```
bool Sound::load(char fileName[])
{
    sound = Mix_LoadWAV(fileName);

    if(sound == NULL)
    {
        printf("Failed to load sound: ");
        printf(fileName);
        printf("\n");

        return false;
    }

    return true;
}

void Sound::free()
{
    if(sound != NULL)
    {
        Mix_FreeChunk(sound);
        sound = NULL;
    }
}

int Sound::play(int loops)
{
    if(sound != NULL)
    {
        return Mix_PlayChannel(-1, sound, loops);
    }
```

```
    else
    {
        return -1;
    }
}
```

Working with Music Files

The `Music` class is very similar to the `Sound` class. The only difference is that this class will be used for music. See Listing 8.33 for the header file for this class.

Listing 8.33: The Music Class Declaration

```
#ifndef MUSIC_H
#define MUSIC_H

#include "Audio.h"
class Music
{
private:
    Mix_Music* music;
public:
    Music();
    ~Music();

    bool load(char fileName[]);
    void free();

    void play(int loops = 0);
    bool isLoaded();
};

#endif
```

Other than a few keywords, this file should look exactly the same as the `Sound` header file seen in Listing 8.34.

Listing 8.34: The Music Class Definition

```
bool Music::load(char fileName[])
{
    music = Mix_LoadMUS(fileName);

    if(music == NULL)
    {
        printf("Failed to load song: ");
        printf(fileName);
        printf("\n");

        return false;
    }
```

```
        return true;
}
void Music::free()
{
    if(music != NULL)
    {
        Mix_FreeMusic(music);
        music = NULL;
    }
}
void Music::play(int loops)
{
    if(music != NULL)
        Mix_PlayMusic(music, loops);
}
```

Testing the Audio System

With every tedious task taken care of, working with audio will be much cleaner. Listing 8.35 demonstrates all of the engine components working together. See Figure 8.5 for a screenshot of the demo.

Listing 8.35: A Game Loop Testing the Audio System

```
while(ProgramRunning())
{
    input.update();
    if(input.keyHit(SDLK_SPACE))
    {
        if(!audio.musicPlaying())
        {
            music.play(-1);
        }
        else
        {
            if(audio.musicPaused())
            {
                audio.resumeMusic();
            }
            else
            {
                audio.pauseMusic();
            }
        }
    }
```

```
int frameStart = SDL_GetTicks();

if(input.keyHit(SDLK_1))
    sounds[0].play();

if(input.keyHit(SDLK_2))
    sounds[1].play();

if(input.keyHit(SDLK_3))
    sounds[2].play();

graphics.clear(0,0,0);
background.draw(0,0, &graphics);
graphics.flip();

int frameTime = SDL_GetTicks()-frameStart;
int delay = FRAME_TIME - frameTime;

if(delay > 0)
    SDL_Delay(delay);
}
```

Building the App

You can find the files necessary to build this app in the BAMGP\. They are located in Source\ Chapter_08\8_5_Audio\. You need to create an SDL project and copy these files

- main.cpp
- Graphics.h
- Graphics.cpp
- Image.h
- Image.cpp
- Input.h
- Input.cpp
- Audio.h
- Audio.cpp
- Sound.h
- Sound.cpp
- Music.h
- Music.cpp

as well as the graphics and audio folders into your project's directory. If you're using Windows, make sure to include the .dll files in the project's directory. This project requires additional .dll files that are specifically used for sound and images, so make sure to include those as well. Your project should be configured properly, as shown in Chapter 1, and all the files should also be properly included. When all is set, you'll be able to build the program and run it on your own. Additionally, a precompiled version is in the Source directory named 8_5_Audio.exe.

Figure 8.5
The audio test.
© Jazon Yamamoto.

TYING THE MAIN ENGINE TOGETHER

At this point, the engine is almost done, but everything must be brought together. The next step will be to combine all components into one simple class. This will be the Game class, and it will initialize all the components of the engine, update the game, and draw the screen. Making games will be a matter of creating a child class derived from the Game class and overriding a few functions. See Listing 8.36 for the header file.

Listing 8.36: The Game Class Definition

```
#ifndef GAME_H
#define GAME_H

#include <SDL/SDL_ttf.h>

#include "Graphics.h"
#include "Input.h"
#include "Audio.h"

class Game
{
private:
    Graphics graphics;
```

```
        Input input;
        Audio audio;
        int fps;
        bool isDone;
public:
        Game();
        ~Game();

        unsigned int getTicks();
        void setFPS(int f);
        void delay(int ticks);
        bool initSystem(char title[], int width, int height, bool fullscreen);
        void freeSystem();
        void run();
        void end();

        virtual bool init();
        virtual void free();
        virtual void update();
        virtual void draw(Graphics* g);

        Graphics* getGraphics();
        Input* getInput();
        Audio* getAudio();
};

#endif
```

This class is composed of two major groups of functions, the first being general-purpose functions and the second being game-specific functions.

General-Purpose Functions

General-purpose functions can be used in different games. Functions like getTicks, setFPS, and delay are pretty self-explanatory. The rest of the general-purpose functions are a bit more complicated. The function initSystem, for example, initializes the entire engine. The function freeSystem cleans up the mess. You can observe their behavior in Listing 8.37.

Listing 8.37: Initializing and Terminating the Game Class

```
bool Game::initSystem(char title[], int width, int height, bool fullscreen)
{
    if(SDL_Init( SDL_INIT_EVERYTHING) == -1)
        return false;

    if(!graphics.init(width, height, fullscreen))
        return false;
```

```
        SDL_WM_SetCaption(title, NULL);

        if(!audio.init())
            return false;

        input.init();

        if(TTF_Init() == -1)
            return false;

        return true;
}
void Game::freeSystem()
{
        input.kill();
        audio.kill();
        TTF_Quit();
        SDL_Quit();
}
```

The function run is crucial to this class since it contains the game loop, regulates the frame rate, and updates the screen. The function end closes the program upon being called. Examine these functions in Listing 8.38 for a more solid understanding of their functionality.

Listing 8.38: Running and Ending a Game

```
void Game::run()
{
        while(!isDone)
        {
                unsigned int frameStart = SDL_GetTicks();

                SDL_Event event;

                while(SDL_PollEvent(&event))
                {
                        if(event.type == SDL_QUIT)
                        {
                                isDone = true;
                                break;
                        }
                }

                input.update();
                update();
                draw(getGraphics());

                getGraphics()->flip();
```

```
        int frameTime = getTicks()-frameStart;
        int delayTime = (1000/fps) - frameTime;

        delay(delayTime);
    }

    free();
    freeSystem();
}
void Game::end()
{
    isDone = true;
}
```

Game-Specific Functions

Game-specific functions are virtual functions that will be overridden by games using this class in order to create different games. There are four game-specific functions: init, free, update, and draw. These will be implemented by different games according to their unique requirements. Every function has a blank body with the exception of init. The default init function creates a blank window using the initSystem function.

Testing the Engine

Testing the game engine will be as easy as writing fewer than 20 lines of code. Take a look at Listing 8.39 for the code to the nice little demo.

Listing 8.39: A Test Game Loop for the Game Class

```
#include "Game.h"

int main(int argc, char *argv[])
{
    Game game;

    if(!game.init())
    {
        game.free();
        return 0;
    }

    game.run();

    return 1;
}
```

Building the App

You can find the files necessary to build this app in the BAMGP\. They are located in `Source\`
`Chapter_08\8_6_GameEngine\`. You need to create an SDL project and copy these files

- `main.cpp`
- `Graphics.h`
- `Graphics.cpp`
- `Image.h`
- `Image.cpp`
- `RasterFont.h`
- `RasterFont.cpp`
- `OutlineFont.h`
- `OutlineFont.cpp`
- `Input.h`
- `Input.cpp`
- `Audio.h`
- `Audio.cpp`
- `Sound.h`
- `Sound.cpp`
- `Music.h`
- `Music.cpp`
- `Game.h`
- `Game.cpp`

into your project's directory. If you're using Windows, make sure to include the `.dll` files in the project's
directory. This project requires additional `.dll` files that are specifically used for sound and images, so
make sure to include those as well. Your project should be configured properly, as shown in Chapter 1,
and all the files should also be properly included. When all is set, you'll be able to build the program
and run it on your own. Additionally, a precompiled version is in the `Source` directory named
`8_6_GameEngine.exe`.

Yes, it is that simple. This is the content of the main function, and until now, this
function has always been a mess! With the new engine, that mess is a thing of the
past! Note that every `main.cpp` file from now on should look almost identical to this.
See Figure 8.6 for a screenshot of the demo. The demo is very minimalistic and
unimpressive, but there is a beast running under it.

Figure 8.6
The engine test.
© Jazon Yamamoto.

ENGINE EXTENSIONS

An *extension* is functionality added to an engine that can be used in different projects. Extensions are always nice to have because they add functionality to the engine without bloating it. A perfect extension to the engine would be one that adds game state functionality. To create it, make a class called GameState to model a game state and a class called StateManager to manage all the different game states. These two classes will interact to elegantly handle game states.

The GameState Class

The GameState class will manage a single game state. In order to have different game states, this class will be inherited from by a child class, and a few functions will be reimplemented in order to create the customized functionality for different game states. Listing 8.40 exhibits the header file for this class.

Listing 8.40: The GameState Class Declaration

```
#ifndef GAMESTATE_H
#define GAMESTATE_H

#include "StateManager.h"

class StateManager;

class GameState
{
private:
    StateManager* manager;
public:
    GameState();
    ~GameState(){};

    virtual void update();
    virtual void draw();

    StateManager* getManager();
    void setManager(StateManager* m);
};

#endif
```

The functions getManager and setManager only provide access to the manager variable. The update and draw functions are just stubs that are to be reimplemented when creating a derivative class.

The StateManager Class

The StateManager class is a bit more interesting. It handles the game states in a clean and elegant way. Instead of having a huge switch statement, this class will have a stack to take care of game states. This makes it possible to have a giant number of game states without having a giant switch statement to handle them all. Take a look at Listing 8.41 for the header file of the StateManager class.

Listing 8.41: The StateManager Class Declaration

```
#ifndef STATEMANAGER_H
#define STATEMANAGER_H

#include <stack>
#include "GameState.h"
#include "Graphics.h"

class GameState;

class StateManager
```

```
{
private:
    std::stack<GameState*> states;
public:
    StateManager(){};
    ~StateManager(){};

    void addState(GameState* s);
    void popState();
    void update();
    void draw(Graphics* g);
    bool isEmpty();
};
```

#endif

This class has a single variable, and it is a stack of game state pointers. The function addState adds a state to the stack. The function popState removes the top state of the stack. The functions update and draw update and draw the top state of the stack. The function isEmpty returns true if the stack is empty. Study the implementation of these functions in Listing 8.42.

Listing 8.42: The StateManager Class Declaration

```
void StateManager::addState(GameState* s)
{
    s->setManager(this);
    states.push(s);
}

void StateManager::popState()
{
    states.pop();
}

void StateManager::update()
{
    if(!states.empty())
    {
        if(states.top() != NULL)
        {
            states.top()->update();
        }
    }
}

void StateManager::draw(Graphics* g)
{
    if(!states.empty())
```

```
        {
            if(states.top() != NULL)
            {
                states.top()->draw(g);
            }
        }
    }
}
bool StateManager::isEmpty()
{
    return states.empty();
}
```

Testing the Game State Mechanism

The following demo will jump from one game state to another when the user presses the spacebar. The first state will be a splash screen to greet the player. It will have a logo coming into the screen from the top and stopping at the center of the screen. Listing 8.43 demonstrates the header file for this game state.

Listing 8.43: The SplashState Class Declaration

```
#ifndef SPLASH_STATE
#define SPLASH_STATE

#include "GameState.h"
#include "Graphics.h"
#include "Image.h"
#include "Input.h"
#include "Sound.h"

class SplashState : public GameState
{
private:
    Input* input;
    Image backgroundImage;
    Image logoImage;
    Sound sound;

    int logoImageY;
    int logoImageX;
    bool soundPlayed;

    static const int TARGET_Y = 300;
public:
    bool init(Input* i, StateManager* m);
    void free();
```

```
    virtual void update();
    virtual void draw(Graphics* g);
};

#endif
```

This game state has its own unique variables and methods. Observe the implementations of these methods in Listing 8.44.

Listing 8.44: The SplashState Class Definition

```
bool SplashState::init(Input* i, StateManager* m)
{
    input = i;
    setManager(m);

    if(!backgroundImage.load("graphics/splash/background.bmp"))
        return false;

    if(!logoImage.load("graphics/splash/logo.bmp"))
        return false;

    if(!sound.load("audio/splash/sound.wav"))
        return false;

    logoImageY = -logoImage.getHeight();
    soundPlayed = false;

    return true;
}

void SplashState::free()
{
    logoImage.free();
    backgroundImage.free();
    sound.free();
}

void SplashState::update()
{
    if(input->keyHit(SDLK_SPACE) || input->keyHit(SDLK_ESCAPE) ||
        input->keyHit(SDLK_RETURN))
    {
        getManager()->popState();
    }
    if(logoImageY < TARGET_Y-logoImage.getHeight()/2)
    {
        logoImageY += 10;
    }
```

```
    else
    {
        if(!soundPlayed)
        {
            sound.play();
            soundPlayed = true;
        }
    }
}
void SplashState::draw(Graphics* g)
{
    backgroundImage.draw(0, 0, g);
    logoImage.draw(g->getWidth()/2 - logoImage.getWidth()/2,
                    logoImageY, g);
}
```

Building the App

You can find the files necessary to build this app in the BAMGP\. They are located in Source\
Chapter_08\8_7_GameState\. You need to create an SDL project and copy these files

- main.cpp
- Graphics.h
- Graphics.cpp
- Image.h
- Image.cpp
- RasterFont.h
- RasterFont.cpp
- OutlineFont.h
- OutlineFont.cpp
- Input.h
- Input.cpp
- Audio.h
- Audio.cpp
- Sound.h
- Sound.cpp
- Music.h
- Music.cpp
- Game.h
- Game.cpp
- StateManager.h

- StateManager.cpp
- GameState.h
- GameState.cpp
- SplashState.h
- SplashState.cpp
- RunState.h
- RunState.cpp
- GameStateDemo.h
- GameStateDemo.cpp

as well as the `graphics` and `audio` folders into your project's directory. If you're using Windows, make sure to include the `.dll` files in the project's directory. This project requires additional `.dll` files that are specifically used for sound and images, so make sure to include those as well. Your project should be configured properly, as shown in Chapter 1, and all the files should also be properly included. When all is set, you'll be able to build the program and run it on your own. Additionally, a precompiled version is in the `Source` directory named `8_7_GameState.exe`.

Notice that this class handles the allocation and deallocation of all of its resources. This makes the class more cohesive. Also notice that this class takes itself off the stack when the user presses certain keys. Figure 8.7 displays a screenshot of this game state.

Figure 8.7
The first game state.
© Jazon Yamamoto.

The second game state will be a mockup of a game running. It will feature a gear turning in the middle of the screen to show that the game is indeed doing some work. Listing 8.45 exposes the code for this class's header file.

Listing 8.45: The RunState Class Declaration

```
#ifndef RUN_STATE
#define RUN_STATE

#include "GameState.h"
#include "Graphics.h"
#include "Image.h"
#include "Input.h"

class RunState : public GameState
{
private:
    Input* input;
    Image backgroundImage;
    Image gearImage;

    static const int IMAGE_FRAMES = 5;

    int imageFrame;
    int frameCounter;
public:
    bool init(Input* i, StateManager* m);
    void free();

    virtual void update();
    virtual void draw(Graphics* g);
};

#endif
```

Much like the previous class, this class has its own assets to take care of. It also has different functionality, so take a look at the implementation of these functions in Listing 8.46.

Listing 8.46: The RunState Class Definition

```
#include "RunState.h"

bool RunState::init(Input* i, StateManager* m)
{
    input = i;
    setManager(m);
```

```
        if(!backgroundImage.load("graphics/run/background.bmp"))
            return false;

        if(!gearImage.load("graphics/run/gear.bmp", 400, 400))
            return false;

        imageFrame = 0;
        frameCounter = 0;

        return true;
}

void RunState::free()
{
        gearImage.free();
        backgroundImage.free();
}

void RunState::update()
{
        if(input->keyHit(SDLK_ESCAPE))
        {
            getManager()->popState();
        }

        frameCounter++;

        if(frameCounter > 5)
        {
            frameCounter = 0;
            imageFrame++;

            if(imageFrame > IMAGE_FRAMES)
                imageFrame = 0;
        }
}

void RunState::draw(Graphics* g)
{
        int x = g->getWidth()/2 - gearImage.getFrameWidth()/2;
        int y = g->getHeight()/2 - gearImage.getFrameHeight()/2;

        backgroundImage.draw(0, 0, g);
        gearImage.draw(x, y, imageFrame, g);
}
```

This game state is illustrated in Figure 8.8.

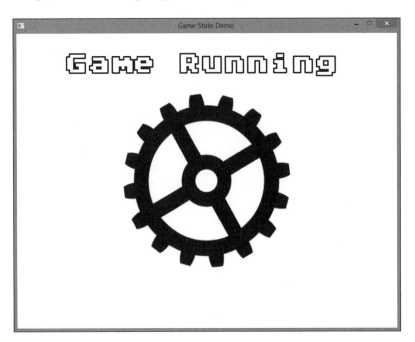

Figure 8.8
The second game state.
© Jazon Yamamoto.

With the new game states, the next step is to create a class deriving from the Game class to put these babies to use. The header file for this class can be examined in Listing 8.47.

Listing 8.47: The GameStateDemo Class Declaration

```
#include "Game.h"
#include "StateManager.h"
#include "RunState.h"
#include "SplashState.h"

class GameStateDemo : public Game
{
private:
    StateManager manager;
    RunState runState;
    SplashState splashState;
public:
    GameStateDemo();
    ~GameStateDemo();
    bool init();
    void free();
```

```
    void update();
    void draw(Graphics* g);
};
```

These methods are implemented as shown in Listing 8.48.

Listing 8.48: The GameStateDemo Class Definition

```
bool GameStateDemo::init()
{
    if(!initSystem("Game State Demo", 800, 600, false))
        return false;

    if(!runState.init(getInput(), &manager))
        return false;

    if(!splashState.init(getInput(), &manager))
        return false;

    manager.addState(&runState);
    manager.addState(&splashState);

    return true;
}

void GameStateDemo::free()
{
    runState.free();
    splashState.free();
}

void GameStateDemo::update()
{
    if(manager.isEmpty())
    {
        end();
        return;
    }

    manager.update();
}

void GameStateDemo::draw(Graphics* g)
{
    manager.draw(g);
}
```

This class sets up the game states and the state. Emptying the state manager will close the program. In any case, take a look at Listing 8.49 for the main.cpp file for this project.

Listing 8.49: The Sample Game State Application

```
#include "GameStateDemo.h"

int main(int argc, char *argv[])
{
    GameStateDemo game;

    if(!game.init())
        game.free();

    game.run();

    return 0;
}
```

This file should look almost identical to the one for the previous demo with the exception of the header and the class used to implement the game object.

Summary

In this chapter, a game engine was designed and developed from scratch. Remember that this engine can always be expanded upon to add functionality that is beyond the scope of this book (such as 3D graphics). The new engine can be used as a basis for countless games. It can also be expanded by creating more extensions to it. Be sure to watch the video tutorial for this chapter since it contains additional information and detailed commentary. Before continuing, make John Carmack proud by completing a few of the following exercises.

Exercises

■ Try re-creating some of the demos from scratch.

■ Try adding new features to each demo. The more you experiment, the more you will generate good ideas for demos and games later.

■ Make an extension. It can be as simple as a new health display bar.

CHAPTER 9

CRAFTING LEVELS WITH TILE MAPS

In the early days of video games, creating large virtual worlds wasn't much more than a fantasy since memory was extremely limited. The graphics for such worlds could potentially consume more memory than any computer had available at the time. This limitation, however, did not stop programmers who wanted to create these worlds. These programmers realized that a large world can be painted using small images that seamlessly repeat themselves across the screen. This technique paved the road for a multitude of games that relied on it to create vast worlds open for exploration. Without hesitation, let's dive head first into tile mapping! In this chapter, you learn how to:

- Create tile maps.
- Draw tile maps.
- Smoothly scroll through maps.
- Create multilayered maps.

TIP

Before getting started, you can check out the video tutorial for this chapter, which is located in BAMGP\ under the Videos directory. The video contains extra material and insights, and reviews the chapter from a high level, so be sure to watch it.

TILE MAPS IN THEORY

A tile map is a large image composed of smaller images arranged in a grid. The smaller images are known as *tiles*. Tiles are usually generic graphics, such as grass, that can be seamlessly drawn on the screen multiple times. This is useful because larger worlds can be painted with a single set of tiles. Furthermore, this also allows you to create large worlds using a minimal amount of memory. This is because a small set of tiles painting a large image would occupy far less memory than a large image file would. This was extremely important for the video game consoles of the late 80s and early 90s. These consoles had severe memory limitations, but using tile maps allowed developers to create large and intricate levels. Figure 9.1 illustrates a room created using tiles.

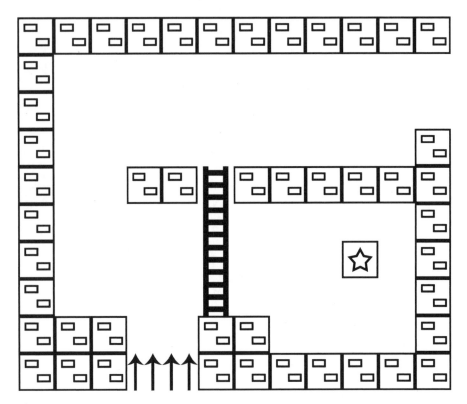

Figure 9.1
A typical tile-mapped room.
© Jazon Yamamoto.

Taking a closer look at the room, you will notice that it was composed of a few tiles that repeat themselves in order to create a bigger picture. You can observe these tiles individually in Figure 9.2.

Figure 9.2
Generic tiles for a platformer video game.
© Jazon Yamamoto.

Using the tile set shown in Figure 9.2, you can create an enormous room with hardly any effort. It should also be pointed out that tiles are typically uniform in size, blend well, and can be repeated seamlessly.

TILE MAPS IN PRACTICE

In practice, a tile map consists of two main components. The first one is a tile set, and the second is the map. The *tile set* is the set of tiles that a map consists of. These tiles can be stored in separate image files, but it is far more convenient to store them in a single file and treat each tile as a frame of the image. This is because it allows you to create a simpler data structure for a map. The map holds the information regarding the placement of the tiles in a room, world, level, and so on. Storing a set of tiles in a single image and accessing them as frames of the image allow the program to store entire maps in a simple integer array. Listing 9.1 exhibits an array holding the information of a tile map.

Listing 9.1: A Sample Map Array

```
int data[] = {1, 1, 1, 1, 1, 1, 1, 1, 1, 1, 1, 1,
              1, 0, 0, 0, 0, 0, 0, 0, 0, 0, 0, 1,
              1, 0, 0, 0, 0, 1, 1, 1, 0, 0, 0, 1,
              1, 0, 0, 0, 0, 0, 0, 0, 0, 0, 0, 1,
              1, 0, 1, 1, 1, 0, 0, 0, 2, 2, 0, 1,
              1, 0, 0, 0, 0, 0, 0, 0, 2, 2, 0, 1,
              1, 1, 1, 1, 1, 1, 1, 1, 1, 1, 1, 1};
```

TIP

Using `int`s to hold tile data is actually quite wasteful since a single `int` is composed of four bytes. Using `unsigned char`s would be more reasonable since they are composed of a single byte and can hold 256 different tiles. This is way more than enough in most cases. The demos in this book use `int`s for the sake of simplicity.

It might be hard to see, but the numbers in the array hold a vague resemblance to a small level in a game. Drawing this map is as simple as creating a `for` loop that draws the map tile-by-tile using the array to acquire the frame number of the current tile. Listing 9.2 demonstrates the algorithm of a map-drawing function.

Listing 9.2: The Tile Drawing Loop

```
for(int y = 0; y < height; y++)
{
    for(int x = 0; x < width; x++)
    {
        int frame = data[y*width+x];
        frame--;
        if(frame >= 0)
            tileSet.draw(x*tileWidth, y*tileHeight, frame, g);
    }
}
```

Building the App

You can find the files necessary to build this app in the BAMGP\. They are located in Source\ Chapter_09\9_1_SimpleTileMap\. You need to create an SDL project and copy these files

- main.cpp
- Map.h
- Map.cpp
- MapDemo.h
- MapDemo.cpp

as well as the Core and the graphics folders into your project's directory. If you're using Windows, make sure to include the .dll files in the project's directory. This project requires additional .dll files that are specifically used for sound and images, so make sure to include those as well. Your project should be configured properly, as shown in Chapter 1, and all the files should also be properly included. When all is set, you'll be able to build the program and run it on your own. Additionally, a precompiled version is in the Source directory named 9_1_SimpleTileMap.exe.

The frame number is altered so that 0 represents the absence of a tile and 1 denotes the first frame of the tile set. This algorithm may be a bit difficult to absorb, but just stare at it for two minutes if you're having difficulty. Figure 9.3 showcases this algorithm in action.

Figure 9.3
Your first venture into drawing maps.
© Jazon Yamamoto.

LOADING A TILE MAP FROM A FILE

It doesn't take a genius to know that storing maps in large arrays directly in the source code could be extremely inconvenient. This would bloat the code and increase compile times, and a recompile would be necessary every single time a map is edited! A better solution is to store maps in a file that can be loaded from memory. The problem is that there isn't a universal tile map format that stores these kind of files, so the program will use a custom one. File formats are typically tedious to work with, but it's always a great learning experience to implement your own. Let's go ahead and create a simple format to store tile maps.

This format has to be simple and easy to work with. It should also be possible to alter a file in this format manually since there aren't any editors out there that will work with this format right out of the box. In all probability, the main editor for this format could be a simple text editor or a rudimentary program coded to create map files. The format displayed in Listing 9.3 will be used for storing map files.

Listing 9.3: A Sample Map File

```
width 10
height 6
tile_width 32
tile_height 32
solid_tiles
1,2
layer1
1, 1, 1, 1, 1, 1, 1, 1, 1, 1, 1
1, 0, 0, 0, 0, 0, 0, 0, 0, 0, 1
(etc.)
layer2
0, 0, 0, 0, 0, 0, 0, 0, 0, 0, 0
0, 0, 0, 0, 0, 0, 0, 0, 0, 0, 0
(etc.)
layer3
0, 0, 0, 0, 0, 0, 0, 0, 0, 0, 0
0, 0, 0, 0, 0, 0, 0, 0, 0, 0, 0
(etc.)
```

TIP

Since this is a custom file format, it can use any file extension. The map files in this book use the `.map` extension.

This format can be read by simply opening the file. There is a total of eight memory fields that this format will directly deal with. The first two, width and height, hold the width and the height of the map. The next two, tile_width and tile_height, hold the size of the tiles. The field labeled as solid_tiles contains a list of tiles that an object can collide with. This feature may not be useful for all games, but it's nice to have as an option. The next three fields are labeled as layer1, layer2, and layer3. This format supports exactly three layers. Multilayer tile mapping is covered later in this chapter. Listing 9.4 demonstrates an early implementation for loading maps. This implementation isn't concerned with solid tiles, and it loads only one layer.

Listing 9.4: The Map Loading Function

```cpp
bool Map::load(char mapName[], char imageName[])
{
    data = NULL;

    std::ifstream in(mapName);

    if(!in.good())
        return false;
```

```cpp
    std::string buffer;

    getline(in, buffer, ' ');
    getline(in, buffer, '\n');
    width = atoi(buffer.c_str());

    getline(in, buffer, ' ');
    getline(in, buffer, '\n');
    height = atoi(buffer.c_str());

    getline(in, buffer, ' ');
    getline(in, buffer, '\n');
    tileWidth = atoi(buffer.c_str());

    getline(in, buffer, ' ');
    getline(in, buffer, '\n');
    tileHeight = atoi(buffer.c_str());

    //Get the line that says 'solid_tiles' and ignore it
    getline(in, buffer, '\n');
    //Get the row containing solid tiles and ignore it
    getline(in, buffer, '\n');
    //Get the row containing 'layer1' and ignore it
    getline(in, buffer, '\n');

    //Get the tile data
    data = new int[width * height];

    int i = 0;
    for(int y = 0; y < height; y++)
    {
        for(int x = 0; x < width; x++)
        {
            char delim = ',';

            if(x == width-1)
                delim = '\n';

            getline(in, buffer, delim);
            data[i] = atoi(buffer.c_str());
            i++;
        }
    }
    in.close();

    //Load Image
    if(!tiles.load(imageName, tileWidth, tileHeight))
        return false;

    return true;
}
```

Building the App

You can find the files necessary to build this app in the BAMGP\. They are located in Source\ Chapter_09\9_2_LoadingTileMaps\. You need to create an SDL project and copy these files

- main.cpp
- Map.h
- Map.cpp
- MapDemo.h
- MapDemo.cpp

as well as the Core and the graphics folders into your project's directory. If you're using Windows, make sure to include the .dll files in the project's directory. This project requires additional .dll files that are specifically used for sound and images, so make sure to include those as well. Your project should be configured properly, as shown in Chapter 1, and all the files should also be properly included. When all is set, you'll be able to build the program and run it on your own. Additionally, a precompiled version is in the Source directory named 9_2_LoadingTileMaps.exe.

The fstream library will be used for easy loading. I won't go too much into detail with the fstream library and how powerful it is because that's beyond the scope of this book. In any case, this function initializes the data in a class called Map. At this point, this class is in an early development phase, but I will be creating a much more robust Map class later on in this chapter. Figure 9.4 shows the demo for this section of the book in action.

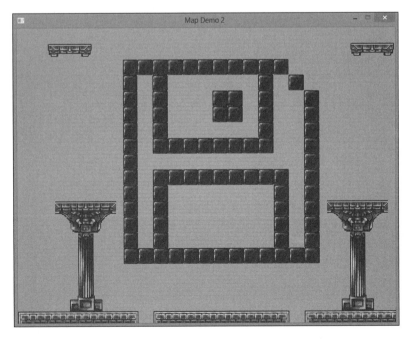

Figure 9.4
A map loaded from a file.
© Jazon Yamamoto.

SCROLLING THROUGH TILE MAPS

In games with large maps, it's important to be able to scroll through them smoothly. This shouldn't take too much effort to implement, but there are some things that you must take into consideration. The previous map-drawing algorithm drew the entire map no matter how big it was. The problem is that with huge maps, there is absolutely no point in drawing tiles that aren't even in the screen! The most intelligent thing to do is to draw only the tiles that are on the screen. The most efficient way of doing this is to start drawing the map where the upper-left corner of the screen is located and only draw enough rows and columns to fill the screen. Listing 9.5 shows the code for the new map-drawing function.

Listing 9.5: A More Advance Drawing Function

```cpp
void Map::draw(int xOffset, int yOffset, Graphics* g)
{
    int startY = yOffset/tileHeight;
    int startX = xOffset/tileWidth;

    int rows = (g->getHeight()/tileHeight) + 2;
    int columns = (g->getWidth()/tileWidth) + 2;

    for(int y = startY; y < startY+rows; y++)
        for(int x = startX; x < startX+columns; x++)
        {
            int frame = -1;

            if(x >= 0 && y >= 0 && x < width && y < height)
                frame = data[y*width+x]-1;

            if(frame >= 0)
                tiles.draw(x*tileWidth - xOffset,
                    y*tileHeight - yOffset,
                    frame, g);
        }
}
```

Building the App

You can find the files necessary to build this app in the `BAMGP\`. They are located in `Source\ Chapter_09\9_3_ScrollingTileMap\`. You need to create an SDL project and copy these files

- `main.cpp`
- `Map.h`
- `Map.cpp`
- `MapDemo.h`
- `MapDemo.cpp`

as well as the Core and the graphics folders into your project's directory. If you're using Windows, make sure to include the .dll files in the project's directory. This project requires additional .dll files that are specifically used for sound and images, so make sure to include those as well. Your project should be configured properly, as shown in Chapter 1, and all the files should also be properly included. When all is set, you'll be able to build the program and run it on your own. Additionally, a precompiled version is in the Source directory named 9_3_ScrollingTileMap.exe.

The new algorithm for drawing maps completely dwarfs the old one! This one is much more sophisticated, and it ensures that only the portion of the map that is currently visible is drawn. This, however, allows for smooth scrolling, which is a staple in the platformer genre of video games. Figure 9.5 demonstrates a screenshot of the demo for this section.

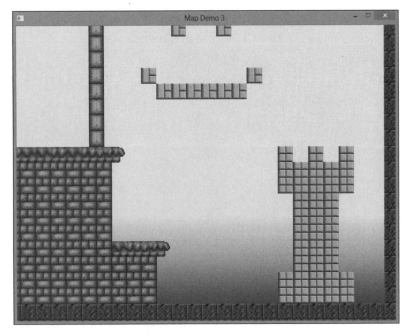

Figure 9.5
A screenshot of a scrollable level.
Source: SpriteLib, created by Ari Feldmen, used under the Common Public License.

LAYERING TILE MAPS

Layering tile maps makes it possible to add more depth into the game. You can layer tile maps by drawing multiple tile maps on top of each other. With multiple layers, you can add a background or a foreground to the current map. This way, tiles can be drawn on top of each other, which can possibly make much more interesting maps.

It's necessary to implement a better method to load maps in order to support multiple layers. Listing 9.6 displays the reimplementation of the load function.

Listing 9.6: A More Advanced Map Loading Function

```
bool Map::load(char mapName[], char imageName[])
{
    layer1 = layer2 = layer3 = solidLayer = NULL;

    ifstream in(mapName);

    if(!in.good())
        return false;

    string buffer;

    loadDimensions(&in);
    loadSolidTiles(&in);

    //Get the tile data
    layer1 = new int[width * height];
    layer2 = new int[width * height];
    layer3 = new int[width * height];
    solidLayer = new int[width * height];

    loadLayer(layer1, &in);
    loadLayer(layer2, &in);
    loadLayer(layer3, &in);
    generateSolidLayer();

    in.close();

    //Load Image
    if(!tiles.load(imageName, tileWidth, tileHeight))
        return false;

    return true;
}
```

The load method has grown into a beast of its own. It is for this reason that it was split into multiple functions that come together as one. Notice the inclusion of a "solid" layer. This layer will work as any other layer, but it will never be drawn on the screen in a real video game. This layer is generated to keep track of the solid tiles. It has an array of its own, and every cell is populated with either a true or a false. A true denotes that the tile in that cell is solid, and a false denotes otherwise. You will be working with the solid layer in the next chapter. You can access the entire implementation of this method in the files that came with this book. Anyway, the drawing function has changed as well. Listing 9.7 displays the new incarnation of the draw function.

Listing 9.7: The Final Map Drawing Function

```cpp
void Map::draw(int layer, int xOffset, int yOffset, Graphics* g)
{
    int* drawLayer = NULL;

    if(layer == 0)
        drawLayer = solidLayer;
    else if(layer == 1)
        drawLayer = layer1;
    else if(layer == 2)
        drawLayer = layer2;
    else if(layer == 3)
        drawLayer = layer3;
    else
        return;

    int startY = yOffset/tileHeight;
    int startX = xOffset/tileWidth;

    int rows = (g->getHeight()/tileHeight) + 2;
    int columns = (g->getWidth()/tileWidth) + 2;

    for(int y = startY; y < startY+rows; y++)
    {
        for(int x = startX; x < startX+columns; x++)
        {
            int frame = -1;

            if(x >= 0 && y >= 0 && x < width && y < height)
                frame = drawLayer[y*width+x]-1;

            if(frame >= 0)
            {
                if(layer == 0)
                {
                    g->drawRect(x*tileWidth - xOffset,
                        y*tileHeight-yOffset,
                        tileWidth, tileHeight, 255, 0, 0);
                }
                else
                {
                    tiles.draw(x*tileWidth - xOffset,
                    y*tileHeight - yOffset,
                    frame, g);
                }
            }
        }
    }
}
```

Building the App

You can find the files necessary to build this app in the BAMGP\. They are located in Source\
Chapter_09\9_4_LayeredTileMap\. You need to create an SDL project and copy these files

- main.cpp
- Map.h
- Map.cpp
- MapDemo.h
- MapDemo.cpp

as well as the Core and the graphics folders into your project's directory. If you're using Windows, make sure to include the .dll files in the project's directory. This project requires additional .dll files that are specifically used for sound and images, so make sure to include those as well. Your project should be configured properly, as shown in Chapter 1, and all the files should also be properly included. When all is set, you'll be able to build the program and run it on your own. Additionally, a precompiled version is in the Source directory named 9_4_LayeredTileMap.exe.

This function has also grown quite large. It draws the desired layer, and it even has the ability to draw the solid layer for debugging purposes. Refer to Figure 9.6 for a screenshot of a demo drawing a multilayered map.

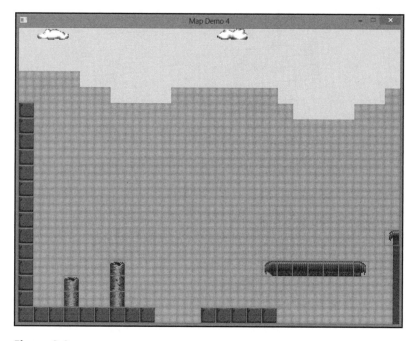

Figure 9.6
A map demonstrating multiple layers in action.
Source: SpriteLib, created by Ari Feldmen, used under the Common Public License.

SUMMARY

Tile maps are awesome! Being able to utilize them efficiently is yet another formidable weapon in anybody's game development arsenal. With a little bit of creativity and minimal effort, you can create vast worlds and intricate levels. Be sure to watch the video tutorial for this chapter since it includes additional commentary and information that will supplement your learning. Before moving on, try completing a few of the following exercises:

Exercises

- Create your own map using your own tile set. Just make sure it can be properly loaded and displayed in a program.

- The solid layer of the map doesn't do much as of now. Try creating a function that checks if a certain coordinate of the map is solid. This would be useful later on.

- Try rolling together a rudimentary map editor. It doesn't have to be too fancy, but it should be more convenient to use than a text editor! (Hint: You can use `printf` as a rudimentary function for outputting text to a file. Using `printf` is vastly inefficient, but it gets the job done. More experienced programmers should use the `fstream` library or write their own library.)

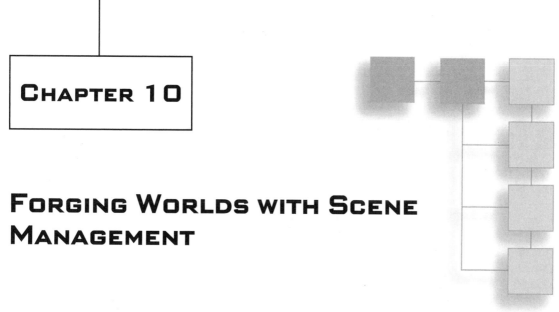

CHAPTER 10

FORGING WORLDS WITH SCENE MANAGEMENT

In the previous chapter, you used tile maps to create virtual environments. These environments were empty and needed a little something to bring life into them. They needed actors to populate them! While populating them with sprites of characters is no mystery, it is optimal to create a standardized way for keeping track of these characters. This can be done through scene management. In this chapter, expect to learn how to:

- Create a scene management class.
- Create a scene node class.
- Add tile maps into the equation.
- Interact with tile maps.

Tip

Before getting started, you can check out the video tutorial for this chapter, which is located in BAMGP/ under the Videos directory. The video contains extra material and insights, and reviews the chapter from a high level, so be sure to watch it.

CRASH COURSE OF SCENE MANAGEMENT

A *scene* is a group of game objects that interact in order to progress gameplay. These objects, sometimes known as actors or scene nodes, could be small soldiers the player controls or maybe aliens the player must shoot out of the sky. Figure 10.1 demonstrates a simple scene with a few game objects populating it.

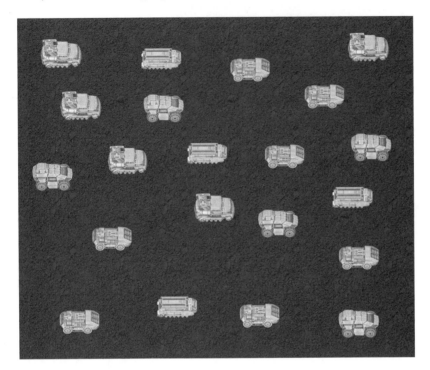

Figure 10.1
A scene filled with vehicles.
Source: Vehicles from 3DRT.com, a world leading developer of real-time CG content.

In the first paddle game, the game objects were the player's paddle, the computer's paddle, and the ball. The interactions between these objects completely defined the game mechanics. The problem is that adding something as simple as a second ball or a power-up can require a tremendous amount of coding. It is of great advantage to have a standardized way of handling game objects because this makes creation of new ones much more straightforward. Enough theory; time to move into the design phase.

DESIGNING THE SCENE MANAGER

To efficiently manage scenes, there will be two classes. One will manage scenes, and another will populate them. These two classes working in conjunction will facilitate the process of creating games filled with interactive objects.

The Scene Class

The Scene class will model a scene and manage it. This class will hold all the objects in the scene, update them, and draw them. It will also take care of cleaning up after itself. You can analyze the header file for this method in Listing 10.1.

Listing 10.1: The Scene Class Definition

```
#ifndef SCENE_H
#define SCENE_H

#include <list>

#include "SceneNode.h"
#include "Rectangle.h"

using namespace std;

class SceneNode;

class Scene
{
private:
    list<SceneNode*> nodes;
public:
    Scene();
    ~Scene();

    void addNode(SceneNode* node);
    void removeNode(SceneNode* node);

    void update();
    void draw(Rectangle* view, Graphics* g);

    list<SceneNode*>* getNodes();
};
```

There are several things in this class that must be explained. The first is that this class is dependent on two classes that haven't been created yet! These are the Rectangle class and the SceneNode class. They will be covered later. The second thing that needs to be explained is the usage of a linked list to store pointers to the game objects. The variable nodes is a linked list that will hold all the scene nodes. Using a linked list is more fitting than using an array because adding a linked list is extremely fast. Arrays have to be resized when adding and removing objects, and this can really grind a computer's gears. Notice that objects are stored as pointers. This creates the ability to allocate scene objects at runtime. Other than that, this class has all the bare bones of a scene manager. Before exploring the guts of these methods, let's cover the other two classes this class works with.

The Rectangle Class

The Rectangle class will be used solely for convenience. This class models an axis-aligned rectangle, and it provides general-purpose operations. These operations could help the program do simple things like finding the rectangle's center or resizing the rectangle. See Listing 10.2 for the header file of the Rectangle class.

Listing 10.2: The Rectangle Class Declaration

```
#ifndef RECTANGLE_H
#define RECTANGLE_H

class Rectangle
{
private:
    int x, y, width, height;
public:
    Rectangle();
    Rectangle(int ax, int ay, int aWidth, int aHeight);
    ~Rectangle();

    void set(int ax, int ay, int aWidth, int aHeight);
    void setPos(int ax, int ay);
    void setSize(int aWidth, int aHeight);
    void setX(int ax);
    void setY(int ay);
    void setX2(int x2);
    void setY2(int y2);

    void setWidth(int aWidth);
    void setHeight(int aHeight);

    int getX();
    int getY();
    int getX2();
    int getY2();
    int getWidth();
    int getHeight();
    int getCenterX();
    int getCenterY();

    bool overlaps(Rectangle rect);
    bool contains(int x, int y);
};

#endif
```

These methods are easy to implement, and they grant you tremendous power. See Table 10.1 for a description of its methods.

Table 10.1 Methods Used in This Class

Method	Description

`void set(`
`  int ax, int ay,`
`  int aWidth,`
`  int aHeight);`
	This method sets all the variables of the rectangle.

`void setPos(` `  int ax, int ay);`	This method sets the position of the upper-left corner of the rectangle.

`void setSize(`
`  int aWidth,`
`  int aHeight);`
	This method sets the size of the rectangle.

`void setX(int ax);`	This method sets the X position of the left edge of the rectangle.
`void setY(int ay);`	This method sets the Y position of the upper edge of the rectangle.
`void setX2(int x2);`	This method sets the X position of the right edge of the rectangle.
`void setY2(int y2);`	This method sets the Y position of the lower edge of the rectangle.
`void setWidth(` `  int aWidth);`	This method sets the width of the rectangle.
`void setHeight(` `  int aHeight);`	This method sets the height of the rectangle.
`int getX();`	This method returns the X coordinate of the left edge of the rectangle.
`int getY();`	This method returns the Y coordinate of the upper edge of the rectangle.
`int getX2();`	This method returns the X coordinate of the right edge of the rectangle.
`int getY2();`	This method returns the Y coordinate of the lower edge of the rectangle.
`int getWidth();`	This method returns the width of the rectangle.
`int getHeight();`	This method returns the height of the rectangle.
`int getCenterX();`	This method returns the X coordinate of the center of the rectangle.
`int getCenterY();`	This method returns the Y coordinate of the center of the rectangle.
`bool overlaps(` `  Rectangle rect);`	This method returns `true` if the rectangle overlaps with `rect`.
`bool contains(` `  int x, int y);`	This method returns `true` if the rectangle contains the point (x, y).

The SceneNode Class

The SceneNode class models game objects. This class is built on top of the Rectangle class. This provides extended functionality, but may limit the game objects to being rectangular in shape when it comes to collision detection. See Listing 10.3 for the SceneNode header file.

Listing 10.3: The SceneNode Class Declaration

```
#ifndef SCENENODE_H
#define SCENENODE_H

#include "Core/Graphics.h"
#include "Scene.h"
#include "Rectangle.h"

class Scene;

class SceneNode : public Rectangle
{
private:
    Scene* scene;
    bool removed;
    int ID;
public:
    SceneNode(int i, int x, int y, int width, int height);
    ~SceneNode();

    void setScene(Scene* s);
    Scene* getScene();

    virtual void update();
    virtual void draw(Rectangle* view, Graphics* g);

    void remove();
    bool isRemoved();

    int getID();
};

#endif
```

This class contains a few methods that are worth noting. The first two, setScene and getScene, provide access to the scene the object belongs to. The methods update and draw update and draw the object. The method remove removes the object from the scene. The last method returns the object's ID number. This number is arbitrary, and it is only used to differentiate between objects of different classes. This class is meant to serve as a base class to custom objects that different games may have.

IMPLEMENTING THE SCENE-MANAGEMENT MECHANISMS

With a general understanding of the purpose of these classes, it is time to implement the methods they're comprised of. Let's start with the Scene class.

Implementing the Scene Class

To begin, take a look at the addNode method in Listing 10.4.

Listing 10.4: The addNode Method

```
void Scene::addNode(SceneNode* node)
{
    node->setScene(this);
    nodes.push_back(node);
}
```

This little method adds a node into the scene. Next, implement removeNode as shown in Listing 10.5.

Listing 10.5: The removeNode Method

```
void Scene::removeNode(SceneNode* node)
{
    if(node != NULL)
    {
        SceneNode* n = node;
        nodes.remove(node);
        delete n;
    }
    else
    {
        while(!nodes.empty())
        {
            removeNode(*nodes.begin());
        }
    }
}
```

This method removes the desired node and deletes it. It also removes every single node in the scene if NULL is passed as an argument. This method can be used to clean up the scene when the program is done with it. The next method updates the scene. Go ahead and analyze it in Listing 10.6.

Listing 10.6: The Scene::update Method

```
void Scene::update()
{
    list<SceneNode*>::iterator it;

    //Remove 'removed' nodes
    for(it = nodes.begin(); it != nodes.end(); it++)
    {
        if((*it)->isRemoved())
        {
            SceneNode* oldNode = (*it);
            it--;
            removeNode(oldNode);
        }
    }

    //Update Nodes
    for(it = nodes.begin(); it != nodes.end(); it++)
    {
        (*it)->update();
    }
}
```

This method updates every single object from the scene. Furthermore, it removes objects that are flagged for removal. The next method draws the entire scene, and it can be examined in Listing 10.7.

Listing 10.7: The Scene::draw Method

```
void Scene::draw(Rectangle* view, Graphics* g)
{
    for(list<SceneNode*>::iterator it = nodes.begin();
        it != nodes.end(); it++)
    {
        (*it)->draw(view, g);
    }
}
```

Notice the parameter called view. This parameter represents the portion of the scene that is to be drawn. Think of this as a camera that can scroll through the scene. The last method, getNodes, returns a pointer to the game object list.

Implementing the SceneNode Class

The constructor for this class is actually very important. You may analyze it in Listing 10.8.

Listing 10.8: The SceneNode Constructor

```
SceneNode::SceneNode(int i, int x, int y,
    int width, int height) :
    Rectangle(x,y,width,height)
{
    ID = i;
    scene = NULL;
    removed = false;
}
```

This initializes the variables inherited from the parent class as well as its own variables. The methods `setScene` and `getScene` provide access to the scene the object belongs to. Furthermore, the `update` method is empty! This is because custom classes will override this method to update objects whichever way is fitting. The `draw` method is actually interesting and can be seen in Listing 10.9.

Listing 10.9: The SceneNode::draw Method

```
void SceneNode::draw(Rectangle* view, Graphics* g)
{
    if(view->overlaps(*this) && g != NULL)
    {
        g->drawRect(getX() - view->getX(), getY() - view->getY(),
            getWidth(), getHeight(), 255, 0, 0);
    }
}
```

This method draws a red rectangle that scrolls as the view scrolls. This might not be useful for video games, but it could be a great tool for debugging and prototyping. The next method, `remove`, flags the object for removal by setting the variable `removed` to `true`. The object will be removed next time the scene is updated. The last two methods, `isRemoved` and `getID`, are just getter methods.

TAKING THE SCENE MANAGER OUT FOR A SPIN

The following demo will test the scene manager. This demo adds a few objects to the scene and allows the users to scroll through the scene. It will also allow the users to add and remove objects with the press of a key. See Listing 10.10 for the header file of this demo's `Game` class derivative.

Listing 10.10: The SceneDemo Class Declaration

```
#ifndef MAPDEMO_H
#define MAPDEMO_H
```

```
#include "Core/Game.h"
#include "Core/Image.h"
#include "Scene.h"
#include "Rectangle.h"

class SceneDemo : public Game
{
private:
    static const int CAM_SPEED = 10;

    Image background;
    Scene scene;
    Rectangle camera;
public:
    SceneDemo();
    ~SceneDemo();
    virtual bool init();
    virtual void update();
    virtual void draw(Graphics* g);
    virtual void free();
};

#endif
```

There are only three member variables. The first, background, will hold an image for
the background. The second, scene, will hold the scene. The third, camera, will hold
the current visible portion of the scene (much like a camera in a movie would). The
code in Listing 10.11 implements the init method.

Listing 10.11: The SceneDemo::init Method

```
bool SceneDemo::init()
{
    if(!initSystem("Scene Demo 1", 800, 600, false))
        return false;

    if(!background.load("graphics//background.bmp"))
        return false;

    camera.set(0,0,800,600);

    return true;
}
```

With the exception of setting the initial position of the view, this method does nothing
new. Listing 10.12 implements the update method.

Listing 10.12: The SceneDemo::update Method

```
void SceneDemo::update()
{
    scene.update();

    Input* in = getInput();

    if(in->keyDown(SDLK_UP))
        camera.setY(camera.getY()-CAM_SPEED);

    if(in->keyDown(SDLK_DOWN))
        camera.setY(camera.getY()+CAM_SPEED);

    if(in->keyDown(SDLK_LEFT))
        camera.setX(camera.getX()-CAM_SPEED);

    if(in->keyDown(SDLK_RIGHT))
        camera.setX(camera.getX()+CAM_SPEED);

    if(in->keyHit(SDLK_SPACE))
    {
        for(int i = 0; i < 10; i++)
        {
            scene.addNode(new SceneNode(0,
                camera.getX() + rand()%1000,
                camera.getY() + rand()%1000, 50, 50));
        }
    }

    if(in->keyHit(SDLK_ESCAPE))
        scene.removeNode(NULL);
}
```

This method is much more interesting. It moves camera around when the arrow keys are pressed. It also allows users to add objects to the scene in a random location and clear the entire scene with the press of a button. The draw method draws the scene and the background. Observe its implementation in Listing 10.13.

Listing 10.13: The SceneDemo::draw Method

```
void SceneDemo::draw(Graphics* g)
{
    background.draw(0, 0, g);
    scene.draw(&camera, g);
}
```

The last method cleans up the demo, and it can be studied in Listing 10.14.

Listing 10.14: The SceneDemo::free Method

```
void SceneDemo::free()
{
    scene.removeNode(NULL);

    background.free();
    freeSystem();
}
```

Building the App

You can find the files necessary to build this app in BAMGP\. They are located in Source\ Chapter_10\10_1_BasicScene\. You need to create an SDL project and copy these files

- main.cpp
- Map.h
- Map.cpp
- Scene.h
- Scene.cpp
- SceneDemo.h
- SceneDemo.cpp
- Rectangle.h
- Rectangle.cpp
- SceneNode.h
- SceneNode.cpp

as well as the Core and the graphics folders into your project's directory. If you're using Windows, make sure to include the .dll files in the project's directory. This project requires additional .dll files that are specifically used for sound and images, so make sure to include those as well. Your project should be configured properly, as shown in Chapter 1, and all the files should also be properly included. When all is set, you'll be able to build the program and run it on your own. Additionally, a precompiled version is in the Source directory named 10_1_BasicScene.exe.

Notice that it removes all the objects in the scene. Failure to do this before the program closes will result in *memory leaks*, which are extremely undesirable. Memory leaks occur when memory that was dynamically allocated isn't deallocated properly. While memory leaks may not always crash a program, they can disrupt a program's behavior in unpredictable ways. This makes them extremely difficult to debug at times. Look at Figure 10.2 for a screenshot of this demo.

Tip

Memory leaks are a common problem in the software development industry. Luckily, there are tools, such as Cppcheck by Daniel Marjamäki, that have been developed to assist a programmer in finding them. These tools can analyze a program's code and find potential bugs (static program analysis), or they can monitor a program while it is running and create a report on leaked memory (dynamic program analysis). Of course, it's always best to quadruple check your code when working with dynamic memory in order to avoid memory leaks altogether.

Figure 10.2
A scene filled with squares.
© Jazon Yamamoto.

STANDARDIZING AND INCORPORATING SPRITES

Populating a scene with squares is a great first step, but squares are boring, and you don't want to make a boring game. The next logical step is to use sprites instead of squares. Let's create a new class to handle sprites.

The Sprite Class

The class for handling sprites will be called Sprite, and its class declaration can be seen in Listing 10.15.

Listing 10.15: The Sprite Class Declaration

```
class Sprite
{
private:
    Image* image;
    int firstFrame;
    int lastFrame;
    int delay;
    int currentFrame;
    int delayCounter;
public:
    Sprite();
    ~Sprite();
    void setImage(Image* i);
    Image* getImage();
    void update();
    void draw(int x, int y, Graphics* g);
    void setAnimation(int f, int l, int d);
    void setFrame(int f);

    int getWidth();
    int getHeight();
};
```

This class is packed with goodies. It will be able to generate a sprite from a pointer to an image and even animate it! The constructor initializes all the int variables to 0 and sets image to NULL. The destructor is empty. The methods setImage and getImage provide access to the image variable. This class also handles animations. The setAnimation method is used to set the sprite's animation parameters. See Listing 10.16 for the code to this method.

Listing 10.16: The Sprite::setAnimation Method

```
void Sprite::setAnimation(int f, int l, int d)
{
    firstFrame = f;
    lastFrame = l;
    delay = d;
    delayCounter = 0;
}
```

This method sets up the variables that will be used to animate a sprite. The variables currentFrame and lastFrame indicate the first and last frame of the animation. The variable called delayCounter works in conjunction with the variable called delay to regulate the speed of the animation. This method only sets up the animation variables, but it doesn't actually update them. The method that updates the animation process is called update. See the implementation of this method in Listing 10.17.

Listing 10.17: The Sprite::update Method

```
void Sprite::update()
{
    delayCounter++;
    if(delayCounter > delay)
    {
        delayCounter = 0;
        currentFrame++;
    }
    if(currentFrame > lastFrame)
        currentFrame = firstFrame;
}
```

The variable called currentFrame determines the frame that will be drawn. This variable is also used in the draw method, as shown in Listing 10.18.

Listing 10.18: The Sprite::draw Method

```
void Sprite::draw(int x, int y, Graphics* g)
{
    if(image != NULL)
    {
        image->draw(x, y, currentFrame, g);
    }
}
```

Another method that is worth noting is the setFrame method. This method sets the entire animation state to one frame, and it can be seen in Listing 10.19.

Listing 10.19: The Sprite::setFrame Method

```
void Sprite::setFrame(int frame)
{
    currentFrame = firstFrame = lastFrame = frame;
    delay = 0;
    delayCounter = 0;
}
```

This could be useful when the sprite doesn't have to be animated but does have to change frames every once in a while. The methods getWidth and getHeight return the width and height of the sprite, respectively.

The Sprite Scene Demo

To generate a scene with sprites, you can create a custom class derived from the SceneNode class. In this case, the class will be called Helicopter, and it will draw an animated helicopter. See the declaration for this class in Listing 10.20.

Listing 10.20: The Helicopter Class Declaration

```
class Helicopter : public SceneNode
{
private:
    Sprite sprite;
    int dir;

    static const int DIR_UP = 0;
    static const int DIR_DOWN = 1;
    static const int DIR_LEFT = 2;
    static const int DIR_RIGHT = 3;

    static const int ANIM_UP_START = 0;
    static const int ANIM_UP_END = 8;
    static const int ANIM_DOWN_START = 9;
    static const int ANIM_DOWN_END = 17;
    static const int ANIM_LEFT_START = 18;
    static const int ANIM_LEFT_END = 26;
    static const int ANIM_RIGHT_START = 27;
    static const int ANIM_RIGHT_END = 35;
public:
    Helicopter(Image* i, int x, int y);
    ~Helicopter();

    void update();
    void draw(Rectangle* view, Graphics* g);
    void setDir(int d);
};
```

The variable sprite will hold the helicopter sprite. The variable dir will hold the direction of the helicopter. All the const int variables hold direction and animation information that you will use later. See the constructor for this class in Listing 10.21.

Listing 10.21: The Helicopter Constructor

```
Helicopter::Helicopter(Image* i, int x, int y) :
    SceneNode(0, x, y, i->getFrameWidth(), i->getFrameHeight())
{
    sprite.setImage(i);
    dir = -1;

    setDir(rand()%4);
}
```

This handles the initialization of the parent class variables as well as the sprite and direction. The next two methods, called update and draw, are pretty self explanatory. See their implementation in Listing 10.22 for a clearer understanding.

Listing 10.22: The Helicopter::update Method

```
void Helicopter::update()
{
    sprite.update();
}
void Helicopter::draw(Rectangle* view, Graphics* g)
{
    sprite.draw(getX() - view->getX(), getY() - view->getY(), g);
}
```

The final method, setDir, is used to set the direction and corresponding animation. Analyze its functionality in Listing 10.23.

Listing 10.23: The Helicopter::setDir Method

```
void Helicopter::setDir(int d)
{
    if(dir != d)
    {
        dir = d;
        if(dir == DIR_UP)
            sprite.setAnimation(ANIM_UP_START,
                                ANIM_UP_END, 0);
        if(dir == DIR_DOWN)
            sprite.setAnimation(ANIM_DOWN_START,
                                ANIM_DOWN_END, 0);
        if(dir == DIR_LEFT)
            sprite.setAnimation(ANIM_LEFT_START,
                                ANIM_LEFT_END, 0);
        if(dir == DIR_RIGHT)
            sprite.setAnimation(ANIM_RIGHT_START,
                                ANIM_RIGHT_END, 0);
    }
}
```

Building the App

You can find the files necessary to build this app in the BAMGP\. They are located in Source\ Chapter_10\10_2_SpriteScene\. You need to create an SDL project and copy these files

- main.cpp
- Map.h
- Map.cpp
- Sprite.h
- Sprite.cpp
- Helicopter.h
- Helicopter.cpp
- Scene.h
- Scene.cpp
- SceneDemo.h
- SceneDemo.cpp
- Rectangle.h
- Rectangle.cpp
- SceneNode.h
- SceneNode.cpp

as well as the Core and the graphics folders into your project's directory. If you're using Windows, make sure to include the .dll files in the project's directory. This project requires additional .dll files that are specifically used for sound and images, so make sure to include those as well. Your project should be configured properly, as shown in Chapter 1, and all the files should also be properly included. When all is set, you'll be able to build the program and run it on your own. Additionally, a precompiled version is in the Source directory named 10_1_SpriteScene.exe.

This method completes the new SceneNode derivative. The little helicopter is ready to be added to a scene. See Figure 10.3 for a screenshot of the demo.

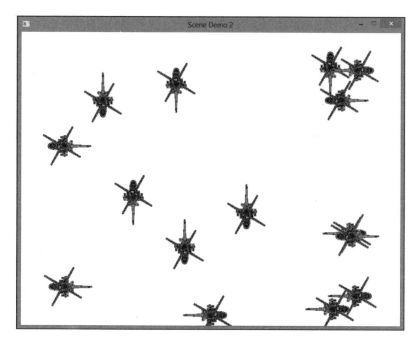

Figure 10.3
Helicopters hovering in the scene.
© Jazon Yamamoto. Source: 3DRT.com.

TILE MAP COLLISION DETECTION

Adding tile-based collision detection to a game object creates a world of new possibilities. This makes it possible to see if an object collided with a map, and it makes the solid layer in the `Map` class useful. This will be accomplished with a class called `MapNode`. This class will extend `SceneNode` and provide a method called `overlapsMap` that will be used to determine if an object has overlapped with the map's solid layer. See Listing 10.24 for a declaration of the class.

Listing 10.24: The MapNode Class Declaration

```
class MapNode : public SceneNode
{
private:
    Map* map;
public:
    MapNode(int i, int x, int y, int width, int height, Map* m);
    ~MapNode();

    virtual void draw(Rectangle* view, Graphics* g);

    bool overlapsMap();
};
```

Objects created from this class are reliant on a pointer to a `Map` object. Collisions will be measured against the solid layer of this tile map in the `overlapsMap` method. See the implementation of this method in Listing 10.25.

Listing 10.25: The MapNode::overlapsMap Method

```cpp
bool MapNode::overlapsMap()
{
    if(map == NULL)
        return false;

    //Check every point from the upper-left
    //corner of the rectangle
    //to the lower-right corner
    for(int x = getX(); x < getX2(); x+= map->getTileWidth())
    {
        for(int y = getY(); y < getY2(); y+= map->getTileHeight())
        {
            if(map->checkSolid(x/map->getTileWidth(),
                                y/map->getTileHeight()))
            {
                return true;
            }
        }

        //Check the bottom edge of the rectangle
        if(map->checkSolid(x/map->getTileWidth(),
                            getY2()/map->getTileHeight()))
        {
            return true;
        }
    }

    //Check the right edge of the rectangle
    for(int y = getY(); y < getY2(); y+= map->getTileHeight())
    {
        if(map->checkSolid(getX2()/map->getTileWidth(),
                            y/map->getTileHeight()))
        {
            return true;
        }
    }

    //Check the bottom-left corner of the rectangle
    return map->checkSolid(getX2()/map->getTileWidth(),
                            getY2()/map->getTileHeight());
}
```

This enormous method may be hard to analyze, but the theory behind it is simple. To determine if the object collided with the map, it checks if a certain group of points in the object overlap the map. These points are arranged in a grid in which every cell is the same size as a single tile in the map. The first `for` loop tests all the points that would fall into the grid and the bottom edge of the object. The second loop traverses through all the points in the left edge of the object. The final `return` statement checks the bottom-right corner of the object. If all the `checkSolid` method calls return `false`, then the object isn't overlapping a solid portion of the map. This method is also used in the new `draw` method to draw the rectangle in a different color when overlapping the map, as demonstrated in Listing 10.26.

Listing 10.26: The `MapNode::draw` Method

```
void MapNode::draw(Rectangle* view, Graphics* g)
{
    if(overlapsMap())
    {
        g->fillRect(getX() - view->getX(), getY() - view->getY(),
            getWidth(), getHeight(), 255, 0, 0);
    }
    else
    {
        g->fillRect(getX() - view->getX(), getY() - view->getY(),
            getWidth(), getHeight(), 0, 0, 255);
    }
}
```

Building the App

You can find the files necessary to build this app in the `BAMGP\`. They are located in `Source\Chapter_10\10_3_MapScene\`. You need to create an SDL project and copy these files

- `main.cpp`
- `Map.h`
- `Map.cpp`
- `MapNode.h`
- `MapNode.cpp`
- `Scene.h`
- `Scene.cpp`
- `SceneDemo.h`
- `SceneDemo.cpp`
- `Rectangle.h`

- `Rectangle.cpp`
- `SceneNode.h`
- `SceneNode.cpp`

as well as the Core and the graphics folders into your project's directory. If you're using Windows, make sure to include the .dll files in the project's directory. This project requires additional .dll files that are specifically used for sound and images, so make sure to include those as well. Your project should be configured properly, as shown in Chapter 1, and all the files should also be properly included. When all is set, you'll be able to build the program and run it on your own. Additionally, a precompiled version is in the Source directory named 10_1_MapScene.exe.

This cool new toy is ready to detect collisions with a map! See Figure 10.4 for a screenshot of the demo for this section.

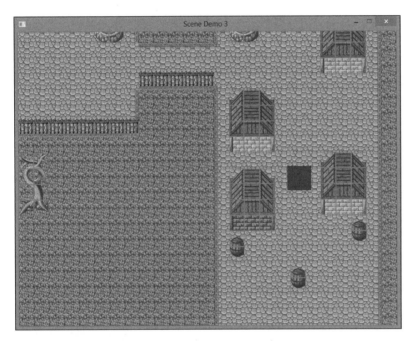

Figure 10.4
An object overlapping a solid tile.
© Jazon Yamamoto.

TILE MAP COLLISION RESPONSE

Up to this point, detecting a collision is possible, but responding to it is just as useful. This is crucial in platformer games and such. There are several ways to respond to a collision, but an extremely useful one is to stop the object in its tracks. If an object in motion is going to collide with a tile in the solid layer of a map, the object should stop in its tracks. It's that simple. Unfortunately, even the simplest ways to do this can be quite convoluted. To handle this type of collision, a method called move will be created to move the object while being mindful of possible collisions. This method will move a MapNode in a desired direction. See Listing 10.27 for the implementation of this method.

Listing 10.27: The MapNode::move Method

```
void MapNode::move(int x, int y)
{
    //If the object isn't solid and the map isn't NULL
    //continue.
    if(!solid || map == NULL)
    {
        setX(getX() + x);
        setY(getY() + y);
        return;
    }

    //First move along the X axis.
    setX(getX() + x);

    //Check for a collision if the object is moving left
    if(x < 0)
    {
        if(overlapsMap())
        {
            //React to the collision
            setX(((getX()/map->getTileWidth()) + 1) *
                    map->getTileWidth());
        }
    }

    if(x > 0)
    {
    //Check for a collision if the object is moving right
        if(overlapsMap())
        {
            //React to the collision
            setX2((getX2()/map->getTileWidth()) *
                    map->getTileWidth() - 1);
        }
    }

    setY(getY() + y);

    if(y < 0)
    {
    //Check for a collision if the object is moving down
        if(overlapsMap())
```

```
        {
            //React to the collision
            setY(((getY()/map->getTileHeight()) + 1) *
                    map->getTileHeight());
        }
    }
    if(y > 0)
    {
    //Check for a collision if the object is moving right
        if(overlapsMap())
        {
            //React to the collision
            setY2((getY2()/map->getTileHeight()) *
                    map->getTileHeight() - 1);
        }
    }
}
```

Building the App

You can find the files necessary to build this app in BAMGP\. They are located in Source\ Chapter_10\10_4_MapCollision\. You need to create an SDL project and copy these files

- ■ main.cpp
- ■ Map.h
- ■ Map.cpp
- ■ MapNode.h
- ■ MapNode.cpp
- ■ Scene.h
- ■ Scene.cpp
- ■ SceneDemo.h
- ■ SceneDemo.cpp
- ■ Rectangle.h
- ■ Rectangle.cpp
- ■ SceneNode.h
- ■ SceneNode.cpp

as well as the Core and the graphics folders into your project's directory. If you're using Windows, make sure to include the .dll files in the project's directory. This project requires additional .dll files that are specifically used for sound and images, so make sure to include those as well. Your project should be configured properly, as shown in Chapter 1, and all the files should also be properly included. When all is set, you'll be able to build the program and run it on your own. Additionally, a precompiled version is in the Source directory named 10_1_MapCollision.exe.

This method handles collision detection and response in a manner that depends on the direction of the object. If the object moves to the right, the position will be updated and tested for collision against the map. If a collision is detected, the object will be moved to the left so that the right edge of the object rests against the solid tile it collided with. The collision-detection algorithm for the rest of the directions works in a similar way. See Figure 10.5 for a screenshot of the demo for this section.

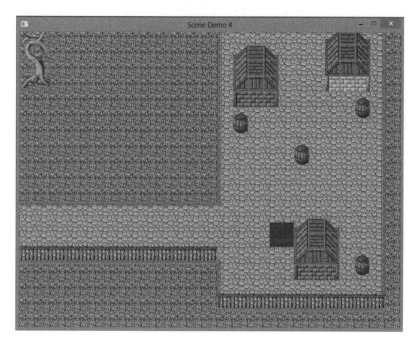

Figure 10.5
An object colliding against a house.
© Jazon Yamamoto.

SUMMARY

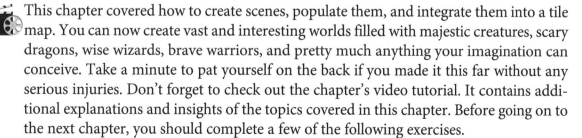

This chapter covered how to create scenes, populate them, and integrate them into a tile map. You can now create vast and interesting worlds filled with majestic creatures, scary dragons, wise wizards, brave warriors, and pretty much anything your imagination can conceive. Take a minute to pat yourself on the back if you made it this far without any serious injuries. Don't forget to check out the chapter's video tutorial. It contains additional explanations and insights of the topics covered in this chapter. Before going on to the next chapter, you should complete a few of the following exercises.

Exercises

■ Modify the `Helicopter` class to make the helicopter go forward. You should see the helicopters disperse when running the demo.

■ Load your own map and add a few little creatures to it. These could be anything, but they should each have distinct behaviors.

■ Create a simple game in which the player has to explore a map, find a key, and take it to a door. This could be the basis of the next great RPG.

CHAPTER 11

INSIDE THE MASS PRODUCTION ZONE WITH FACTORIES AND SCRIPTS

With scene management out of the way, this chapter focuses on the power of creation. The goal is to simplify the process of defining new objects to populate scenes. This can easily be achieved with unified object creation. This concept makes it possible to expand upon games with minimal effort. In this chapter, expect to learn about:

- Unified object creation.

- Implementing factories.

- Implementing scripting systems.

Tip

Before getting started, you can check out the video tutorial for this chapter, which is located in BAMGP\ under the Videos directory. The video contains extra material and insights, and reviews the chapter from a high level, so be sure to watch it.

UNIFIED OBJECT CREATION

Unified object creation is the process of creating different objects from a single object. This object is often called a *factory*. Although this may not be suitable for most cases, it is perfect for scene node objects. This is because these objects are often created in a similar fashion, and creating them all from a single factory can eliminate code redundancies. This may seem vague, but it is an abstract concept, and putting this theory into practice is the best way to master this subject.

233

USING FACTORIES

When unifying object creation, factories are powerhouses that put objects together. Think of a factory as an object with the sole purpose of creating other objects. Factories are in charge of ensuring that objects are created properly. They can also be used to manage the resources that will be used by the objects it creates. These resources can be images, sounds, and so on. Unfortunately, factories are not very portable, and they tend to function properly only with the program for which they were created.

Putting Factories into Practice

For demonstrational purposes, you'll see how to create a simple factory. This factory will be able to create four different objects. These objects will all be scene nodes, and they will be dropped into a scene at the press of a button. Go ahead and examine the factory's header file in Listing 11.1.

Listing 11.1: The Factory Class Definition

```
#ifndef FACTORY_H
#define FACTORY_H

#include "Core/Image.h"
#include "Core/Map.h"
#include "Core/SceneNode.h"

#include "Flier.h"
#include "Walker.h"

enum{ENTITY_SLUG, ENTITY_SOLDIER, ENTITY_RIDER, ENTITY_FLIER};

class Factory
{
private:
    Map* map;

    Image soldierImage;
    Image slugImage;
    Image riderImage;
    Image flierImage;
public:
    bool init(Map* m);
    void free();

    SceneNode* create(int entity, int x, int y);
};

#endif
```

At the top, there are two files that will be included. These are header files of scene node classes that this factory will use to create objects. They are flier objects and walker objects. The flier object is a non-player character (NPC) that will fly over all the other objects at the top of the screen, and the walker object is an NPC that walks on the ground, going left and right. Also notice the enumerated definitions at the top of the code that begin with ENTITY_(NAME). These definitions are used as identification numbers to the types of objects that will be available for creation.

There are three methods in this class. The init method loads all the files the factory needs to create objects, and it requires a reference to the map being used. The free method releases all the resources acquired by the factory. The method that creates objects is the create method. This method returns the reference to an object created by the factory, and it requires three parameters. The first is the identification number of the object (it should always be the ENTITY_(NAME) enumerations that were defined earlier). The latter two indicate the object's position. Listing 11.2 demonstrates the method's definition.

Listing 11.2: The Factory::create Method

```
SceneNode* Factory::create(int entity, int x, int y)
{
    switch(entity)
    {
        case ENTITY_SOLDIER:
            return new Walker(&soldierImage, x, y, map);
            break;
        case ENTITY_SLUG:
            return new Walker(&slugImage, x, y, map);
            break;
        case ENTITY_RIDER:
            return new Walker(&riderImage, x, y, map);
            break;
        case ENTITY_FLIER:
            return new Flier(&flierImage, x, y, map);
            break;
        default:
            return new SceneNode(1, x, y, 50, 50);
    }
}
```

This method is very nice because it hides all the ugly code that goes into object creation, and it ties everything into one single method. Keep in mind that any object can create scene objects as long as it has access to the factory object (this can be accomplished with a pointer). Take a look at this method being used in a demo in Listing 11.3.

Listing 11.3: The `FactoryDemo::update` Method

```
void FactoryDemo::update()
{
    Input* in = getInput();

    updateCamera();

    if(in->keyHit(SDLK_1))
        buttonSelection = 0;

    if(in->keyHit(SDLK_2))
        buttonSelection = 1;

    if(in->keyHit(SDLK_3))
        buttonSelection = 2;

    if(in->keyHit(SDLK_4))
        buttonSelection = 3;

    if(in->mouseHit(Input::MOUSE_LEFT))
    {
        int x = in->getMouseX() + camera.getX();
        int y = in->getMouseY() + camera.getY();

        switch(buttonSelection)
        {
            case 0:
                scene.addNode(factory.create(ENTITY_SOLDIER,x,y));
                break;
            case 1:
                scene.addNode(factory.create(ENTITY_SLUG,x,y));
                break;
            case 2:
                scene.addNode(factory.create(ENTITY_RIDER, x,y));
                break;
            case 3:
                scene.addNode(factory.create(ENTITY_FLIER, x,y));
                break;
            default:
                break;
        }
    }

    scene.update();
}
```

Building the App

You can find the files necessary to build this app in the BAMGP\. They are located in Source\ Chapter_11\11_1_Factories\. You need to create an SDL project and copy these files

- main.cpp
- Factory.h
- Factory.cpp
- FactoryDemo.h
- FactoryDemo.cpp
- Flier.h
- Flier.cpp
- Walker.h
- Walker.cpp

as well as the Core and the graphics folders into your project's directory. If you're using Windows, make sure to include the .dll files in the project's directory. This project requires additional .dll files that are specifically used for sound and images, so make sure to include those as well. Your project should be configured properly, as shown in Chapter 1, and all the files should also be properly included. When all is set, you'll be able to build the program and run it on your own. Additionally, a precompiled version is in the Source directory named 11_1_Factories.exe.

This demo allows users to select a desired object that they want to add to the scene by pressing the 1–4 keys on the keyboard. Users can then add the desired object by clicking on the desired location in the scene. Figure 11.1 shows a screenshot of this demo.

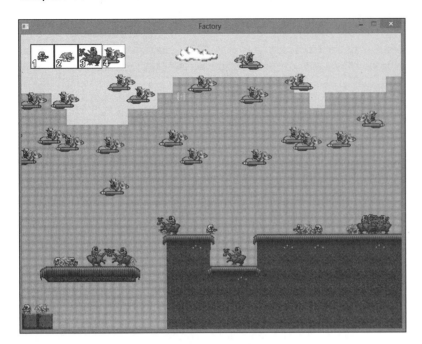

Figure 11.1
Objects manually dropped into a scene.
© Jazon Yamamoto. Source: Ari Feldman.

USING SCRIPTING SYSTEMS

In terms of computer programming, a *script* is a text file containing code that is to be interpreted and executed by a program. This is useful because it makes it possible to change a program's behavior without recompiling it. Scripts can actually be very powerful. There are scripting languages, such as Python, that are powerful enough to create fully functional desktop applications. For the purpose of this book, a simple script interpreter will be developed to make it easier to define how games will behave.

In general, scripts are mainly used to add objects to a scene. Most scripts in this book mainly resemble the code in Listing 11.4.

Listing 11.4: A Sample Script

```
addObject 100 200
addObject 200 300
addObject 100 300
```

This is the equivalent of calling a function and passing in two parameters. Keep in mind that the functionality the scripts have will be very limited, but this alone would provide sufficient power for many things. It is also possible to have if statements, for loops, and data structures implemented into the scripting system, but this would be too advanced to cover in this book.

The Scripting System

For demonstrational purposes, the following demo creates a script interpreter that specifically focuses on adding different objects to a scene upon execution. Listing 11.5 contains a sample of a script that program will be able to execute.

Listing 11.5: An Actual Script

```
rider 4967 555
rider 4867 282
soldier 5346 538
soldier 5508 542
slug 5842 547
slug 6114 560
slug 6302 507
rider 6761 394
rider 6941 394
flier 7792 153
flier 7591 124
```

The script interpreter will read and execute each line from the script file, one line at a time. Each line begins with a command name followed by a parameter list. In this case, the command names are the names of scene objects that will be added to the scene. The parameters indicate their initial positions. Listing 11.6 demonstrates a method that loads a script from a file and starts executing it line-by-line.

Listing 11.6: The ScriptDemo::load Method

```
bool ScriptDemo::load()
{
    ifstream in("script.txt"); //load script

    if(!in.good())
    {
        return false;
    }

    while(!in.eof())
    {
        parseLine(&in);
    }

    in.close();

    return true;
}
```

This method loads a script, makes sure it's valid, and then calls parseLine until there are no more lines in the script. The parseLine method reads the current line of the string and adds the corresponding objects to the scene at their corresponding locations. Examine its code in Listing 11.7.

Listing 11.7: The ScriptDemo::parseLine Method

```
void ScriptDemo::parseLine(ifstream* in)
{
    char command[64];
    (*in)>>command;

    if(!strcmp(command, "soldier"))
    {
        int x;
        int y;

        (*in)>>x;
        (*in)>>y;

        scene.addNode(factory.create(ENTITY_SOLDIER, x, y));
    }

    if(!strcmp(command, "slug"))
    {
        int x;
        int y;

        (*in)>>x;
        (*in)>>y;

        scene.addNode(factory.create(ENTITY_SLUG, x, y));
    }

    if(!strcmp(command, "rider"))
    {
        int x;
        int y;

        (*in)>>x;
        (*in)>>y;

        scene.addNode(factory.create(ENTITY_RIDER, x, y));
    }

    if(!strcmp(command, "flier"))
    {
        int x;
        int y;
```

```
        (*in)>>x;
        (*in)>>y;
        scene.addNode(factory.create(ENTITY_FLIER, x, y));
    }
}
```

Building the App

You can find the files necessary to build this app in the BAMGP\. They are located in Source\ Chapter_11\11_2_Scripting\. You need to create an SDL project and copy these files

- `main.cpp`
- `Factory.h`
- `Script.cpp`
- `ScriptDemo.h`
- `FactoryDemo.cpp`
- `Flier.h`
- `Flier.cpp`
- `Walker.h`
- `Walker.cpp`
- `script.txt`

as well as the `Core` and the `graphics` folders into your project's directory. If you're using Windows, make sure to include the `.dll` files in the project's directory. This project requires additional `.dll` files that are specifically used for sound and images, so make sure to include those as well. Your project should be configured properly, as shown in Chapter 1, and all the files should also be properly included. When all is set, you'll be able to build the program and run it on your own. Additionally, a precompiled version is in the `Source` directory named `11_2_Scripting.exe`.

This method is capable of adding four different types of objects to the scene. Notice that there is no error checking, so faulty scripts can lead an application to behave in a strange manner. Remember that scripts can be much more robust than this, and they can even contain commands to change the screen resolution, change the current game state, and define the initial state of a game's level or even how levels will be arranged. See Figure 11.2 for a screenshot of the demo for this section.

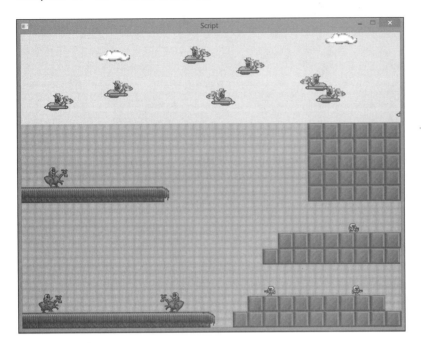

Figure 11.2
Object scripted into a scene.
© Jazon Yamamoto. Source: Ari Feldman.

Tip

If you're interested in learning more about scripting, there are many books available, including the classic one, *Game Scripting Mastery*, by Alex Varanese. You can find it on Amazon and other online retailers. The book covers very advanced scripting, parsing, compiler, and interpreter design, as well as virtual machines.

SUMMARY

This was a rather short chapter, but it demonstrated two techniques that are commonly used for object creation. These techniques are essential for making complete games. It's a shame that the code demonstrated in this section is not very reusable, but the theory behind it is invaluable. The next chapter will be the final frontier for this book. It will put into practice everything that has been covered so far, and this chapter served mainly as a stepping stone to what is to come. Be sure to watch the video tutorial for this chapter; it contains extra commentary to supplement your learning. Before continuing on to the final frontier, complete a few of the following exercises.

Exercises

- Add a custom object for the factory to make. One that the user can control would definitely be interesting.

- Pass a reference of the factory to an object, and make that object spawn more objects. Perhaps the flying object could drop little soldiers onto the ground.

- Add a custom command to the script interpreter. This command should add 10 random objects to the scene.

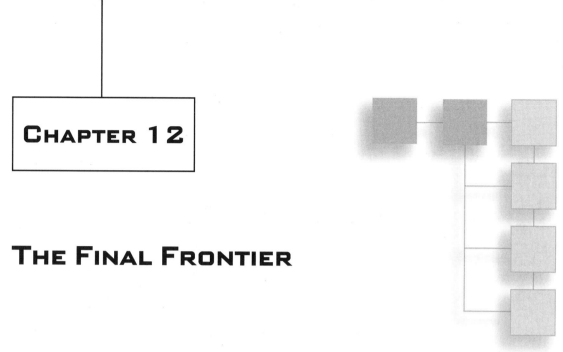

CHAPTER 12

THE FINAL FRONTIER

Congratulations. You have arrived at the final frontier. This is the last stretch of the book where everything comes together. This chapter takes everything that was covered and uses it on a final project. This project is more intricate than anything else in this book, but if you covered all the previous chapters, you're more than ready for this challenge. Working on this project will teach you more about:

- Effectively using the game engine.
- Using scrolling tile maps in a game.
- Utilizing scene management to handle game objects.
- Putting factories to work on object production.
- Polishing a game.
- Last minute details.

Tip

Before getting started, you can check out the video tutorial for this chapter, which is located in BAMGP/ under the Videos directory. The video contains extra material and insights, and reviews the chapter from a high level, so be sure to watch it.

THE DESIGN OF *CONFLICT ANDROMEDA*

This game actually has two design goals. The first is to make a game that is simple, easy to understand, and easy to code. The second is to make the game look and feel like a real arcade game. In the end, I chose a space shoot 'em up game. This genre is well established and has remained popular in the arcade for decades. There are two main types of shoot 'em up games—vertical ones and horizontal ones. Vertical shoot 'em up games position the players at the bottom of the screen, and they fight waves of enemies approaching from the top of the screen, as pictured in Figure 12.1.

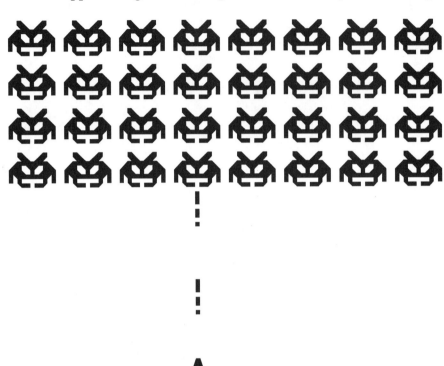

Figure 12.1
A vertical shooter.
© Jazon Yamamoto.

Horizontal shoot 'em up games position the players at the left of the screen as they fight waves of enemies coming in from the right, as demonstrated in Figure 12.2.

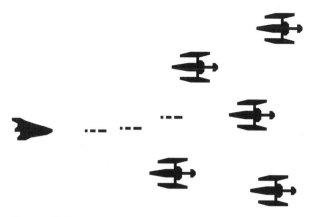

Figure 12.2
A horizontal shooter.
© Jazon Yamamoto.

Typically, there are bosses at the end of each level, which are enemies that are much more difficult to kill than the average enemy. Levels usually end when the player manages to kill these bosses. Bosses are supposed to be intimidating.

The game in this chapter takes a horizontal gameplay approach. It also has generic enemy units and a boss. There will be a scrolling background and even obstacles in the background. Figure 12.3 shows what the game will look like in the middle of a boss fight.

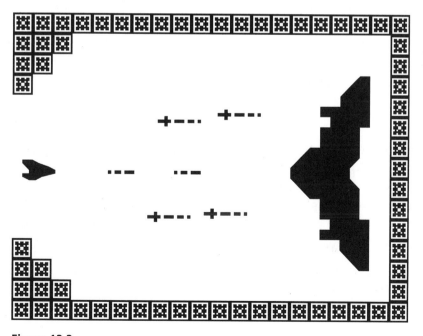

Figure 12.3
The player is fighting a boss.
© Jazon Yamamoto.

The Game's Story

In modern days, every great game has a story. This rule almost goes completely without an exception. The game in this chapter is called *Conflict Andromeda*. Its story goes like this:

> The year is 2562 C.E. Humanity has outgrown its home planet and has been forced to expand to different sectors of the universe in search of planets that are fit for habitation. In the midst of this search, contact was made with a strange substance that could mimic simple forms of life. Human researchers found this substance during a mining mission in a deserted planet in the outer edges of the Andromeda galaxy. Ever since its discovery, this substance has been used to construct ecosystems in a previously uninhabitable planet. This planet is called the Atlas Ring. A second planet was made inhabitable by more traditional means, but this planet cannot support nearly as much life as the Atlas Ring. This second planet is called the Zeta Colony. With time, both planets have prospered, formed governments, and conducted trade, but after decades of progress, the Atlas Ring has begun to falter. The substance that once supported life in it began to create completely new forms of life. These forms of life understand humanity, including its strengths and weaknesses. They enslaved humanity in the Atlas Ring, created a sizable army, and launched an attack against the Zeta Colony. The Zeta Colony launched a counterattack with their last remaining pilot, Zack Heizenshmit. He was an extremely skilled pilot and probably the best that the galaxy has known. The only problem is that he has only three lives…

As cheesy as it may be, this story gets the job done and sets up the field for some intense gameplay.

Gameplay

With the core mechanics laid out, it's time to hammer out more specifics. The player will have three lives at the beginning of the game. If he loses all three lives, he will be sent back to the beginning. Enemies will enter from the right side of the screen, and the player can shoot them down from the left. There will also be checkpoints. If a player progresses past a checkpoint and then dies, he will be sent back to the checkpoint, and all the enemies will be reset. At the end of the level, there will be a boss. This boss will be much more difficult than any previous enemies. It will also be much more intricate and behave in a manner that is less predictable than a regular enemy. The player will win the game upon defeating the final boss.

CREATING THE MENU SYSTEM

This game will have a cool menu system with a fancy background. Upon launching the program, the user will be greeted with the menu screen shown in Figure 12.4. Background music will accompany this menu to prepare the player for action. The menu will have the following three options: Start Game, Credits, and Exit.

Figure 12.4
The menu screen.
Source: Spaceship from 3DRT.com, world leading developer of real-time CG content.

Clicking on the Start Game option will start the game. At this point, the game state will be changed, and the player will be dropped right into action. The Credits option will send the player to an alternate state. This state will display the credits of the people who worked on it. The user will be able to exit this state and return to the main menu by pressing the spacebar. Take a look at Figure 12.5 for a screenshot of the Credits state.

Figure 12.5
The Credits screen.
Source: Spaceship from 3DRT.com, world leading developer of real-time CG content.

The last option will exit the game. It is also the only way to exit the game. Many computer game developers choose to do it this way, and this game follows suit.

CREATING THE PLAYER

The player will control humanity's last chance of survival. This will be in the form of a compact spaceship with superior defense and offense. The spaceship will be able to absorb a great deal of damage (including head-on collisions with spaceships that are similar in size). It is equipped with a gun that fires orbs of energy that deal damage to enemy vessels. The player will be implemented in two classes. There will be an abstract player class, which deals with keeping track of lives, checkpoints, and so on. The player object class keeps track of the scene node that the player controls.

The Abstract Player

The abstract player will keep track of the number of lives the player has and his spawn points. It is interesting to note that this class also handles input and acts as a controller for the player object. All the input is handled in this class. This makes it possible to have multiple player objects that act independently of each other! This class is also in charge of drawing the heads-up display (HUD). The HUD will display the player's health bar and number of lives left. See Listing 12.1 for the declaration of this class. Objects instantiated from this class should be drawn and updated in the game loop.

Listing 12.1: The Player Class Declaration

```
class Player
{
private:
    static const int LIFEBAR_WIDTH = 300;
    static const int LIFEBAR_HEIGHT = 30;
    static const int LIFEBAR_X = 10;
    static const int LIFEBAR_Y = 10;
    static const int LIVES_PANEL_X = 10;
    static const int LIVES_PANEL_Y = 50;
    static const int LIVES_SPACING = 75;

    Image lifeCounterImage;
    PlayerEntity* entity;
    Rectangle* camera;
    int deathDelay;
    int lives;
public:
    bool init();
    void free();

    void setEntity(PlayerEntity* n);
    void setCamera(Rectangle* r);
    void update(Input* i, Level* l);
    void draw(Graphics* g);
    void scroll(int x);
    int getLives();
};
```

The Player Object

The player object will be a scene node that represents the actual entity that the user controls. It will be able to fire energy orbs, move up, down, left, and right, and it will die when it collides with a solid section of the map or when its health reaches zero. This entity is controlled by the abstract player through the use of a few methods. These methods are declared in Listing 12.2.

Listing 12.2: The PlayerEntity Declaration

```cpp
class PlayerEntity : public MapNode
{
private:
    static const int ENTITY_WIDTH = 120;
    static const int ENTITY_HEIGHT = 60;
    static const int ACCEL = 3;
    static const int GUN_COOLDOWN_TIME = 6;
    static const int MAX_VEL = 10;
    static const int NUM_FRAMES = 7;

    EntityFactory* factory;
    Sprite sprite;
    Rectangle* camera;

    int xVel;
    int yVel;
    int startX;
    int startY;
    int health;
    int gunCooldown;
public:
    PlayerEntity(Image* image, Map* m, Rectangle* c,
        int x, int y, EntityFactory* f);
    ~PlayerEntity();

    void moveUp();
    void moveDown();
    void moveLeft();
    void moveRight();
    void shoot();
    void respawn();
    void setSpawn(int x, int y);
    int getSpawnX();

    void damage(int d);
    int getHealth();

    void update();
    void draw(Rectangle* view, Graphics* g);
};
```

Updating the Player

The player is updated in two separate classes. Listing 12.3 shows the code for the update method of the abstract player class.

Listing 12.3: The Player::update Method

```cpp
void Player::update(Input* i, Level* l)
{
    if(entity != NULL)
    {
        if(i->keyDown(SDLK_UP))
        {
            entity->moveUp();
        }

        if(i->keyDown(SDLK_DOWN))
        {
            entity->moveDown();
        }

        if(i->keyDown(SDLK_LEFT))
        {
            entity->moveLeft();
        }

        if(i->keyDown(SDLK_RIGHT))
        {
            entity->moveRight();
        }

        if(i->keyDown(SDLK_SPACE))
        {
            entity->shoot();
        }

        if(entity->getHealth() <= 0)
        {
            if(deathDelay == 0)
            {
                lives--;
            }

            deathDelay++;

            if(deathDelay >= 60)
            {
                deathDelay = 0;
                entity->respawn();
                camera->setCenterX(entity->getSpawnX());
                l->reset();
            }
        }
    }
}
```

The first half of this class updates the player object based on user input. The last segment of the class resets the level and respawns the player when he loses a life. There is a small delay that occurs before the level is reset, and it allows the player to realize that he lost. The player object class has a simple implementation as well, but it's lengthy, and there's not much to learn from it, so it won't be analyzed here.

Drawing the Player

Drawing the player consists of drawing the actual player object and generating a HUD to inform the player about his ship's remaining health and the number of lives left. The player's health is displayed by a health bar. This bar is drawn as a gradient that fades from green to red. The HUD will also draw a small spaceship icon under the health bar for each life the player has remaining. See Listing 12.4 for the code that draws the HUD.

Listing 12.4: The `Player::draw` Method

```
void Player::draw(Graphics* g)
{
    int barWidth = entity->getHealth()*3;

    //Draw the gradient bar
    for(int i = 0; i < barWidth; i++)
    {
        int colorMod = ((float)i/LIFEBAR_WIDTH)*255;

        g->drawRect(LIFEBAR_X+i, LIFEBAR_Y, 1, LIFEBAR_HEIGHT,
            255-colorMod, colorMod, 0);
    }

    //Draw a border around the gradient bar
    g->drawRect(LIFEBAR_X, LIFEBAR_Y,
        LIFEBAR_WIDTH, LIFEBAR_HEIGHT,
        255, 255, 255);
    g->drawRect(LIFEBAR_X-1,LIFEBAR_Y-1,
        LIFEBAR_WIDTH+2, LIFEBAR_HEIGHT+2,
        0, 0, 0);

    //Draw the ship icons
    for(int i = 0; i < lives; i++)
    {
        lifeCounterImage.draw(LIVES_PANEL_X+LIVES_SPACING*i,
            LIVES_PANEL_Y, g);
    }
}
```

The player's ship is drawn from the sprite sheet on Figure 12.6. The frame is selected according to the player's vertical velocity. The middle frame is drawn when the player's vertical velocity is zero. The frames to the right of the middle frame are drawn when the player's velocity is less than zero, and the left frames are drawn when the player's velocity is greater than zero.

Figure 12.6
The player's sprite sheet.
Source: Spaceship from 3DRT.com, world leading developer of real-time CG content.

The code in Listing 12.5 implements the player's frame-selection algorithm, which is located in the player object's update method.

Listing 12.5: The Player's Frame-Selection Algorithm

```
int middleFrame = NUM_FRAMES/2;

if(yVel == 0)
{
    sprite.setFrame(middleFrame);
}
else if(yVel > 0)
{
    float ratio = ((float)yVel/MAX_VEL));
    sprite.setFrame(middleFrame + 1 + (NUM_FRAMES/2)*ratio);
}
else
{
    float ratio = ((float)yVel/MAX_VEL));
    sprite.setFrame(middleFrame + (NUM_FRAMES/2)*ratio);
}
```

This algorithm is complicated. The first part gets the middle frame. If the vertical velocity is zero, then the middle frame is selected. Otherwise, a frame is selected by computing the ratio of the current velocity and the maximum velocity and multiplying that by half the number of frames. This value is added to the middle frame value to compute the value for the final frame.

CREATING THE LEVEL

The level is composed of a scene manager and a tile map. Each level has a boss. The level will be over when the boss is defeated. The header file for the `Level` class can be studied in Listing 12.6.

Listing 12.6: The Level Class Declaration

```cpp
#include "EntityFactory.h"
#include "BossEntity.h"

using namespace std;

class Level
{
private:
    BossEntity* boss;
    EntityFactory* factory;
    Map map;
    Scene scene;

    int spawnX;
    int spawnY;

    char filename[256];

    void parseLine(ifstream* in, EntityFactory* f);
public:
    bool load(char fn[], EntityFactory* factory);
    void free();
    void reset();

    void update();
    void draw(Rectangle* view, Graphics* g);

    BossEntity* getBoss();
    Map* getMap();
    Scene* getScene();
    int getSpawnX();
    int getSpawnY();
};
#endif
```

Level Script

Levels will be scripted to specify the map file to use, as well as the player's spawn position and the location of the enemies in the level. Listing 12.7 demonstrates a sample of a level script.

Listing 12.7: A Sample Level Script

```
graphics/maps/level1.map
graphics/maps/tiles.bmp
411
393
checkpoint 16311 393
checkpoint 29761 357
alien_scout 2048 201
alien_scout 2048 472
alien_scout 3109 197
alien_boss 38128 416
```

The first two lines of the script specify the map file and the map's tile image. The next two lines specify the player's spawn position. This is followed by a list of entities that will populate the scene. Each script will contain one boss and a few generic enemies. The script will be interpreted by the Level class in order to generate the desired level.

CREATING THE ALIEN SCOUTS

Alien scouts are the meat of the enemy army. They are fast, easy to produce, and create damage by colliding against the player. Unlike the player, they don't explode on impact against the map, and this can be used to their advantage. Their drawback is that they are stupid and move in a predictable pattern.

Alien Scout Behavior

Alien scouts are scene nodes that are spawned when the level is loaded or reset. They are idle until they enter the screen. Upon entering the screen, they will begin to fly to the left in a sine wave pattern. If they exit the screen through the left edge, they will be removed from the scene. The code to update them is shown in Listing 12.8.

Listing 12.8: The AlienScoutEntity::update Method

```cpp
void AlienScoutEntity::update()
{
    if(health <= 0)
    {
        remove();
        return;
    }
    if(active)
    {
        cycle+=PI/20;
```

```
    if(cycle > 2*PI)
        cycle = 0;

setY(startY + sin(cycle)*ENTITY_HEIGHT);
setX(getX()-ENTITY_SPEED);

if(!overlaps(*camera))
    remove();

std::list<SceneNode*>* nodes = getScene()->getNodes();

for(list<SceneNode*>::iterator it = nodes->begin();
    it != nodes->end(); it++)
{
    if((*it)->getID() == ENTITY_PLAYER && overlaps(**it))
    {
        PlayerEntity* player = (PlayerEntity*)(*it);

        player->damage(5);
        getScene()->addNode(
            factory->makeEntity(ENTITY_EXPLOSION,
            getCenterX(), getCenterY()));
        remove();
    }
}
    }
    else
    {
        if(overlaps(*camera))
            active = true;
    }
}
```

Drawing an Alien Scout

The alien scout is drawn using the animation strip in Figure 12.7. The frame is selected according to the scout's vertical velocity.

Figure 12.7
The scout's sprite sheet.

Source: Spaceship from 3DRT.com, world leading developer of real-time CG content.

Its drawing method can be analyzed in Listing 12.9.

Listing 12.9: The `AlienScoutEntity::draw` Method

```
void AlienScoutEntity::draw(Rectangle* view, Graphics* g)
{
    if(active)
    {
        if(image != NULL)
        {
            int x = getCenterX() - getWidth()/2 - view->getX();
            int y = getCenterY() - getHeight()/2 - view->getY();
            int frame = NUM_FRAMES/2 + sin(cycle)*NUM_FRAMES/2;

            image->draw(x, y, frame, g);
        }
    }
}
```

CREATING THE BOSS

The boss is the final enemy the player will face. The player will win the level when he defeats the boss. Unlike alien scouts, the boss can take a lot more damage. It can also shoot at the player and even spawn alien scouts to act as projectiles and shields! This entity is much larger and more detailed than any other entity. The sprite used for this entity is displayed in Figure 12.8.

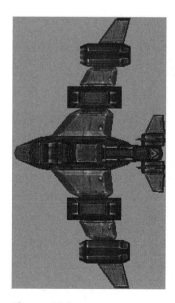

Figure 12.8
The boss sprite.

Source: Spaceship from 3DRT.com, world leading developer of real-time CG content.

This entity has four different states. It has a moving state in which it will move up and down. It will switch to an attack state in which it fires projectiles at the player. If the player deals enough damage, it will enter the panic state. During panic state, the boss will attack the player much more frequently and much more relentlessly. When the player finally kills the boss, it will go into the dying state. In this state, it will stop attacking and exit the screen. Upon exiting the screen, the game will end, and the player will be victorious. Each state is updated accordingly in the boss's update method, as shown in Listing 12.10.

Listing 12.10: The BossEntity::update Method

```
void BossEntity::update()
{
    if(active)
    {
        if(health <= 0)
            state = STATE_DYING;
        switch(state)
        {
            case STATE_MOVING:
                updateMoving();
                break;
            case STATE_ATTACKING:
                updateAttacking();
                break;
            case STATE_PANIC:
                updatePanic();
                break;
            case STATE_DYING:
                updateDying();
                break;
        }
    }
    else
    {
        if(overlaps(*camera))
            active = true;
    }
}
```

The Boss's Moving State

The moving state is the simplest of states. In this state, the boss will move vertically and randomly switch into the attacking state. This state will also put the boss in panic state if its health drops below a certain value. The code for the method that updates the boss in this state is shown in Listing 12.11.

Listing 12.11: The `BossEntity::updateMoving` Method

```
void BossEntity::updateMoving()
{
    setY(getY()+yVel);
    if(getY() < camera->getY())
    {
        yVel = ENTITY_SPEED;
    }
    if(getY2() > camera->getY2())
    {
        yVel = -ENTITY_SPEED;
    }
    if(rand()%100 == 1)
    {
        state = STATE_ATTACKING;
        attackCounter = 0;
    }
    if(health <= 200)
    {
        panicCounter = 0;
        state = STATE_PANIC;
    }
}
```

The Boss's Attacking State

In this state, the boss will launch a few waves of attacks before finally returning to the moving state. These attacks include energy orbs and waves of alien scouts. The code for this state is shown in Listing 12.12.

Listing 12.12: The `BossEntity::updateAttacking` Method

```
void BossEntity::updateAttacking()
{
    attackCounter++;
```

```
if(attackCounter == 10)
{
    for(int i = 0; i < getHeight(); i+= getHeight()/5)
    {
        getScene()->addNode(factory->makeEntity(
            ENTITY_ENEMY_BULLET,
            getX(), getY()+i));
    }
}

if(attackCounter > 20)
{
    setY(getY()+yVel);

    if(getY() < camera->getY())
    {
        yVel = ENTITY_SPEED;
    }

    if(getY2() > camera->getY2())
    {
        yVel = -ENTITY_SPEED;
    }
}

if(attackCounter == 30)
{
    for(int i = 0; i < getHeight(); i+= getHeight()/5)
    {
        getScene()->addNode(factory->makeEntity(
            ENTITY_ALIEN_SCOUT,
            getX(), getY()+i));
    }
}

if(attackCounter >= 50)
{
    for(int i = 0; i < getHeight(); i+= getHeight()/10)
    {
        getScene()->addNode(factory->makeEntity(
            ENTITY_ENEMY_BULLET,
            getX(), getY()+i));
    }

    state = STATE_MOVING;
}
}
```

The Boss's Panic Mode

In this mode, the boss realizes he's going to lose and begins to throw everything he can against the player. This is the most complicated state and lengthiest in code. Its code is shown in Listing 12.13.

Listing 12.13: The BossEntity::updatePanic Method

```
void BossEntity::updatePanic()
{
    getScene()->addNode(factory->makeEntity(
        ENTITY_SILENT_EXPLOSION,
        getX() + rand()%getWidth(),
        getY() + rand()%getHeight()));

    panicCounter++;

    if(panicCounter > 100)
        panicCounter = 0;


    setY(getY()+yVel);

    if(getY() < camera->getY())
    {
        yVel = ENTITY_SPEED;
    }

    if(getY2() > camera->getY2())
    {
        yVel = -ENTITY_SPEED;
    }

    if(panicCounter %5 != 0)
        return;

    if(health < 0)
    {
        remove();
    }

    if(panicCounter > 10 && panicCounter < 30)
    {
        getScene()->addNode(factory->makeEntity(
            ENTITY_ENEMY_BULLET,
            getX(),
            getY()+(rand()%getHeight())));
    }

    if(panicCounter > 30 && panicCounter < 60 && rand()%4)
```

```
    {
        getScene()->addNode(factory->makeEntity(
            ENTITY_ALIEN_SCOUT,
            getX(),
            getY()+(rand()%getHeight())));
    }
    if(panicCounter > 60 && panicCounter < 100 && rand()%4)
    {
        getScene()->addNode(factory->makeEntity(
            ENTITY_ALIEN_SCOUT,
            getX(),
            getY()+(rand()%getHeight())));

        getScene()->addNode(factory->makeEntity(
            ENTITY_ENEMY_BULLET,
            getX(),
            getY()+(rand()%getHeight())));
    }
}
```

This state is very chaotic and quickly fills up the screen with bullets and alien scouts. Its effects are shown in Figure 12.9.

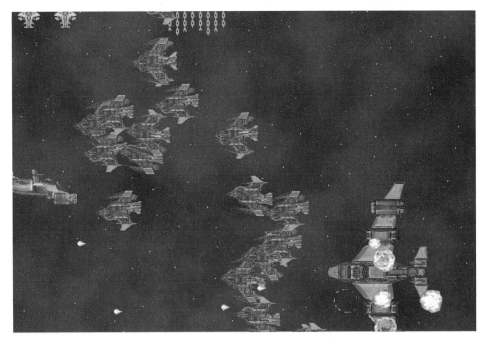

Figure 12.9
The boss is in panic state.
Source: Spaceship from 3DRT.com, world leading developer of real-time CG content.

The Boss's Dying State

The boss enters the dying state when the player has inflicted enough damage to kill him. In this state, the boss will stop attacking and exit the screen through the right edge before finally being declared dead. When the boss is declared dead, the level will end, and the player will emerge victorious. The dying state is implemented in Listing 12.14.

Listing 12.14: The BossEntity::updateDying Method

```cpp
void BossEntity::updateDying()
{
    deathCounter++;

    for(int i = 0; i < rand()%10; i++)
        getScene()->addNode(factory->makeEntity(
                            ENTITY_SILENT_EXPLOSION,
                            getX() + rand()%getWidth(),
                            getY() + rand()%getHeight()));

    setX(getX()+2);

    setX(getX()+2-rand()%4);
    setY(getY()+2-rand()%4);

    if(!overlaps(*camera))
    {
        dead = true;
    }
}
```

CREATING THE BULLET SYSTEM

The bullets are an important aspect of this game. In the bullet system, you're going to create a scene node class called BulletEntity to represent a projectile. There will be player bullets, which only damage enemy entities, and enemy bullets, which only damage the player. Player bullets will fly toward the right of the screen, while enemy bullets fly toward the left. Player bullets will be spawned when the player presses the spacebar. Listing 12.15 demonstrates the class declaration for the BulletEntity class.

Listing 12.15: The BulletEntity Class Declaration

```cpp
class BulletEntity : public MapNode
{
private:
    static const int ENTITY_WIDTH = 20;
    static const int ENTITY_HEIGHT = 20;
```

```
    static const int PLAYER_BULLET_FRAME = 0;
    static const int ENEMY_BULLET_FRAME = 1;
    static const int SPEED = 30;

    bool enemyBullet;
    EntityFactory* factory;
    Image* image;
    Rectangle* camera;
    Sound* sound;
public:
    BulletEntity(Image* i, Sound* s, Map* m, Rectangle* c,
        EntityFactory* f, int x, int y, bool enemy);
    ~BulletEntity();
    void update();
    void draw(Rectangle* view, Graphics* g);
};
```

Updating the Bullets

Bullets have a few main behaviors. If the bullet was fired by an enemy, it will fly toward the left of the screen at half speed. Bullets can also interact with several different objects. Enemy bullets can damage the player. Player bullets can damage enemy units. Any bullet that touches the map will be destroyed. See Listing 12.16 for the code to the update method of the BulletEntity class.

Listing 12.16: The BulletEntity::update Method

```
void BulletEntity::update()
{
    int moveX = SPEED;

    if(enemyBullet)
    {
        moveX*=-1;
        moveX/=2;
    }

    setX(getX()+moveX);

    if(overlapsMap())
    {
        remove();
        getScene()->addNode(factory->makeEntity(ENTITY_EXPLOSION,
            getX(), getY()));
        return;
    }
```

```
    if(!camera->overlaps(*this))
        remove();

    if(!enemyBullet)
    {
        std::list<SceneNode*>* nodes = getScene()->getNodes();

        for(list<SceneNode*>::iterator it = nodes->begin();
            it != nodes->end(); it++)
        {
            if((*it)->getID() == ENTITY_ENEMY && overlaps(**it))
            {
                AlienScoutEntity* alien =
                    (AlienScoutEntity*)(*it);

                alien->damage(5);

                getScene()->addNode(factory->makeEntity(
                    ENTITY_EXPLOSION, getX(), getY()));
                remove();
            }

            if((*it)->getID() == ENTITY_BOSS && overlaps(**it))
            {
                BossEntity* boss = (BossEntity*)(*it);

                boss->damage(5);

                getScene()->addNode(factory->makeEntity(
                    ENTITY_EXPLOSION, getX(), getY()));
                remove();
            }
        }
    }
    else
    {
        std::list<SceneNode*>* nodes = getScene()->getNodes();

        for(list<SceneNode*>::iterator it = nodes->begin();
            it != nodes->end(); it++)
        {
            if((*it)->getID() == ENTITY_PLAYER && overlaps(**it))
            {
                PlayerEntity* player = (PlayerEntity*)(*it);

                player->damage(5);
                remove();
            }
        }
    }
}
```

CREATING THE SPECIAL EFFECTS

There are several special effects included in the game that haven't been discussed. They are simple but achieve neat effects. These effects enhance the game's presentation by making it look a little flashier.

Parallax Scrolling Background

Parallax scrolling is a cool technique used in 2D video games. This technique utilizes multiple layers of backgrounds that move at different speeds to create the illusion of depth. Figure 12.10 illustrates a scene decomposed into three layers.

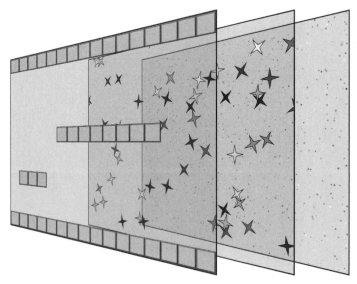

Figure 12.10
A scene decomposed into three layers.
© Jazon Yamamoto.

The first is a tile map, and it would move at the same speed as the camera. The second would represent stars that are relatively close to the player. This layer would scroll a bit slower than the camera. The last layer represents stars that are very far from the camera. These stars scroll at a much slower rate than the stars that are closer. This technique adds depth to the background and makes the game look more believable without doing a lot of work.

Explosions

Explosions always make games look a lot cooler. There will be several types of explosions. The first are small explosions. These make no sounds, and they are emitted by the player and boss when their health drops a certain level. There are also large explosions, which emit an explosion sound when they occur. The last type of explosions are the silent ones. These explosions look exactly the same as the large explosions but don't make a sound. This is to make it possible to fill the screen with explosions without clogging all the audio channels. Explosions are basically scene nodes holding sprites that play a single animation before being deleted. All explosions are handled by the ExplosionEntity class. Listing 12.17 holds this class's update method.

Listing 12.17: The ExplosionEntity::update Method

```
void ExplosionEntity::update()
{
    frame++;

    if(frame >= NUM_FRAMES)
    {
        remove();
    }

    sprite.setFrame(frame);
    sprite.update();
}
```

CREATING THE GAME'S GRAPHICS

This game has more intricate graphics than any of the previous ones. For this game, actual 3D models were used to create the sprites. Using 3D models for 2D games was common practice in the 1990s, when real-time 3D graphics on PCs were in their primitive era. Blizzard's *Starcraft* is an example of a game that used sprites made from 3D models. In this game, sprites were produced by rendering a model into an animation strip in several different angles. This can be done by using Milkshape 3D.

Milkshape 3D

Milkshape 3D is a really nice 3D modeling program. It started off as a third-party modeling program for Valve's *Half-Life* game, but it quickly became a popular general-purpose modeling application due to its low price and user friendliness. This program can be bought for a bargain price at **http://chumbalum.swissquake.ch/**, and it can be used to create and animate models. It can also be used to create sprite sheets by taking screenshots of models and exporting them to a paint program. Figure 12.11 displays a screenshot of Milkshape 3D being used to create an enemy sprite.

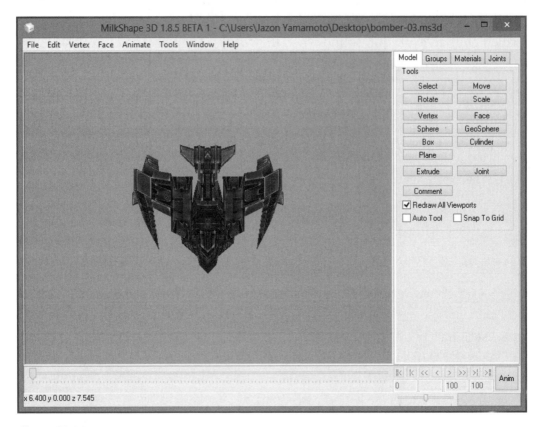

Figure 12.11
Working with Milkshape 3D.
Source: Milkshape 3D ®, a registered trademark of chUmbaLum sOft.

Tip

Milkshape 3D itself can't render 3D models directly into sprite sheets. To render sprite sheets, you simply open a model and take screenshots by pressing Ctrl+Print Screen.

Paint.NET

After taking screenshots of the models, you can touch them up and arrange them into a sprite sheet by using an image-editing program. Paint.NET is a fully functional program that is very useful for editing these sprites. It is packed with features, and it's easy to learn and use. It's not as extensive as Adobe's Photoshop, but it's free, and it has a plug-in system that allows the user to expand its functionality. Figure 12.12 shows Paint.NET being used to edit a sprite made from a screenshot of Milkshape 3D.

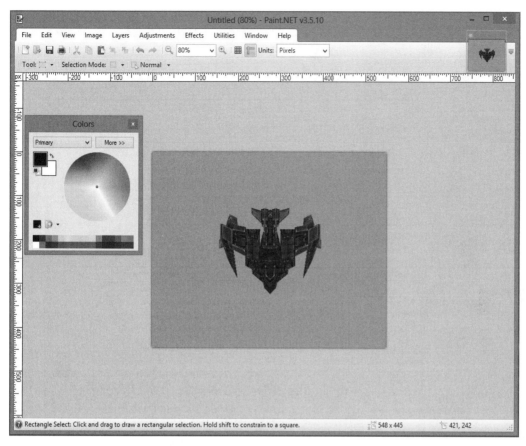

Figure 12.12
Editing a screenshot of Milkshape 3D with Paint.NET.

Source: Paint.NET ®, a registered trademark of dotPDN LLC.

After obtaining all the necessary screenshots, the sprite can be edited a little bit and finally rendered into a sprite sheet, as shown in Figure 12.13.

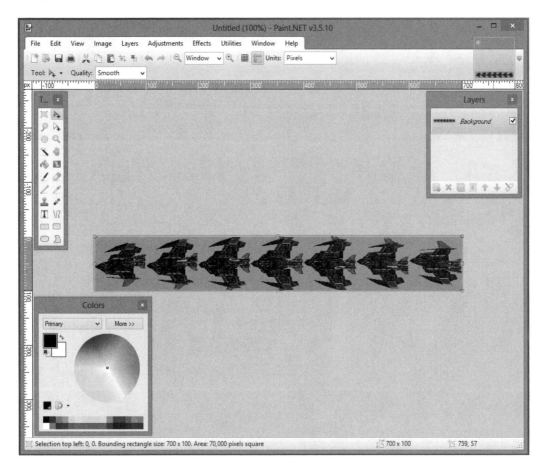

Figure 12.13
The finalized sprite sheet.

Source: Paint.NET ®, a registered trademark of dotPDN LLC. Milkshape 3D.

PUTTING IT ALL TOGETHER

Up to this point, you have several parts of a complete game, and it is time to create the game's class. The game's class will be called SpaceGame, and its declaration is shown in Listing 12.18.

Listing 12.18: The SpaceGame Class Declaration

```
class SpaceGame : public Game
{
private:
    const static int SCREEN_WIDTH = 1024;
    const static int SCREEN_HEIGHT = 768;
```

```
    StateManager stateManager;
    MainMenuState mainMenuState;
    RunState runState;
public:
    bool init();
    void free();
    void update();
    void draw(Graphics* g);
};
```

This class contains a few variables, and its functionality is relatively simple. It consists of a state manager and a couple of states. The implementation of this class's methods can be observed in Listing 12.19.

Listing 12.19: A Few SpaceGame Methods

```
bool SpaceGame::init()
{
    if(!initSystem("Conflict: Andromeda",
        SCREEN_WIDTH, SCREEN_HEIGHT, true))
    {
        return false;
    }

    if(!mainMenuState.init(getInput(), getAudio(),
        this, &runState))
    {
        return false;
    }

    setFPS(60);
    stateManager.addState(&mainMenuState);

    return true;
}

void SpaceGame::free()
{
    mainMenuState.free();
    freeSystem();
}

void SpaceGame::update()
{
    stateManager.update();
}
```

```
void SpaceGame::draw(Graphics* g)
{
    stateManager.draw(g);
}
```

This class initially puts the game into the main menu state. From this state, the player can navigate to the run game state, view the credits, or exit the program.

Tip

This is a real game and not just a demo. Going fullscreen with 60 frames per second really completes the experience.

The RunGame State

The RunGame state is the single most important state of the game. This state is also the most complicated and lengthiest in code. The declaration of its class is shown in Listing 12.20.

Listing 12.20: The RunState Class Declaration

```
class RunState : public GameState
{
private:
    Image background1;
    Image background2;
    Image background3;

    Audio* audio;
    Input* input;
    Music song;

    EntityFactory factory;
    GameOverState gameOverState;
    GameEndingState gameEndingState;
    Level level;
    Player player;
    PauseState pauseState;
    Rectangle camera;

    bool loadFiles();
    void freeFiles();
    void drawBackground(Graphics* g);
    bool initLevel();
```

```
public:
    bool init(Input* i, Audio* a, int width, int height);
    void free();
    void update();
    void draw(Graphics* g);
};
```

This state contains the level, the entity factory, and the player objects. It is the central part of the entire game, and it is a beast in terms of complexity. Initializing the game alone is a very complicated process. Luckily, you can split the init method into several methods to make the process more manageable. Listing 12.21 consists of the code for this method.

Listing 12.21: The RunState::init Method

```
bool RunState::init(Input* i, Audio* a, int width, int height)
{
    camera.set(0, 0, width, height);

    if(!loadFiles())
        return false;

    if(!gameEndingState.init(this, i))
        return false;

    if(!gameOverState.init(this,i))
        return false;

    if(!pauseState.init(this, i))
        return false;

    if(!player.init())
        return false;

    if(!factory.init())
        return false;

    factory.setCamera(&camera);
    player.setCamera(&camera);

    if(!initLevel())
        return false;

    input = i;
    audio = a;

    song.play(-1);

    return true;
}
```

The update method for this class is simple compared to the init method. Although there is actually a lot of stuff happening in the update method, all the complicated procedures are handled by other objects. This method can be seen in Listing 12.22.

Listing 12.22: The RunState::update Method

```
void RunState::update()
{
    camera.setX(camera.getX()+10);

    if(camera.getX2() >= level.getMap()->getTotalWidth())
        camera.setX2(level.getMap()->getTotalWidth());
    else
        player.scroll(10);

    player.update(input, &level);
    level.update();

    if(input->keyHit(SDLK_ESCAPE))
    {
        getManager()->addState(&pauseState);
    }

    if(player.getLives() <= 0)
    {
        getManager()->addState(&gameOverState);
    }

    if(level.getBoss()->isDead() || input->keyHit(SDLK_a))
    {
        getManager()->addState(&gameEndingState);
    }
}
```

This method updates the player and the level and then checks if the game state should be changed. This is a complicated process, but the framework you created makes it much more manageable.

BALANCING GAMEPLAY

After coding the entire game and going back to play through it, it's easy to determine if it's fun or not. This is the first chance to test the mechanics and see if they work. It is common for games to be extensively tested after they are finished to make sure that the game is fun. At this point, you forget about coding and focus on playing. Before putting the finished stamp on the game, there are a few things to look into.

Optimal Difficulty Curve

Have you ever played a game that kicked your butt in the first 20 minutes? This is very frustrating, and it alienates players. It is important to make the first few minutes of the game easy enough for anybody to get through and then gradually increase the difficulty. Games should start out easy and end with blistering difficulty. The easy start will give players time to learn the mechanics, and the difficult ending will ensure a satisfying experience. The difficulty curve for a game should resemble the one in Figure 12.14.

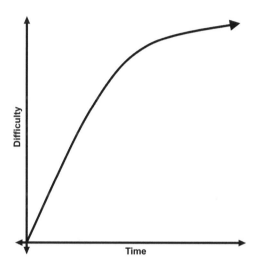

Figure 12.14
The ideal difficulty curve.
© Jazon Yamamoto.

When the player first starts playing, he will be focused more on which button does what. After a few minutes, the focus will shift to the new tricks he can learn and make use of. When the player has mastered the game, he will play by reflex, and the game can reach its maximum difficulty.

Last-Minute Tweaking

When the code is done, it's wise to go back through the game and play it a few times. When I did this with this game, I found several issues. At this late stage, going back and adding new features is not an option. Instead, I tweaked a few variables.

To start, the player fired bullets too quickly. A player completely cleared the screen with a brief press of the spacebar. To fix this, the cooldown for the player's gun was increased. Now the boss was too hard to kill. To fix this, the boss attacked less often but spawned more enemies and bullets.

At this stage of game creation, you should be able to make small tweaks in order to correct simple issues. It's better not to add new features to fix small errors. These features should have been thought about during the design phase and should be added only if they are important enough. Remember that the most important part of creating games is finishing them.

Tip

In a professional environment, adding features at this point could mean delays in the release of the video game. Players hate this, and publishers hate this. Remember that boring games can be made into fun ones by simply tweaking a few variables.

FINAL THOUGHTS AND MUSINGS

It's hard, but it's over. After so much work, it's time to sit back and enjoy the video game. Take a minute to high-five yourself or pat yourself on the back. While the game might not be very impressive, and it's possible to beat it in about five minutes, it can very easily be expanded upon. Some features that would improve gameplay are power-ups, multiple levels, a larger array of enemies, and so on. All these features can be implemented with a minimal amount of work, thanks to the engine it was built on. From now on, the only limitations are those imposed by your imagination. With the power of creation, feel free to move on and venture into the amazing world of game creation. Figure 12.15 displays a screenshot of this game's hero valiantly defeating the alien boss.

Building the App

You can find the files necessary to build this app in the BAMGP/. They are located in Source/Chapter_12/12_1_SpaceGame/. You need to create an SDL project and copy these files

- main.cpp
- AlienScoutEntity.h
- AlienScoutEntity.cpp
- BossEntity.h
- BossEntity.cpp
- BulletEntity.h
- BulletEntity.cpp
- Button.h
- Button.cpp
- CheckpointEntity.h
- CheckpointEntity.cpp

- CreditsState.h
- CreditsState.cpp
- EntityDef.h
- EntityFactory.h
- EntityFactory.cpp
- ExplosionEntity.h
- ExplosionEntity.cpp
- GameEndingState.h
- GameEndingState.cpp
- GameOverState.h
- GameOverState.cpp
- Level.h
- Level.cpp
- MainMenuState.h
- MainMenuState.cpp
- PauseState.h
- PauseState.cpp
- Player.h
- Player.cpp
- PlayerEntity.h
- PlayerEntity.cpp
- RunState.h
- RunState.cpp
- SpaceGame.h
- SpaceGame.cpp

as well as the `Core` and the `graphics` folders into your project's directory. If you're using Windows, make sure to include the `.dll` files in the project's directory. This project requires additional `.dll` files that are specifically used for sound and images, so make sure to include those as well. Your project should be configured properly, as shown in Chapter 1, and all the files should also be properly included. When all is set, you'll be able to build the program and run it on your own. Additionally, a precompiled version is in the `Source` directory named `12_1_SpaceGame.exe`.

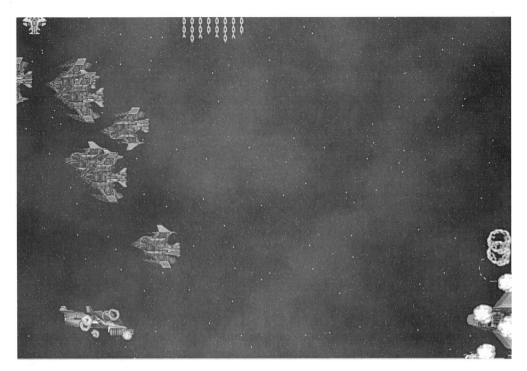

Figure 12.15
Low on health, but still managed to kill the boss!
© Jazon Yamamoto.

Summary

Remember to watch the final video tutorial for additional insight regarding this chapter and the book as a whole. Congratulations for making it this far and understanding all the concepts presented in this book. Lots of ground was covered by dividing and conquering. From beginner-level topics to advanced ones, enough information was presented in this book to create an amazing game. So what's next? You can check out the bonus chapter, Chapter 13. It covers SDL 2.0, which will eventually replace SDL 1.2.

Also, you can go out there and start creating games. Start creating masterpieces and awe the world with your creations. There is a whole planet out there waiting for you to conquer it. So what are you waiting for? Go out there and show the world what you got! Thanks for reading. I hope to play your video games soon.

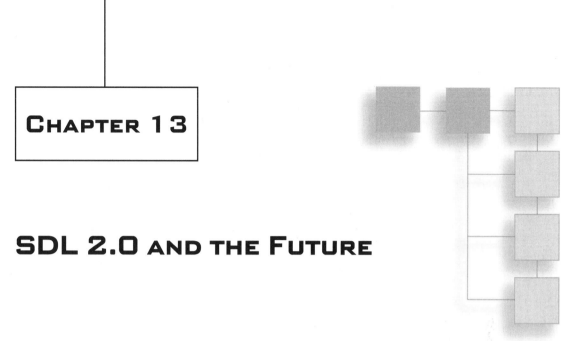

CHAPTER 13

SDL 2.0 AND THE FUTURE

Although this book is just about over, the adventure continues. As I write this, SDL 2.0 has been released after a few years in development. Naturally, the technology hasn't quite proven itself yet, unlike its older brother, and will take some time to gain ground. But game developers should still be forward thinkers and explore the new library. Keep in mind that SDL 1.2 is still the core of many game engines and commercial games. Furthermore, it runs on quite a few more platforms. But as time progresses, SDL 2.0 will eventually replace its predecessor. With all this in consideration, let's get a glimpse of the future. This bonus chapter covers the following topics:

- Changes in the API.
- Adapting the code.
- Using some of the new features.

Tip

Before getting started, you can check out the video tutorial for this chapter, which is located in BAMGP\ under the Videos directory. The video contains extra material and insights, and reviews the chapter from a high level, so be sure to watch it.

WHAT'S NEW IN SDL 2.0?

There are some notable features worth mentioning, and one of them is support for multiple windows. While most games tend to use only one window, this makes it possible to make tools such as map editors and animation editors using SDL. Previously, making these tools on SDL was clunky since everything had to fit in one window.

Another new feature is a new 2D rendering API. While the traditional method is still there, the new rendering API takes advantage of hardware acceleration, and it can perform a few new effects such as clipping, color blending, and stretching. Even though this was possible in SDL 1.2, the keyword is hardware acceleration. *Hardware acceleration* is the usage of special hardware to conduct graphical operations much more efficiently. Most devices that SDL 2.0 can run on are equipped with harder acceleration capabilities. In short, hardware acceleration makes games run faster and allows them to grow in terms of graphical complexity. This, however, comes at a cost since the new API is more complicated and not as beginner friendly.

Other features were added to enhance mobile development with SDL. These include direct support of touchscreens and battery life information.

The rest of the new features are more technically involved. They include 32-bit audio, an assert macro, and atomic operations, to name a few. These are beyond the scope of this book.

WHAT WAS LEFT BEHIND?

There were a few functions that did not survive the jump to the new platform. Although some of these functions were used throughout this book, there are replacement functions that accomplish the same goal. Table 13.1 illustrates the removed functions and their replacements. I will go further into detail in the following section.

Table 13.1   Removed Functions and Their Replacements

Old Function	New Function
SDL_SetVideoMode	SDL_CreateWindow
SDL_DisplayFormat	SDL_ConvertSurface
SDL_SetCaption	SDL_SetWindowTitle
SDL_GetKeyState	SDL_GetKeyboardState
SDL_WarpMouse	SDL_WarpMouseInWindow

© Jazon Yamamoto.

INSTALLING SDL 2.0

Installing SDL 2.0 isn't different from installing SDL 1. The only difference is the files you need and some of the compiler settings.

Installing on Windows

The new SDL 2.0 files can be found at **http://libsdl.org/download-2.0.php**. You will want to download the file called `SDL2-devel-2.0.1-mingw.tar.gz`, as shown in Figure 13.1.

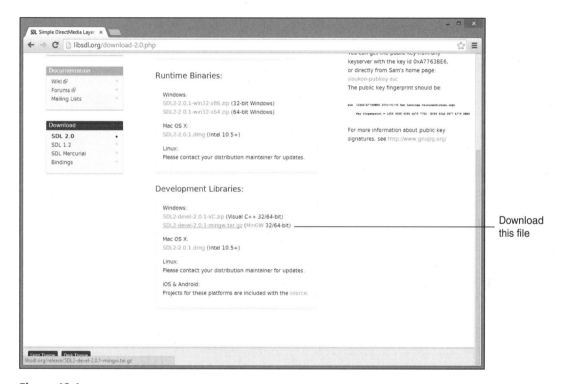

Figure 13.1
The download link.
Source: Google Chrome is a registered trademark of Google Inc., used with permission.

After that, extract it using a tool such as WinRAR and open the containing folder. SDL will come with two versions upon download. The one that is compatible with MinGW is in a folder called `i686-w64-mingw32`. Using the other version labeled as `x86_64-w64-mingw32` leads to compiling errors that are hard to get any information out of. Trying to link the wrong library can drive a software guru crazy, so make sure you're using the right one.

Create a folder in the root of your hard drive (in most cases, it's in the C:\ directory) called SDL2-2.0.1 and copy the contents from i686-w64-mingw32 into that new folder. My installation looks like Figure 13.2. Pay particular attention to the part at the top where the directory is displayed.

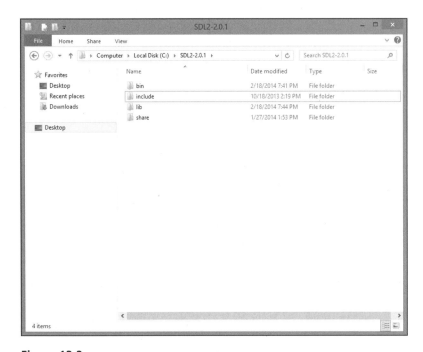

Figure 13.2
My SDL 2.0 installation in my main drive.
Source: Windows 8 File Explorer, © Microsoft Corporation. Used with permission from Microsoft.

The extension libraries can be installed the same way as the ones from SDL 1.2. The SDL 2.0 libraries can be downloaded from the following links:

http://www.libsdl.org/projects/SDL_image/

http://www.libsdl.org/projects/SDL_mixer/

http://www.libsdl.org/projects/SDL_ttf/

Make sure you download the development libraries for `MinGW 32/64-bit`. Figure 13.3 shows the correct download link for the `SDL_image` library.

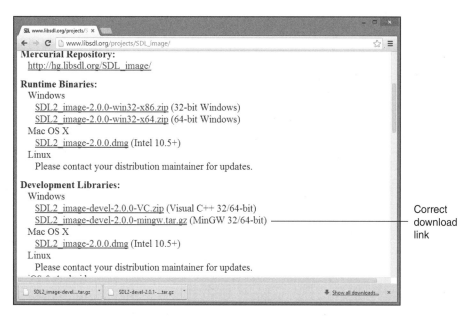

Figure 13.3
The correct download link for the `SDL_image` library.
© Jazon Yamamoto. Source: 3DRT.com.

Once the libraries are downloaded, copy the contents of each library and paste them in the directories of the SDL installation that share the same name. (For example, in the `SDL_Image` library, upon downloading and extracting, take the contents in `SDL_Image\include` and paste them into `C:\SDL2-2.0.1\include` and take the contents in `SDL_Image\lib` and paste them in `C:\SDL2-2.0.1\lib`. Repeat this process for `SDL_mixer` and `SDL_ttf`.) Once this is done, `include\SDL2` and the `lib` directories of the SDL2 installation should resemble Figure 13.4.

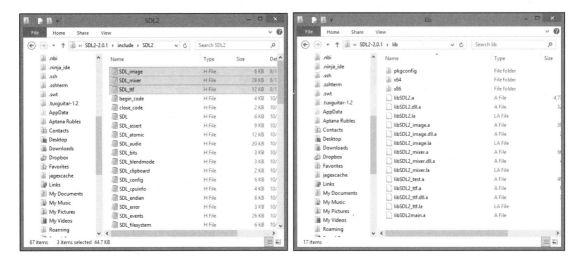

Figure 13.4
The include\SDL2 and the lib directories of the SDL2 installation.

Source: Windows 8 File Explorer, © Microsoft Corporation. Used with permission from Microsoft.

After SDL 2.0 has been installed, you can configure Code::Blocks. First, add the folders called include and lib to Code::Block's search directories under Settings → Compiler → Search Directories (much like you did in Chapter 1). This is shown in Figure 13.5.

Figure 13.5
The compiler and linker search directories.

Source: Code::Blocks Studio.

Next, clear the Other Linker Options box in the Linker Settings tab and add the following linker options:

```
-lmingw32 -lopengl32 -lSDL2main -lSDL2 -lSDL2_image -lSDL2_ttf -lSDL2_mixer
```

The options window should look like Figure 13.6.

Figure 13.6
The Linker Settings tab.
Source: Code::Blocks Studio.

Installing on Linux

Again, installing on Linux is much easier, and you can follow the instructions in Chapter 1 to install the Synaptic Package Manager and Eclipse. To install SDL 2.0, first you need to run a few command-line arguments from the terminal, which download the SDL 2.0 library files. Open the Terminal program and enter the following command (see Figure 13.7):

```
sudo add-apt-repository ppa:zoogie/sdl2-snapshots
```

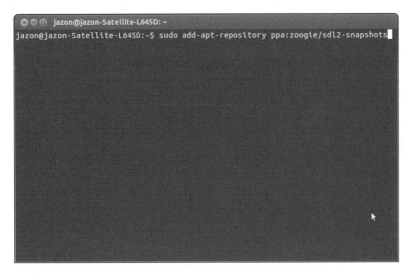

Figure 13.7
Linux command needed for installing on Linux.
Source: Ubuntu running Terminal, by Canonical Group Limited.

Press Enter to confirm. This will require entering the root password. Next, enter the command (see Figure 13.8):

```
sudo apt-get update
```

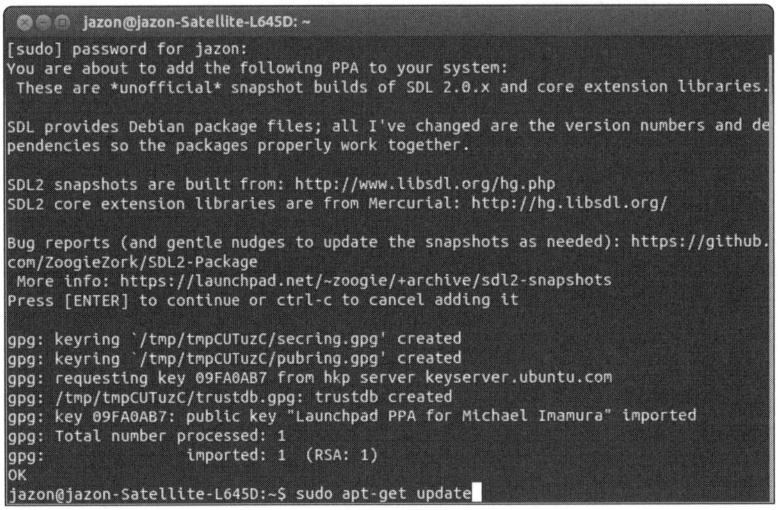

Figure 13.8
The Linux `sudo` command.
Source: Ubuntu running Terminal, by Canonical Group Limited.

Now, open the Synaptic Package Manager. At the top-right corner, there is a large Reload button. Click on it and wait until all the libraries have been updated. Once that is done, mark the following libraries for installation:

- `libsdl2`
- `libsdl2-dev`
- `libsmpeg0`
- `libsmpeg-dev`
- `libsdl2-mixer`
- `libsdl2-mixer-dev`
- `libsdl2-image`
- `libsdl2-image-dev`
- `libsdl2-ttf`
- `libsdl2-ttf-dev`

If you already installed `libsmpeg-dev` and `libsmpeg0` in Chapter 1, then you may skip these. There is no need to mark them for reinstallation. Once all the libs have been marked, click on the Apply button in the top bar of the window and apply all the changes. When the changes have been applied, you may close the Synaptic Package Manager. Once you're done downloading all the packages, open Eclipse, create a new project, and click on Project → Properties. In this window, click on C/C++ Build → Settings. Under the Tool Settings tab, click on GCC C++ Linker → Libraries. In the Libraries panel, add the following libraries: `SDL2`, `SDL2_image`, `SDL2_mixer`, and `SDL2_ttf`. The result should resemble Figure 13.9. Note that you must do this for every SDL 2.0 project you create in Eclipse.

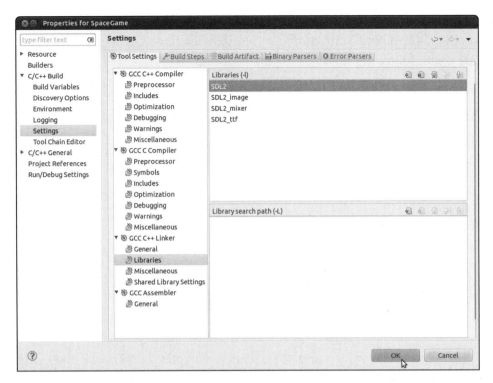

Figure 13.9
Adding libraries in the Libraries panel of Eclipse.
Source: Eclipse, © The Eclipse Foundation.

Porting Your Code

This section demonstrates the old way of doing things and the new way, side by side. Any drastic changes are commented upon. Keep in mind that BAMGP\ also contains the source code for all the demos in this book, completely ported to SDL 2.0.

Tip

Unfortunately, SDL 2.0 on Linux does not support the .mp3 file format when playing sounds. The .mp3 files from the new demos in this book were converted to a different file format, and the code was adjusted to compensate for this change. Other than that small detail, the new demos function as the original ones do.

Including SDL 2.0

Including SDL 2.0 is actually different from including SDL 1.2; however, this difference is minor. The following strip of code includes SDL 1.2:

```
#include <SDL/SDL.h>
```

The following line of code replaces the old one:

```
#include <SDL2/SDL.h>
```

Not a big difference, but still necessary.

Creating a Window

Previously, creating a window was a matter of calling a single function, but with multiple window support, that function is now obsolete. Furthermore, the new way of creating windows makes it possible to specify their location and visibility. Here is what window creation looks like in SDL 1.2:

```
int main(int arc, char* args[])
{
    SDL_Init( SDL_INIT_EVERYTHING );
    SDL_Surface* backbuffer = SDL_SetVideoMode(800,
                                               600,
                                               32,
                                               SDL_SWSURFACE);

    /*Game Code*/
    SDL_Quit();
}
```

Now, it looks a bit different:

```
int main(int arc, char* args[])
{
    SDL_Init( SDL_INIT_EVERYTHING );
    SDL_Window* window = SDL_CreateWindow("SDL!!!",
                                          SDL_WINDOWPOS_UNDEFINED,
                                          SDL_WINDOWPOS_UNDEFINED,
                                          800, 600, SDL_WINDOW_SHOWN);

    SDL_Surface* backbuffer = SDL_GetWindowSurface(window);

    /*Game Code*/

    SDL_DestroyWindow(window);
    SDL_Quit();
}
```

All right, not much has changed. The difference is that now a window is created, and the backbuffer is obtained from that window. When the program is done, it is also necessary to destroy that window. Usually, I would put a table with descriptions of the new functions used, but I'll hold on until the end of this section to list all the new functions in one place. For now, let's move on.

Flipping the Backbuffer

Since there can be multiple windows, you can't just call SDL_Flip to draw the backbuffer onto the screen. Each window must be updated individually using the function SDL_UpdateWindowSurface, as shown here:

```
SDL_UpdateWindowSurface(window);
```

The new function makes it possible to update windows independently of each other. This is not a big change, but a change nonetheless.

Loading Images

The process of loading images hasn't actually changed, but the way images are processed after loading them has. If you recall, images were loaded, then optimized, and finally, color-keyed. The original image-loading function had a piece of code that looked like this:

```
imageLoaded = IMG_Load(fileName);

    if(imageLoaded != NULL)
    {
        processedImage = SDL_DisplayFormat(imageLoaded);
        SDL_FreeSurface(imageLoaded);

        if(processedImage != NULL)
        {
            Uint32 colorKey = SDL_MapRGB(processedImage->format, 255, 0, 255);
            SDL_SetColorKey(processedImage, SDL_SRCCOLORKEY, colorKey);
        }

    }
```

The function SDL_DisplayFormat is gone, and the function SDL_SetColorKey has been slightly modified. In order to optimize the image, you can now use SDL_ConvertSurface, and instead of using SDL_SRCCOLORKEY, just use the flag SDL_TRUE. The new code looks like so:

```
imageLoaded = IMG_Load(fileName);

if(imageLoaded != NULL)
```

```
{
    processedImage = SDL_ConvertSurface(imageLoaded, Backbuffer->format, 0);
    SDL_FreeSurface(imageLoaded);

    if(processedImage != NULL)
    {
        Uint32 colorKey = SDL_MapRGB(processedImage->format, 0xFF, 0, 0xFF);
        SDL_SetColorKey(processedImage, SDL_TRUE, colorKey);
    }
}
```

Remember that all the new functions are listed in Table 13.2, which appears at the end of this section.

Changing the Window Title

Changing the title of a window is really easy. Instead of calling `SDL_WM_SetCaption`, you can use the following line of code:

```
SDL_SetWindowTitle(window, "The New Title");
```

See? That wasn't too bad. Now you can set the title of any window you want.

Buffered Keyboard Input

This is one of the more annoying changes. It simply causes inconveniences, but it's not too bad. The function `SDL_GetKeyState` has been replaced by `SDL_GetKeyboardState`. These two functions are almost identical. The only difference is how the keys are accessed with the newer function. Here is an example of the old function in action:

```
Uint8* keys = SDL_GetKeyState(NULL);

if(keys[SDLK_ESCAPE])
    gameOver = true;
```

By comparison, the new version looks more like this:

```
Uint8* keys = SDL_GetKeyboardState(NULL);

if(keys[SDL_SCANCODE_ESCAPE])
    gameOver = true;
```

While the parameters of the functions remain the same, the array returned by the new function shouldn't be accessed by the old `SDLK_*` key codes. They are now accessed by the `SDL_SCANCODE_*` key codes. This is very annoying since it's now necessary to track down every single `SDLK_*` code and change it to the corresponding new one when porting code from SDL 1.2 to SDL 2.0. Failing to do so will create runtime errors and not compile-time errors. Fortunately, you don't have to memorize new key codes. You can just change the prefix from `SDLK_` to `SDL_SCANCODE_`.

Warping the Mouse

While this feature wasn't used much, it's still worth mentioning. Warping the mouse now requires a pointer to a window, so keep that in mind. Instead of using `SDL_WarpMouse`, the program has to use `SDL_WarpMouseInWindow`. Alas, the code for mouse warping looks like so:

```
SDL_WarpMouseInWindow(window, x, y);
```

Easy enough right?

Summary of New Functions

For the most part, porting from SDL 1.2 to SDL 2.0 is not very difficult. Only a few functions have changed, but this was for the sake of adding flexibility and multiple window support. As promised, Table 13.2 details the new functions used in this chapter.

Table 13.2 New SDL Functions

SDL Function	Description

`SDL_Window* SDL_CreateWindow(`
`    const char* title,`
`    int x,`
`    int y,`
`    int w,`
`    int h,`
`    Uint32 flags);`
	This function creates a window for you to work with. The first parameter is the title, and the parameters x and y indicate the position of the window on the screen. Passing `SDL_WINDOWPOS_UNDEFINED` for x and y will place the window in an arbitrary location on the screen. The parameters w and h will indicate the size of the window in terms of width and height, respectively. The final parameter indicates the status of the window. The values you're interested in are `SDL_WINDOW_SHOWN`, which displays the created window, and `SDL_WINDOW_FULLSCREEN`, which creates a fullscreen window.

`void SDL_DestroyWindow(` `    SDL_Window* window);`	This function cleans up the window you created earlier. This must be done for every window before quitting the application.
`SDL_Surface *SDL_GetWindowSurface(` `    SDL_Window* window);`	This function returns the surface of the specified window. In this case, this is used as the backbuffer.
`int SDL_UpdateWindowSurface(` `    SDL_Window* window);`	This function draws the provided window's backbuffer onto the screen.

```SDL_Surface *SDL_ConvertSurface(SDL_Surface *src, SDL_PixelFormat *fmt, Uint32 flags);```	This function converts the src surface to the pixel format provided in parameter number 2. The last parameter is always 0. It's sort of strange, but that's what it says in the official documentation.
```int SDL_SetColorKey(SDL_Surface *surface, Uint32 flag, Uint32 key)```	While this function hasn't changed, the value SDL_SRCCOLORKEY no longer exists and has been replaced by SDL_TRUE.
```void SDL_SetWindowTitle(SDL_Window* window, const char* title);```	This function sets the desired window's title to the string provided in parameter number 2.
```Uint8* SDL_GetKeyboardState(int* numkeys)```	This function is almost a carbon copy of SDL_GetKeyState. The difference is that the array it returns is to be accessed by SDL_SCANCODE_* values instead of SDLK_* values.
```void SDL_WarpMouseInWindow(SDL_Window* window, int x, int y);```	This function warps the mouse to the appropriate window and at the appropriate coordinates.

© Jazon Yamamoto.

Tip

Remember that all the demos made in this book were redone in SDL 2.0. They can all be found in BAMGP\ under Extras\SDL2_Demos.

Building the App

You can find the files necessary to build any the previous apps in BAMGP\. They are located in Extras\ SDL2_Demos\. You need to create an SDL project for each app and copy the following files all the source and header files as well as any of the resource folders into your project's directory. If you're using Windows, make sure to include the SDL 2.0 .dll files in the project's directory. Your project should be configured properly, as shown in earlier in this chapter, and all the files should also be properly included. When all is set, you'll be able to build the program and run it on your own. Additionally, there are precompiled versions the Source directory of each demo.

Introduction to the Mighty Rendering API

Although the methods for drawing graphics that were introduced in this book are still viable and always will be, the rendering API introduced in SDL 2.0 has a variety of features that prove to be useful in a number of applications. The new rendering API is actually quite fancy, and it boasts a number of features that can make a game more graphically interesting. Although I won't go deep into detail of every single aspect of the API, this section does cover all the most important features the API has to offer.

The new API provides the ability to draw hollow and filled rectangles, as well as draw lines. This was possible before, but now, there's less coding on the programmer's end. This isn't a fancy feature, but it's nice to have. A more interesting feature is the ability to stretch, rotate, flip, and "dye" images. Doing this would be terribly slow in SDL 1.2, but SDL 2.0 takes advantage of hardware acceleration to speed up the process. *Hardware acceleration* is the process of using specialized hardware to help a computer do a set of operations at blazing speeds. Using hardware acceleration in effect enables programmers to clutter the screen with fancy graphics without a drastic performance drop! Of course, this doesn't mean unlimited power. Everything has its limits.

Although the rendering API provides more power, it is not as flexible as the previous approach. In the previous approach, there was direct access to the backbuffer. You could manually modify each pixel on it. The rendering API removes this ability, but the power it provides makes the trade-off worth it in most cases. The new rendering API takes a more modern approach to rendering graphics, but the old methods are more traditional.

Initializing the Rendering Device

To make use of the new graphical functionality provided in SDL 2.0, a rendering device must be created separately from the windows on which it operates. Before creating a rendering device, you will need a handle to store it. The following line of code creates a handle to a rendering device:

```
SDL_Renderer* renderer = NULL;
```

Boom! Now, you can create a rendering device. Note that you need to call SDL_Init and create a window before you create a rendering device. You can create a rendering device using the following line of code:

```
renderer = SDL_CreateRenderer(window, -1,
                    SDL_RENDERER_ACCELERATED |
                    SDL_RENDERER_PRESENTVSYNC);
```

I'll explain this line in detail at the end of this section. For now, it's worth mentioning that you set two flags. The first flag, SDL_RENDERER_ACCELERATED, tells SDL to create a renderer with hardware acceleration. This may not always be possible, but it should work on most PCs and a variety of mobile devices since hardware acceleration is so ubiquitous. The second flag, SDL_RENDERER_PRESENTVSYNC, is actually pretty cool. It synchronizes the frame rate to the device's default frame rate. This ensures that games will have the most fluid motion possible!

All right, now it's time to have the render do something useful like clear the screen. The following lines of code clear the screen:

```
SDL_SetRenderDrawColor(renderer, 100, 0, 250, 255);
SDL_RenderClear(renderer);
```

The first line of code sets the renderer's draw color. Basically, if the render has to draw anything that requires a color, it will use the active color. Whenever you clear the screen, you have to specify the draw color again since you can't always assume the draw color hasn't changed since the last frame. The second line of code simply fills the screen with the draw color.

Now, it's time to flip the screen. Since you're not working directly with a surface anymore, there's a different way of doing this. To flip the screen, call the following function:

```
SDL_RenderPresent(renderer);
```

When you're finally finished using the renderer, you must destroy it. This is accomplished by the following line of code:

```
SDL_DestroyRenderer(renderer);
```

Sweet! Now put it all together and make a small demo out of this. Listing 13.1 illustrates the most basic usage of the new rendering API.

Listing 13.1: Creating a Rendering Device

```
//Include the SDL 2 header file
#include <SDL2/SDL.h>

int main(int args, char* argvs[])
{
    //Set up variables
    SDL_Window* window = NULL;
    SDL_Renderer* renderer = NULL;

    //Initialize SDL
    if(SDL_Init(SDL_INIT_EVERYTHING) == -1)
```

```
    {
        return 0;
    }

    //Create the window
    window = SDL_CreateWindow("SDL 2 Test",
                                SDL_WINDOWPOS_UNDEFINED,
                                SDL_WINDOWPOS_UNDEFINED,
                                800,
                                600,
                                SDL_WINDOW_SHOWN);

    //Error Checking
    if(window == NULL)
    {
        SDL_Quit();
        return 0;
    }

    //This creates our rendering device, which we use now to handle graphics for us.
    renderer = SDL_CreateRenderer(window, -1,
                                    SDL_RENDERER_ACCELERATED |
                                    SDL_RENDERER_PRESENTVSYNC);

    bool isRunning = true;

    //The game loop
    while(isRunning)
    {
        //Check if the user pressed the exit button
        SDL_Event event;

        if(SDL_PollEvent(&event))
        {
            if(event.type == SDL_QUIT)
            {
                isRunning = false;
            }
        }

        //Set the drawing color
        SDL_SetRenderDrawColor(renderer, 100, 0, 250, 255);

        //Clear the screen
        SDL_RenderClear(renderer);

        //Draw the screen. This replaces SDL_Flip in SDL 1.2
        //and SDL_UpdateWindowSurface in SDL 2 if we weren't
        //working with a rendering context
        SDL_RenderPresent(renderer);
    }
```

```
    //We have to clean up the renderer when we're done with it
    SDL_DestroyRenderer(renderer);

    //Clean up the window
    SDL_DestroyWindow(window);

    //And quit :)
    SDL_Quit();

    return 1;
}
```

Building the App

You can find the files necessary to build this app in BAMGP\. They are located in Extras\
Bonus_Chapter_Demos\Bonus_1_RendererSetup\. You need to create an SDL project and copy the
main.cpp into your project's directory. If you're using Windows, make sure to include the .dll files in
the project's directory. Your project should be configured properly, as shown earlier in this chapter, and
all the files should also be properly included. When all is set, you'll be able to build the program
and run it on your own. Additionally, a precompiled version is in the Output directory named
Bonus_1_RendererSetup.exe.

The results can be admired in Figure 13.10.

Figure 13.10
A majestic canvas!

© Jazon Yamamoto.

Table 13.3 explains the functions used in this demo.

Table 13.3 New SDL Functions

SDL Function	Description

`SDL_Renderer*`
`   SDL_CreateRenderer(`
`   SDL_Window* window,`
`   int index,`
`   Uint32 flags);`
	This function creates a rendering device on the specified window. The first parameter specifies a window, the second a rendering driver. Stick to using -1 every time for this because that selects the first driver supporting the requested flags. The final parameter specifies flags. It is possible to select multiple flags. Select `SDL_RENDERER_ACCELERATED` to speed up drawing and `SDL_RENDERER_PRESENTVSYNC` to lock the frame rate to the screen's frame rate. This function returns a valid rendering device upon success and `NULL` on failure.

`int SDL_SetRenderDrawColor(`
`   SDL_Renderer* renderer,`
`   Uint8 r,`
`   Uint8 g,`
`   Uint8 b,`
`   Uint8 a);`
	This function sets the draw color on the specified renderer. This includes an RGB value and an alpha value. The color specified will be used when drawing primitives and clearing the screen. This function return 0 on success or a negative error code on failure.

`int SDL_RenderClear(` `   SDL_Renderer* renderer);`	This function fills the renderer with the color set by `SDL_SetRenderDrawColor`. It returns 0 on success or a negative value on failure.
`void SDL_RenderPresent(` `   SDL_Renderer* renderer);`	This function draws the content from the renderer onto the screen. This is similar to `SDL_Flip` or `SDL_UpdateWindowSurface`.
`void SDL_DestroyRenderer(` `   SDL_Renderer* renderer);`	This function destroys the renderer. This must be done for every single renderer created when you're done using it.

DRAWING PRIMITIVES

The fancy rendering device comes with a few functions that allow programs to draw primitive graphics. Start out by plotting pixels. Once the device has been created, you can plot pixels using the following line of code:

```
SDL_RenderDrawPoint(Renderer, x, y);
```

This will draw a pixel in the indicated coordinate. The color of the pixel will be the color set in the function SDL_SetRenderDrawColor. Remember that this time around, you need to specify it in RGBA format! The difference is that RGBA stands for *Red Green Blue Alpha*. RGB was covered in Chapter 3, but the A part is new. The alpha value of a pixel represents how opaque that pixel is. An alpha value of 255 makes a pixel completely opaque while a 0 value makes it completely transparent. A value like 127 makes the pixel seem somewhat transparent. Games commonly use this to create cool effects like lighting and shadows, but that's actually quite advanced and beyond the scope of this book.

With the ability to draw pixels in place, it's time to master rectangle drawing. As usual, there are solid and hollow rectangles, and the following lines of code are used to draw them:

```
SDL_RenderFillRect(Renderer, &rect);
SDL_RenderDrawRect(Renderer, &rect);
```

The first line draws a solid rectangle, while the latter one draws a hollow rectangle. The first parameter is a pointer to the renderer, and the second is a pointer to the SDL_Rect structure that will be drawn on the screen. The last primitive drawing operation is a bit more interesting. The following line of code draws a line from point A to point B:

```
SDL_RenderDrawLine(Renderer, x1, y1, x2, y2);
```

This code takes two sets of coordinates and draws a line between them.

All of the knowledge acquired here can be put together into a small demo showing off all kinds of cool effects. Listing 13.2 contains the code of the primitive drawing demo.

Listing 13.2: Drawing Primitives

```
//Include the SDL 2 header file
#include <SDL2/SDL.h>
#include <cstdlib>

//Set up variables
SDL_Window* Window = NULL;
SDL_Renderer* Renderer = NULL;

bool InitSDL();
void CleanUp();
void DrawScreen();

int main(int args, char* argvs[])
{
    bool isRunning = true;
```

```
    if(!InitSDL())
    {
        CleanUp();
        return false;
    }

    //The game loop
    while(isRunning)
    {
        //Check if the user pressed the exit button
        SDL_Event event;

        if(SDL_PollEvent(&event))
        {
            if(event.type == SDL_QUIT)
            {
                isRunning = false;
            }
        }

        //Draw The Screen
        DrawScreen();
    }

    //Clean Everything up :)
    CleanUp();

    return 1;
}

bool InitSDL()
{
    //Initialize SDL
    if(SDL_Init(SDL_INIT_EVERYTHING) == -1)
    {
        return false;
    }
    //Create the window
    Window = SDL_CreateWindow("SDL 2 Primitives!",
                            SDL_WINDOWPOS_UNDEFINED,
                            SDL_WINDOWPOS_UNDEFINED,
                            800, 600, SDL_WINDOW_SHOWN);

    //Error Checking
    if(Window == NULL)
    {
        return false;
    }
```

```
        //This creates our rendering device, which we use now
        //to handle graphics for us.
        Renderer = SDL_CreateRenderer(Window, -1,
                                        SDL_RENDERER_ACCELERATED |
                                        SDL_RENDERER_PRESENTVSYNC);

        if(Renderer == NULL)
        {
            return false;
        }

        return true;
}

void CleanUp()
{
        //We have to clean up the renderer when we're done with it
        SDL_DestroyRenderer(Renderer);

        //Clean up the window
        SDL_DestroyWindow(Window);

        //And quit :)
        SDL_Quit();
}

void DrawScreen()
{
        //Clear the screen
        SDL_SetRenderDrawColor(Renderer, 255, 255, 250, 255);
        SDL_RenderClear(Renderer);

        //Draw 10 rectangles across the screen
        SDL_SetRenderDrawColor(Renderer, 100, 200, 87, 255);
        for(int i = 0; i < 10; i++)
        {
            SDL_Rect rect;

            rect.x = 80*i + 10;
            rect.y = 10;
            rect.w = 7*i;
            rect.h = 7*i;

            SDL_RenderDrawRect(Renderer, &rect);
        }

        //Fill 10 Rectangles across the Screen
        SDL_SetRenderDrawColor(Renderer, 255, 80, 50, 255);
```

```
for(int i = 0; i < 10; i++)
{
    SDL_Rect rect;

    rect.x = 80*i + 10;
    rect.y = 90;
    rect.w = 7*i;
    rect.h = 7*i;

    SDL_RenderFillRect(Renderer, &rect);
}

//Draw 10 lines across the screen
SDL_SetRenderDrawColor(Renderer, 0, 0, 0, 255);

for(int i = 0; i < 10; i++)
{
    int x1 = i*80 + 10;
    int y1 = 170;
    int x2 = i*87 + 10;
    int y2 = 240;

    SDL_RenderDrawLine(Renderer, x1, y1, x2, y2);
}

for(int i = 0; i < 8000; i++)
{
    int x = i/10;
    int y = 250 + rand()%20;

    SDL_SetRenderDrawColor(Renderer, i%255, (x*x)%255, y%255, 255);

    SDL_RenderDrawPoint(Renderer, x, y);
}

SDL_RenderPresent(Renderer);
}
```

Building the App

You can find the files necessary to build this app in BAMGP\. They are located in Extras\ Bonus_Chapter_Demos\Bonus_2_RendererPrimitives\. You need to create an SDL project and copy the main.cpp file into your project's directory. If you're using Windows, make sure to include the .dll files in the project's directory. Your project should be configured properly, as shown earlier in this chapter, and all the files should also be properly included. When all is set, you'll be able to build the program and run it on your own. Additionally, a precompiled version is in the Output directory named Bonus_2_RendererPrimitives.exe.

Figure 13.11 displays a screenshot of the demo in all its blazing glory.

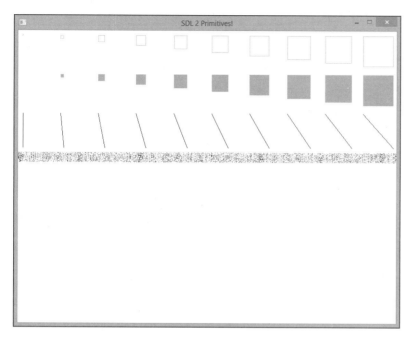

Figure 13.11
Drawing primitives in their everlasting glory.
© Jazon Yamamoto.

Table 13.4 examines the functions used in this demo.

Table 13.4 New SDL Functions

SDL Function	Description

`int SDL_RenderDrawPoint(`
`  SDL_RenderDrawPoint* renderer,`
`  int x,`
`  int y);`
	This function draws a single pixel at the specified coordinate. It returns 0 on success and a negative value on failure.

`int SDL_RenderFillRect(`
`  SDL_Renderer* renderer,`
`  SDL_Rect* rect);`
	This function draws a filled rectangle at the specified rectangle on the renderer. It returns 0 on success and a negative value on failure.

`int SDL_RenderDrawRect(`
`  SDL_Renderer* renderer,`
`  SDL_Rect* rect);`
	This function draws a hollow rectangle at the specified rectangle on the renderer. It returns 0 on success and a negative value on failure.

(Continued)

Table 13.4 New SDL Functions (*Continued*)

SDL Function	Description

```int SDL_RenderDrawLine(```
    ```SDL_Renderer* renderer,```
    ```Int x1,```
    ```Int y2,```
    ```Int x2,```
    ```Int y2);```
	This function draws a line on the specified renderer from point (x1, y1) to point (x2, y2). It returns 0 on success and a negative value on failure.

© Jazon Yamamoto.

DRAWING IMAGES

Drawing primitives is cool and all, but unless you're a master in modern arts, it'll hardly make a game interesting with just rectangles, lines, and points. You can take things further by drawing images.

Previously, images were drawn by loading them into a surface and drawing that surface onto the backbuffer. The new API comes with different and more interesting methods of working with images. Instead of drawing images by using surfaces, you can do so by using textures! Okay, so what's a texture and why is it better than a surface? While the concept of a texture can span a few pages, perhaps even a few chapters in a 3D game programming book, just think of it as a surface that can be stretched and "dyed" (dyeing images is covered later in this chapter). Like many other components in SDL, to create a texture, you need a handle. The following line of code creates a texture handle:

```
SDL_Texture* texture = NULL;
```

Textures must be created from surfaces. To do so, you can load an image into a surface and then create the texture from that surface using the following line of code:

```
texture = SDL_CreateTextureFromSurface(Renderer, surface);
```

Assume the `surface` variable was preloaded with an image. Now you can draw the image on the screen using the following line of code:

```
SDL_RenderCopy(Renderer, texture, &sourceRect, &destRect);
```

The first two parameters simply specify a renderer and a texture. The last two parameters are more complicated. `sourceRect` specifies the source rectangle. This rectangle specifies the portion of the image that is to be drawn. The last parameter, `destRect`, determines the rectangle on the screen where the texture will be drawn. If this rectangle is smaller than sourceRect, the texture will actually be shrunk to fit that rectangle, and if it's larger, it will be stretched to fill it. This is called *scaling*. Pretty cool huh?

Finally, when you're done with a texture, destroy it using the following line of code:

```
SDL_DestroyTexture(texture);
```

Being able to scale images in real time is really cool, and it allows programmers to be really creative. Before the rise of 3D engines, a popular approach to create the illusion of 3D characters was to scale a character's sprite according to the player's distance. The farther away a player was from a character, the smaller the character's sprite would be drawn. This was the approach taken in games such as *Doom* and *Wolfenstein* by id Software. The following demo makes use of this technique to make it appear as if an enemy is pacing back and forth. Note that the perspective in the demo is not perfect, and this is just a rudimentary approach to simulating 3D graphics. Instead of typing the entire 270 lines of source code for this demo, I just show the most interesting functions in Listing 13.3.

Listing 13.3: Drawing Textures

```
void UpdateGame()
{
    MonsterFrameDelayCounter++;
    if(MonsterFrameDelayCounter > MonsterFrameDelay)
    {
        MonsterFrame++;
        MonsterFrameDelayCounter = 0;
    }
    if(MonsterFrame >= MonsterAnimEnd)
    {
        MonsterFrame = MonsterAnimBegin;
    }
    if(MonsterWalkingForward)
    {
        MonsterDistance--;
    }
    else
    {
        MonsterDistance++;
    }
```

```
    if(MonsterDistance < 10)
    {
        MonsterWalkingForward = false;
        MonsterAnimBegin = MONSTER_WALK_BACK_START;
        MonsterAnimEnd = MONSTER_WALK_BACK_END;
    }

    if(MonsterDistance > 200)
    {
        MonsterWalkingForward = true;
        MonsterAnimBegin = MONSTER_WALK_FRONT_START;
        MonsterAnimEnd = MONSTER_WALK_FRONT_END;
    }

    float StretchFactor = float(200-MonsterDistance)/200;
    StretchFactor*=StretchFactor;

     MonsterDestRect.w = MONSTER_MIN_WIDTH +
                         StretchFactor*
                         (MONSTER_MAX_WIDTH - MONSTER_MIN_WIDTH);
     MonsterDestRect.h = MONSTER_MIN_HEIGHT +
                         StretchFactor*
                         (MONSTER_MAX_HEIGHT - MONSTER_MIN_HEIGHT);
    MonsterDestRect.x = CLIENT_WIDTH/2 - MonsterDestRect.w/2;
    MonsterDestRect.y = 50+CLIENT_HEIGHT/2 - MonsterDestRect.h/2;
}

void DrawScreen()
{
    //Clear the screen
    SDL_SetRenderDrawColor(Renderer, 255, 255, 250, 255);
    SDL_RenderClear(Renderer);

    //Draw the background on the entire screen
    SDL_RenderCopy(Renderer, Background, NULL, NULL);

    //Draw the monster
    SDL_RenderCopy(Renderer, MonsterSprite[MonsterFrame], NULL, &MonsterDestRect);

    //Draw the screen. This replaces SDL_Flip in SDL 1.2 and SDL_UpdateWindowSurface
    //in SDL 2 if we weren't working with a rendering context
    SDL_RenderPresent(Renderer);
}
SDL_Texture* LoadTexture(char* filename)
{
    SDL_Texture* texture = NULL;
    SDL_Surface* surface = NULL;

    surface = SDL_LoadBMP(filename);
```

```
if(surface != NULL)
{
    //Let's color key the surface
    Uint32 colorKey = IMG_Load(surface->format, 255, 0, 255);
    SDL_SetColorKey(surface, SDL_TRUE, colorKey);

    texture = SDL_CreateTextureFromSurface(Renderer, surface);
    SDL_FreeSurface(surface);
}

if(texture == NULL)
{
    SDL_ShowSimpleMessageBox(SDL_MESSAGEBOX_ERROR,
                             "Error!",
                             "Failed to load texture!", Window);
}

return texture;
}
```

Building the App

You can find the files necessary to build this app in BAMGP\. They are located in Extras\ Bonus_Chapter_Demos\Bonus_3_RendererImages\. You need to create an SDL project and copy the main.cpp file as well as the graphics folder into your project's directory. If you're using Windows, make sure to include the .dll files in the project's directory. Your project should be configured properly, as shown earlier in this chapter, and all the files should also be properly included. When all is set, you'll be able to build the program and run it on your own. Additionally, a precompiled version is in the Output directory named Bonus_3_RendererImages.exe.

There are three function definitions in this demo. The first one, UpdateGame, runs once per cycle in the game loop. In a video game, this is where all the logic takes place. The second function, DrawScreen, draws the screen every frame. The last function loads a texture from a file. This demo draws a cloud that stretches and shrinks while a monster runs in place on the screen. The monster's image is scaled by a factor of 200 percent. Figure 13.12 displays a monster about to eat you.

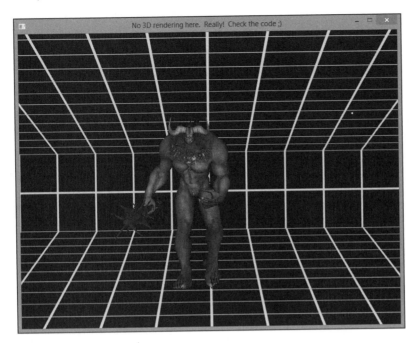

Figure 13.12
A monster out to eat you.
Source: Monster from DEXSOFT-Games (**www.3dmodels-textures.com**).

Table 13.5 explains the functions used in this section.

Table 13.5   New SDL Functions

SDL Function	Description

`SDL_Texture* SDL_CreateTextureFromSurface(`
`    SDL_Renderer* renderer,`
`    SDL_Surface* surface);`
	This creates a texture on the specified renderer and from the specified surface. It returns a valid texture on success and `NULL` on failure.

`int SDL_RenderCopy(`
`    SDL_Renderer* renderer,`
`    SDL_Texture* texture,`
`    SDL_Rect* srcrect,`
`    SDL_Rect* dstrect);`
	This function stretches a portion of a texture specified by `srcrect` onto a portion of the content of a renderer specified by `dstrect`. It returns 0 on success and a negative value on failure.

`void SDL_DestroyTexture(` `    SDL_Texture* texture)`	This function destroys a texture. It is necessary to do so whenever you are done using a texture you created.

ADVANCED IMAGE DRAWING

Drawing images was pretty fun, and being able to stretch them opens up many possibilities. Now, let's play around by rotating images. To draw rotated images, you use SDL_RenderCopy's bigger brother, SDL_RenderCopyEx. This cool new function takes a few more parameters but makes it possible to rotate an image and even flip it! To use it, simply replace SDL_RenderCopy and add the missing parameters like so:

```
SDL_RenderCopyEx(Renderer, Cloud, &Source Rect, &DestRect,
                 Angle, &RotationCenter, SDL_FLIP_NONE);
```

The last three parameters in this function were added to give programmers the power to rotate and flip the images they draw. The image will be rotated counterclockwise when drawn by a degree equivalent to Angle. In other words, if Angle is equal to 45°, the image will be drawn rotated by 45° degrees counterclockwise.

The second variable that should be noted is RotationCenter. This variable is a pointer to a SDL_Point (which is like SDL_Rect, but without width and height components). If this variable is equal to NULL, then the image will be rotated about the center. Otherwise, it will be rotated about the point specified by RotationCenter. This may sound confusing, but imagine placing your index finger on a sheet of paper while turning the paper with your other hand. The point at which your index finger is placed is the center of rotation specified by RotationCenter.

The last parameter specifies the flipping procedure. There are several possibilities for this. The one pictured previously, SDL_FLIP_NONE, draws the image as is. It is also possible to draw the image "flipped" horizontally by using SDL_FLIP_HORIZONTAL and vertically by using SDL_FLIP_VERTICAL. The former one draws the image flipped about the y-axis and the latter one draws the image flipped about the x-axis. This is useful because it is possible to draw a character once and flip it to draw it facing the opposite direction.

With the ability to rotate sprites, it is now possible to make more complicated demos. In the demo for this section, the player controls a spaceship. Unlike previous demos, it is now possible to rotate that spaceship and maneuver it with 360 degrees of freedom. You can press Left/Right to turn the spaceship and Up/Down to make it go forward or backward. Figure 13.13 displays the screenshot of the demo for this section.

Figure 13.13
A scaled spaceship rotating on the screen.
Source: Spaceship from 3DRT.com, a world leading developer of real-time CG content.

Building the App

You can find the files necessary to build this app in BAMGP\. They are located in Extras\
Bonus_Chapter_Demos\Bonus_4_AdvancedImages\. You need to create an SDL project and copy
the main.cpp file as well as the graphics folders into your project's directory. If you're using
Windows, make sure to also include the .dll files in the project's directory. Your project should be
configured properly, as shown earlier in this chapter, and all the files should also be properly included.
When all is set, you'll be able to build the program and run it on your own. Additionally, a precompiled
version is in the Output directory named Bonus_4_AdvancedImages.exe.

ALPHA BLENDING AND COLOR MODULATION (DYEING IMAGES)

Aside from resizing, flipping, and rotating images, you can also blend them and modulate their color. These effects use the color data of textures to produce interesting results. Alpha blending gives you the ability to adjust the level of transparency of an image, and color modulation allows you to alter the overall color of an image. These operations are equally awesome, but first let's talk about alpha blending.

Alpha Blending

Alpha blending is the process of applying an alpha value to an image. This alpha value determines the image's transparency. If you recall the primitives section of this chapter, it was possible to draw primitives that were partially transparent. This concept also applies to images. It is now possible to declare an alpha value for an image (using textures, of course) that will set the level of transparency of an image. Using this novel technique, you can experiment with fancy effects like fading images into the screen or out of the screen. Anything is possible with a little creativity.

To draw a transparent image on the screen, first load a texture and set its alpha value. This can be accomplished using the function `SDL_SetTextureAlphaMod`. This function takes two parameters. The first one is a handle to the texture, and the second is the alpha value. The alpha value ranges from 0 to 255, with 0 being completely transparent (invisible) and 255 being completely opaque. Using intermediate values will result in images that are somewhat transparent. Keep in mind that you can always make textures completely opaque after applying transparency. The following code displays the function in action:

```
SDL_SetTextureBlendMode(Texture, SDL_BLENDMODE_BLEND);
SDL_SetTextureAlphaMod(Texture, 127);
SDL_RenderCopyEx(Renderer, Texture, &DestRect, &SrcRect);
```

You might have noticed I snuck a function called `SDL_SetTextureBlendMode` into this code sample. This function sets the texture's blend mode. There are four blend modes that SDL 2.0 supports, but `SDL_BLENDMODE_BLEND` is the most common. This mode makes the image transparent or opaque, depending on the alpha value.

There are other possible blend modes like `SDL_BLENDMODE_NONE`, which disables alpha blending completely (and even ignores the color key if there is one). Another blend mode is `SDL_BLENDMODE_ADD`. This mode is very similar to `SDL_BLENDMODE_BLEND` but generally results in lighter colors. The final mode is `SDL_BLENDMODE_MOD`. This is a more complicated mode and generally not as popular as the former, but I'll cover it anyway. This mode essentially calculates the RGB values by multiplying the source image's (the texture) RGB values by the destination's (the backbuffer) corresponding RGB values. Figure 13.14 shows the demo where all these modes are displayed; it appears at the end of this section.

Color Modulation (Dyeing Images)

Color modulation is the process of selecting an RGB value that will influence the color levels of an image. This may sound very broad and abstract, but to simplify matters, imagine picking an RGB value of (0, 255, 0). This value creates an extremely saturated green. By setting that RGB value as an image's modulation color, you can effectively make that image greener. By selecting a red RGB value, you can make that image redder. This may be hard to visualize on text, but just think of it as dyeing an image. The code used to set an image's modulation color can be examined here:

```
SDL_SetTextureColorMod(Texture, 0, 255, 0);
SDL_RenderCopy(Renderer, Texture, &DestRect, &SrcRect);
```

I suggest you experiment with code modulation, not just to understand it better, but also because it's mighty fun to mess around with.

Figure 13.14 contains a screenshot of a color modulation and alpha blending demo. The demo for this section makes use of alpha blending and color modulation to create particles. A *particle* is a small graphical object with complex behavior. Individually, a particle is dull, but things get interesting when there are multiple particles on the screen. Particles can be used in games to simulate rain, snow, fire, and many other advanced special effects. In this demo, particles are spawned at the position of the cursor. They appear with random color modulation, velocities, acceleration, and sizes. They also have a certain life span. As the particles' lives end, they fade (using alpha blending) until they completely disappear. When a particle is dead, it is recycled and respawned at the mouse position. By clicking the left mouse button, you can change the blending operators and see what each of them looks like.

Building the App

You can find the files necessary to build this app in BAMGP\. They are located in Extras\ Bonus_Chapter_Demos\Bonus_5_RendererBlending\. You need to create an SDL project and copy main.cpp and the graphics folders into your project's directory. If you're using Windows, make sure to also include the .dll files in the project's directory. Your project should be configured properly, as shown earlier in this chapter, and all the files should also be properly included. When all is set, you'll be able to build the program and run it on your own. Additionally, a precompiled version is in the Output directory named Bonus_5_RendererBlending.exe.

Figure 13.14
A blending sampler.
© Jazon Yamamoto.

Table 13.6 explains the new functions used in this section.

Table 13.6   New SDL Functions

SDL Function	Description

`int SDL_SetTextureBlendMode(`
`    SDL_Texture* texture,`
`    SDL_BlendMode blendMode);`
	This function sets the blending mode for the specified texture. The first parameter specifies the texture. The second specifies the blend mode. Passing `SDL_BLENDMODE_NONE` for the second parameter disables alpha blending. Passing `SDL_BLENDMODE_BLEND` enables alpha blending. `SDL_BLENDMODE_ADD` enables additive blending. `SDL_BLENDMODE_MOD` enables modulation blending.

`int SDL_SetTextureAlphaMod(`
`    SDL_Texture* texture,`
`    Uint8 alpha);`
	This function sets the alpha value for an image. If alpha blending is enabled, passing 0 will make the image completely transparent, and passing 255 will make it completely opaque. Intermediate values will make the image somewhat transparent.

(Continued)

Table 13.6 New SDL Functions (*Continued*)

SDL Function	Description

int SDL_SetTextureColorMod(
    SDL_Texture* texture,
    Uint8 r,
    Uing8 g,
    Uint8 b);
	This function sets the color modulation RGB value of a texture. That texture's RGB values will be multiplied by the specified RGB value when drawn, resulting in an image that has a color influenced toward the RGB value specified.

© Jazon Yamamoto.

SUMMARY

Wow, this chapter was an exciting look into the future! While this isn't the definitive guide to SDL 2.0, it is enough to not only port the games made in this but also to enhance them! Of course, keep in mind that the added functionality makes for a more complicated game engine design, but it also provides more possibilities. Don't forget to check out the chapter's video tutorial. It contains additional explanations and insights of the topics covered in this chapter. To ensure mastery of the subjects presented in this chapter, try to complete a few of the following exercises.

Exercises

- Create multiple windows. It's not impossible anymore; just make sure you destroy them all.

- Redesign some of the game engine to add support for some of the new features (for example, add transparency and rotation to sprites).

- Mess around with color modulation. It is possible to use two images to draw a single sprite. One of the images can represent the character, and the other one can represent the character's clothing. By drawing the clothing on top of the character, it is possible to modulate the color of the clothes and have many characters with different colored clothes from two single bitmaps! Isn't this cool? This is a technique used in many popular 2D RTS games.

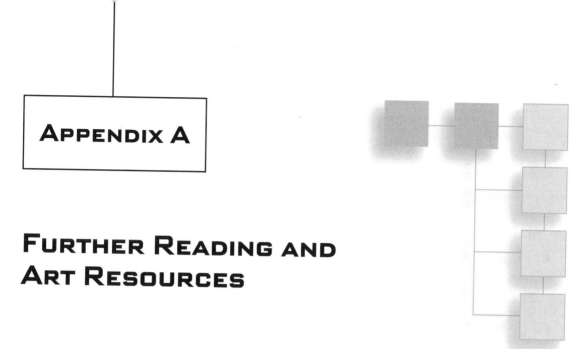

APPENDIX A

FURTHER READING AND ART RESOURCES

Although I have tried to cover as much as I could in this book, there are topics that haven't been covered, or at least not in great detail. Some of these topics include 3D game programming, mobile game programming, and even game console design. This appendix lists some print and online resources covering a huge array of game programming aspects. These resources are useful to game developers.

Books

There are many books out there that can enhance your learning. Some of the ones I found most useful are the following:

- *Effective C++ Third Edition,* Scott Meyers, Addison-Wesley, 2005—For those who haven't yet mastered C++, this book proves to be an effective (no pun intended) source of information. This book is commonly cited as a must-have for any professional C++ programmer.

- *Tricks of the Windows Game Programming Gurus 2nd Edition,* André LaMothe, Sams Publishing, 2002—This book covers advanced aspects of game programming in great detail. It was released over a decade ago, but it still proves to be an invaluable source of knowledge, since math is still math.

- *Beginning OpenGL Programming 2nd Edition,* Luke Benstead, Course Technology PTR, 2009—Those who want to venture in 3D game programming should start with this book. This book teaches all the fundamentals of using OpenGL and delves into the basics of 3D game programming. It has great pacing, and all the information is presented very clearly.

- *Programming Role Playing Games with DirectX 2nd Edition*, Jim Adams, Course Technology PTR, 2004—This book covers the specific aspects of programming role-playing games (RPGs). It does a magnificent job at outlining all the theories behind RPG design. It also covers DirectX and 3D engine development. This book covers very advanced topics, but reading it is very satisfying.

- *Beginning Android Games*, Mario Zechner, Apress, 2011—This book is directed to those who want to develop mobile games on the Android platform. With a booming mobile indie game industry, reading this book could prove to be a highly productive activity.

- *The Black Art of Video Game Console Design*, André LaMothe, Sams Publishing, 2005—This book is for those who are interested in hardcore game programming at a hardware level. It teaches how to actually design and build a video game console from scratch. This book is the only one of its kind, and it does a great job at explaining every single topic. Be warned that this book covers difficult topics, but the author does a great job at explaining every detail.

ONLINE SOURCES

There are many online sources that can either complement your learning or provide you with invaluable information.

Jazon Yamamoto

http://jazon-yamamoto.com/

This is my personal website, and it contains information related to game programming as well as additional information on this book. Be sure to check it out for updates.

SDL

http://www.libsdl.org

This is the home site of the Simple DirectMedia Layer. Here, you can expect to find programming resources, as well as the development files and updates to the library. This site also hosts the SDL documentation. This is useful for those who want to learn SDL topics that were not covered in this book.

CPlusPlus

http://www.cplusplus.com

This website is packed with features detailing C++. It has a set of tutorials that are extremely helpful for those who are still learning how to program. It is also a great reference site since it hosts a lot of C++ standard library documentation along with a few code examples.

GameDev

http://www.gamedev.net

This is one of the must-visit websites for game programmers. It is home to a forum board that is very active. It is a great place to get to know other coders, and it is host to a magnitude of articles and tutorials. I've made quite a few friends on this website, and some of my favorite indie games came from its community.

Gamasutra

http://www.gamasutra.com

This website is constantly updated with game development news. It is a great place to research exactly what is going on in the game development industry. It also hosts tutorials that are very useful and cover a wide range of topics. This is great for aspiring indie programmers who need inspiration, want to read more about the life of an average game developer, or want more information about the current state of the industry.

DevMaster

http://www.devmaster.net

This website is a great resource for game programmers who are interested in learning advanced techniques for making games. It has a simple layout, and it is easy to navigate. It is very similar to GameDev, but it has its unique charm.

ART RESOURCES

I'm a programmer and not much of an artist, so I like to use resources made by others to ensure quality art. The following websites contain high-quality art resources.

FroGames

http://www.frogames.net/

This site is home to a few content packs to start making games right away. They are mostly 3D models, but they can be turned into sprites easily.

3D Models-Textures

http://www.3dmodels-textures.com/

This site has more variety in models, and it also includes textures as well as complete environments. This website has high-quality models at very attractive prices.

Open Clip Art

http://openclipart.org/

This site contains all sorts of icons and glyphs that can be used for free (make sure to read their licenses, of course, since there may be some restrictions).

Open Game Art

http://opengameart.org/

This site is filled with all kinds of assets for video games (including music and sound effects!). The problem is that they are all from different authors, and there are no minimum quality standards for this site. However, if you dig around, you can find the gems.

FreeSound

http://www.freesound.org/

Here you can find a great variety of audio files. They have different licenses. Make sure to dig around to find the sounds that fit with your game.

Open Font Library

http://openfontlibrary.org/

This is another awesome site. It contains many fonts that you can use in your games as well as other applications. They are of high quality and visually appealing.

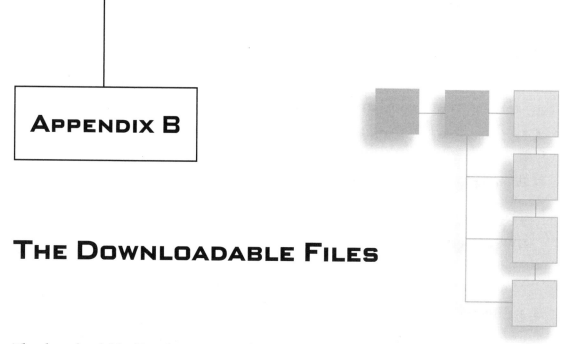

APPENDIX B

THE DOWNLOADABLE FILES

The downloadable files that come with this book are packed with resources that will be extremely useful to any game programmer.

All of the files necessary to set up a game development environment can be obtained from the following web page: **http://cengageptr.com/Topics/TitleDetail/1305110382**. Simply locate the "Companion Downloads" link and click on it to be redirected to a download page.

Alternatively, the files can also be downloaded from **http://www.jazon-yamamoto .com/bamgp**. They are contained in a .zip file named BAMGP.zip. Download the .zip file and extract it anywhere on your hard drive. This will make it easier to explore and experiment with the files in the future. As a convention, I refer to the root directory of the files as BAMGP\.

You'll find the following resources in the downloads:

- *Source code*—The source code to every demo or game can be found here. Due to the nature of SDL, this code can be built using Windows, Linux, Mac OS, and pretty much anything that can compile C++ applications. The demos from the first few chapters usually only contain one source file. The demos from the latter chapters are much larger and contain more source files.

- *Video tutorials*—Every chapter in this book has a video tutorial to go along with it. Video tutorials explain some things in more detail or demonstrate how to modify the source code that comes with each chapter. Be sure to check these out, since they add information that cannot be conveyed as clearly through text.

- *The SDL 1.2 library files*—These are the development files. They are required in order to compile SDL applications.

The following tools are used in this book:

- *Code::Blocks*—This is a free compiler that is well suited for programming games. It is constantly updated, and it has proved to be a robust tool.

- *Paint.NET*—This is an image-editing program. It is useful for making and editing sprites. It is fully featured, and there is a large community of users behind it. I prefer to use Paint.NET over Adobe's Photoshop for quick image editing and spriting, since it has a simpler interface but still offers great features.

- *Audacity*—This is an audio-editing program. It can be used to work with video game sounds. It is free, easy to use, and has a wide range of features.

- *Milkshape 3D demo*—This is a demo to the awesome 3D modeling program. It is good for 30 days, but after that, it will not save the models created in it. It's easier to learn than other programs out there, and it can be used as a great starting point for aspiring artists.

Figure B.1 shows a directory tree of the companion files for this book.

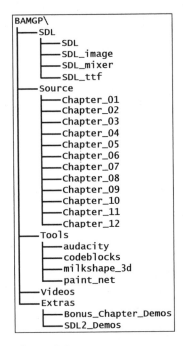

Figure B.1
The BAMGP\ directory tree.

© Jazon Yamamoto.

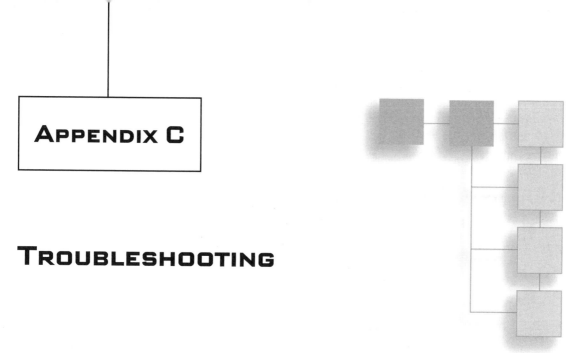

Appendix C

Troubleshooting

Murphy's law states that "anything that can go wrong, will go wrong." This applies to any process that is repeated multiple times. This is a technical book, and it requires the users to perform many tasks perfectly step-by-step in order to have everything work. This section of the book deals with common errors that you might come across when you're reading this book. If none of the methods suggested here work, you can find additional information at **http://jazon-yamamoto.com/bamgp**. It is also possible to email me directly at `info@jazon-yamamoto.com`.

Problems Installing Code::Blocks on Windows

If Code::Blocks fails to install on Windows, rerun the installer with administrator permissions. This is done by right-clicking on the installer and selecting Run as Administrator.

Problems Compiling with Code::Blocks

There are a ton of factors that can lead to compiling failures. There are two common messages that appear when compiling under Code::Block fails. The message `Fatal error CXXXX: Cannot include 'SDL.h'` indicates that SDL hasn't been installed properly. Refer back to Chapter 1 for instructions of installing SDL. The message `[Linker error] undefined reference to 'SDL_function'` indicates the Additional Linker Options were not set or that the `SDL\lib` folder is not linked to Code::Blocks or doesn't contain the necessary library files.

PROBLEMS COMPILING WITH ECLIPSE

Problems with Eclipse can be more varied. If you're having problems compiling with Eclipse, make sure you downloaded the SDL libraries using the Synaptic Package Manager. Also, make sure you installed the additional Eclipse components for C++ development.

PROBLEMS RUNNING THE DEMOS

There is a possibility that the demos in this book might not run on some computers. If any of the demos fails to run, make sure your graphic drivers are up to date. There may also be issues with fullscreen demos that are not present in windowed demos. If a fullscreen demo crashes, try recompiling it to run in windowed mode.

PROBLEMS LOADING FILES IN LINUX

Another common problem is being unable to load file in Linux that would load normally in Windows. This is because Linux is case-sensitive when it comes to file paths. `File.txt` is not the same as `file.txt` in Linux. Furthermore, Linux uses forward slashes in file paths, and Windows traditionally uses backslashes. Forward slashes still work on Windows, but backslashes don't work on Linux. In short, make sure file paths use forward slashes and all the lower- and uppercases match.

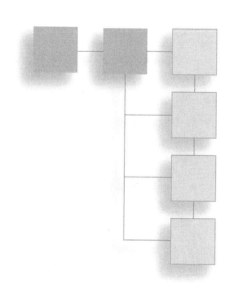

ASCII TABLE

DEC	HEX	Symbol	DEC	HEX	Symbol	DEC	HEX	Symbol
0	00	null	17	11	◄	34	22	"
1	01	☺	18	12	↕	35	23	#
2	02	☻	19	13	‼	36	24	$
3	03	♥	20	14	¶	37	25	%
4	04	♦	21	15	§	38	26	&
5	05	♣	22	16	▬	39	27	'
6	06	♠	23	17	↨	40	28	(
7	07	•	24	18	↑	41	29	)
8	08	◘	25	19	↓	42	2A	*
9	09	○	26	1A	→	43	2B	+
10	0A	◎	27	1B	←	44	2C	,
11	0B	♂	28	1C	∟	45	2D	-
12	0C	♀	29	1D	↔	46	2E	.
13	0D	♪	30	1E	▲	47	2F	/
14	0E	♫	31	1F	▼	48	30	0
15	0F	☼	32	20	space	49	31	1
16	10	►	33	21	!	50	32	2

(Continued)

(*Continued*)

DEC	HEX	Symbol	DEC	HEX	Symbol	DEC	HEX	Symbol
51	33	3	80	50	P	109	6D	m
52	34	4	81	51	Q	110	6E	n
53	35	5	82	52	R	111	6F	o
54	36	6	83	53	S	112	70	p
55	37	7	84	54	T	113	71	q
56	38	8	85	55	U	114	72	r
57	39	9	86	56	V	115	73	s
58	3A	:	87	57	W	116	74	t
59	3B	;	88	58	X	117	75	u
60	3C	<	89	59	Y	118	76	v
61	3D	=	90	5A	Z	119	77	w
62	3E	>	91	5B	[	120	78	x
63	3F	?	92	5C	\	121	79	y
64	40	@	93	5D	]	122	7A	z
65	41	A	94	5E	^	123	7B	{
66	42	B	95	5F	_	124	7C	|
67	43	C	96	60	`	125	7D	}
68	44	D	97	61	a	126	7E	~
69	45	E	98	62	b	127	7F	⌂
70	46	F	99	63	c	128	80	€
71	47	G	100	64	d	129	81	Ç
72	48	H	101	65	e	130	82	‚
73	49	I	102	66	f	131	83	ƒ
74	4A	J	103	67	g	132	84	„
75	4B	K	104	68	h	133	85	…
76	4C	L	105	69	i	134	86	†
77	4D	M	106	6A	j	135	87	‡
78	4E	N	107	6B	k	136	88	ˆ
79	4F	O	108	6C	l	137	89	‰

DEC	HEX	Symbol	DEC	HEX	Symbol	DEC	HEX	Symbol
138	8A	Š	168	A8	¨	198	C6	Æ
139	8B	‹	169	A9	©	199	C7	Ç
140	8C	Œ	170	AA	ª	201	C9	É
141	8D	ì	171	AB	«	202	CA	Ê
142	8E	Ž	172	AC	¬	203	CB	Ë
143	8F	Å	173	AD	¡	204	CC	Ì
144	90	É	174	AE	®	205	CD	Í
145	91	'	175	AF	¯	206	CE	Î
146	92	'	176	B0	°	207	CF	Ï
147	93	"	177	B1	±	208	D0	Ð
148	94	"	178	B2	²	209	D1	Ñ
149	95	•	179	B3	³	210	D2	Ò
150	96	–	180	B4	´	211	D3	Ó
151	97	—	181	B5	µ	212	D4	Ô
152	98	~	182	B6	¶	213	D5	Õ
153	99	™	183	B7	·	214	D6	Ö
154	9A	š	184	B8	¸	215	D7	×
155	9B	›	185	B9	¹	216	D8	Ø
156	9C	œ	186	BA	º	217	D9	Ù
157	9D	¥	187	BB	»	218	DA	Ú
158	9E	ž	188	BC	¼	219	DB	Û
159	9F	Ÿ	189	BD	½	220	DC	Ü
160	A0	á	190	BE	¾	221	DD	Ý
161	A1	¡	191	BF	¿	222	DE	Þ
162	A2	¢	192	C0	À	223	DF	ß
163	A3	£	193	C1	Á	224	E0	à
164	A4	¤	194	C2	Â	225	E1	á
165	A5	¥	195	C3	Ã	226	E2	â
166	A6	¦	196	C4	Ä	227	E3	ã
167	A7	§	197	C5	Å	228	E4	ä

(Continued)

(*Continued*)

DEC	HEX	Symbol	DEC	HEX	Symbol	DEC	HEX	Symbol
229	E5	å	238	EE	î	247	F7	÷
230	E6	æ	239	EF	ï	248	F8	ø
231	E7	ç	240	F0	ð	249	F9	ù
232	E8	è	241	F1	ñ	250	FA	ú
233	E9	é	242	F2	ò	251	FB	û
234	EA	ê	243	F3	ó	252	FC	ü
235	EB	ë	244	F4	ô	253	FD	ý
236	EC	ì	245	F5	õ	254	FE	þ
237	ED	í	246	F6	ö	255	FF	ÿ

INDEX